T0355419

The Meaning of Thought

For Leona Maya

The Meaning of Thought

Markus Gabriel

Translated by Alex Englander and Markus Gabriel

polity

Originally published in German as *Der Sinn des Denkens* © Ullstein Buchverlage GmbH, Berlin. Published in 2018 by Ullstein Verlag

This English edition © 2020 by Polity Press

The translation of this work was funded by Geisteswissenschaften International – Translation Funding for Humanities and Social Sciences from Germany, a joint initiative of the Fritz Thyssen Foundation, the German Federal Foreign Office, the collecting society VG WORT and the Börsenverein des Deutschen Buchhandels (German Publishers & Booksellers Association)

Excerpt from: Durs Grünbein, *Zündkerzen. Gedichte.* © Suhrkamp Verlag Berlin 2017.

Polity Press
65 Bridge Street
Cambridge CB2 1UR, UK

Polity Press
101 Station Landing
Suite 300
Medford, MA 02155, USA

ISBN-13: 978-1-5095-3836-2

A catalogue record for this book is available from the British Library.

Typeset in 10.5 on 12pt Sabon by
Servis Filmsetting Limited, Stockport, Cheshire
Printed and bound in Great Britain by TJ Books Limited

For further information on Polity, visit our website:
politybooks.com

Technology, the little titanic mistake, is
Nothing that saves humanity from itself

Durs Grünbein

Contents

Acknowledgements

This book was made possible through the support of a number of people and institutions, to all of which I owe a debt of gratitude. First and foremost, I would like to thank the Alexander von Humboldt Stiftung and the Université Paris 1 Panthéon-Sorbonne. I completed the manuscript while I was guest professor at the Sorbonne, which was enabled by a Feodor Lynen fellowship for experienced researchers. The research project that led to *The Meaning of Thought* is concerned with fictional objects – that is, with the question of the extent to which those objects that we imagine and tell stories about really exist. Answering this question means further elaborating the framework of New Realism, in which, as I've made clear elsewhere, fictional objects are quite welcome, just like unicorns. I would also like to thank my own university, the University of Bonn, for granting me a generous period of leave so that I could take up the research grant in Paris.

In this connection, thanks are due to the CNRS, to the president of the University of Paris 1, Professor Georges Haddad, and to the rector of the University of Bonn, Prof. Dr. Dr. h.c. Michael Hoch for their support in founding a new research centre on New Realism (Centre de Recherches sur les Nouveaux Réalismes, CRNR), funded by the CNRS and partner universities. A key focus of this centre is the prospects for a realist philosophy of perception, a topic I have had the pleasure of being able to pursue with the philosophers Jocelyn Benoist and Quentin Meillassoux. Considerable thanks are due to Jocelyn Benoist in particular, to whom I owe the inspiration for trying to overcome the subject–object split already at the level of perception, so as to arrive at a realist understanding of the sensible. Benoist's own recent work constitutes one of the most important contributions to this goal.

I would also like to thank the senate of the Republic of Chile for the invitation to their Congresso Futuro. It was at this event

ix

that I had the opportunity to get to know Giulio Tononi, whose non-reductionist, realist theory of consciousness gets us beyond the subject–object dichotomy on the terrain of neuroscientific research. Unfortunately, I had completed the manuscript of the book before I was able to visit Tononi's lab in Madison, Wisconsin, in May 2018, which meant that the fruits of our conversations did not find their way into the book.

Thanks are also due to my colleagues at the Center for Science and Thought (CST) at the University of Bonn and at the International Center for Philosophy NRW for many days of conversation about the topics of the book. Ulf-G. Meissner, Michael N. Forster and Jens Rometsch deserve particular mention: for many months, I have had the pleasure of discussing with them which form should be taken by a realist theory of perception and thought. In addition, I had the opportunity to run an immensely stimulating seminar in Bonn together with Jocelyn Benoist and Charles Travis on the manuscript of Charles's new work on Frege, in which he defends the existence of an '*invisible realm*' against the error of a linguistic reading of the reality of thought. One day, I might reveal to Charles that behind Frege stands the good old project of an 'invisible church',[1] which is called German idealism.

I would also like to express my gratitude to the team working at my chair: Walid Faizzada, Marin Geier, Mariya Halvadzhieva, Jens Pier, Jens Rometsch and Jan Voosholz, for their comments on an earlier version of the book and for their help in putting together and preparing the final manuscript.

Preface

The present book is the concluding part of a trilogy that began with *Why the World Does Not Exist* and continued with *I am Not a Brain*. Yet I have written it so that it can be understood without any acquaintance with its two predecessors. All three books have the same intended audience: anyone who likes to engage in philosophical thinking. And it is precisely this phenomenon, thinking, that is my topic in this book. Over the course of the following pages I will develop a theory of (human) thought that anyone should be able to understand.

Thought is perhaps *the* central concept of philosophy. Ever since Plato and Aristotle, philosophy has been understood as a science that thinks about thinking. Thinking about thinking is the origin of logic. Logic, in turn, is one of the foundations of our digital civilization, as, were it not for advances in philosophical logic in the nineteenth century, computer science would never have developed. In this regard, George Boole (1815–1864) and Gottlob Frege (1848–1925) were especially influential. Both were mathematicians, logicians and philosophers, and both set out a theory of thought which they used as the basis for developing the first systems of symbolic logic, the systems which underlie contemporary computer science. They thus did much to prepare the way for the digital revolution of our own day.

You are about to read a philosophical book free from opaque technical jargon. To follow the central arguments, there is no need to have worked your way through the technical aspects of logic. The main thesis I am going to advance is that human thought is a sense organ. Thinking is aesthetic (in the best case, something pleasurable) and not an exercise of force, discipline, punishment or blind, creativity-stifling rule-following. On the contrary: philosophical thought is a creative process, which is why philosophers such as the Romantics or Friedrich Nietzsche even went so far as to (try to) push it into the same camp as poetry.

Yet philosophy is ultimately neither quite like mathematics nor quite like poetry (or indeed any other art form). It borders on both domains, forming a point of intersection between the two.

Philosophy is the most general way of thinking about our thinking. It is more general still than mathematics, which is itself a form of language and thought that serves as a foundation for the natural sciences and technology. However, while not utterly unrelated to them, mathematics doesn't give us the foundation of poetry, painting, religion, music or philosophy. What unites *all* of these highly sophisticated human phenomena is our sense of thought, and the structure and nature of this sense are the object (and subject) of philosophy. For philosophy is thought thinking itself.

At the same time, philosophy is much closer to the concrete phenomena of our everyday lives than many believe. It wants to get to the bottom of our experience and perception. It is not just in the business of building models that help us better predict and steer the anonymous course of nature or the behaviour of living beings such as ourselves; rather, it aims at wisdom. And, ultimately, the love of wisdom requires a more precise knowledge of all those fields of reality that we don't (yet) know about. This is why Socrates understood philosophy as knowledge of our ignorance, without which wisdom is unattainable.

Thought is the interface between natural and psychological reality. To this extent, it ties together the topics of the previous two books of this trilogy: the world (which doesn't really exist) and the self (which is not identical with the brain). In part, thinking means establishing and recognizing connections. In thought, we link together widely disparate realities and manufacture new ones.

Thinking is not some ethereal process floating far above reality, finding its home solely in the ivory tower. This is why philosophy shouldn't be reduced to an academic parlour game, in which professional philosophers take competing positions on intimidatingly technical arguments with the aid of high-spec analytic tools. In the logic lectures he gave at the University of Königsberg, no less a thinker than Immanuel Kant distinguished between a 'scholastic concept' and a 'worldly concept' of philosophy.[1] The scholastic concept is systematic theory construction, the craft practised and handed down in philosophy departments, institutes and seminars. It addresses the architecture of those fundamental concepts without which we could not grasp our own rationality. Kant gave this process the same name as his famous book: he called it a *Critique of Pure Reason*.

By contrast, the worldly concept is concerned with the 'final ends of human reason',[2] which ultimately includes the question of what or who the human being is. And it therefore also has to ask what exactly our human capacity for thinking consists in. Are we merely an insignificant part of nature? Perhaps an especially clever animal? Perhaps even an animal blinded by its own intelligence? Or is the human being a privileged witness to a non-sensory, immaterial reality?

> This high concept gives philosophy *dignity*, i.e. an absolute worth. And actually it is philosophy, too, which alone has only *inner* worth, and which first gives a worth to all other cognitions.[3]

All of the great philosophers – to name a few at random: Laozi, Plato, Aristotle, Immanuel Kant, Georg Wilhelm Friedrich Hegel, Friedrich Nietzsche, Jean-Paul Sartre, Edith Stein and Judith Butler – have inscribed themselves in our cultural memory through their contributions to the worldly concept of philosophy. We do not possess a single academic treatise by Plato. Yet, in his surviving dialogues, we find some of the deepest philosophical thoughts ever to be articulated, all in the simple language of everyday conversations.

In recent decades, Germany (not to mention other places that are yet to develop a public philosophical culture) has unfortunately witnessed a partial deterioration in its culture of public philosophical debate. One of the theses I want to advance here is that naturalism bears the chief responsibility for this decline. *Naturalism* is the view that all genuine knowledge and progress can be reduced to a combination of natural science and technological mastery of the survival conditions of human beings. Yet this is a fundamental error, a dangerous delusion, which haunts us in the form of various ideological crises: in the return of religion (which frankly never really went away) as an explanatory model in the grand style; in the demagogic seductions of so-called populists, who invoke lost national identities (which never actually existed); and in the crises of the public sphere that have arisen through the defining medium of the internet. Naturalism is incapable of addressing these urgent topics: starting from a misguided conception of the human mind, it cannot even understand the appeal of religion or the power of human rhetoric. Without new efforts of philosophical thought, our intellectual negotiation of all these crises will come up short. Without ethical reflection, advances in natural science and technology do not lead automatically to the improvement of human life. Rather, unbridled progress is currently destroying our planet, and this ought to be an impetus to reflection and a change of course. We should not forget that, over the last two hundred years, philosophically uninformed naturalism and its unjustified belief in pure scientific and technological progress have led to weapons of mass destruction as well as to actual mass destruction.

Today, as in all ages in which our species has graced the Earth, the human being itself is at stake, and, with it – due to the sheer technological power it wields – the continued existence of life on our planet. Philosophy can only face up to this challenge by developing new tools and thought models, with the help of which we can come to a greater knowledge of reality. Today, philosophy is a form of resistance against the lie of a 'post-truth' age. For philosophy is opposed to the senseless assertion of alternative facts, to conspiracy theories and ungrounded apocalyptic scenarios, lest all these get out of control and the not too distant future does in fact witness the end of humanity.

I will therefore be arguing in what follows for a contemporary, enlightened humanism – a humanism that defends the intellectual and ethical capacities of the human being against our post- and trans-humanist despisers.

A chief aim of this trilogy is to introduce the fundamental theoretical commitments of New Realism to an audience beyond the walls of the academy. New Realism is my proposal for overcoming the basic intellectual errors to which we continue to succumb, much to the harm of our society and our own humanity. A particularly insidious member of this set is the rampant 'fear of truth', to quote Hegel, that characterizes our age, or the 'fear of knowledge' that the American philosopher Paul Boghossian (b. 1957) diagnosed in his own critique of the errors underlying postmodernity. Among these are the conceits that there is no truth, no objective facts or objective reality.[4]

As I said, I will not be presupposing any knowledge of the previous two books of the trilogy. Each of these can be read as a more or less stand-alone work. In the few places where it might be necessary, though, I will repeat some of the ideas introduced in the previous books so that the reader has a fully adequate picture of the overall intellectual terrain being covered.

The principal function of philosophical books is to provoke the reader to think for herself. What we can learn from philosophy is how to get in view and then reflect upon our prejudices and unspoken assumptions concerning the essential questions of humanity, such as *What or who are we as human beings really? What distinguishes us from other animals?* Or: *Can computers think?*

At the end of the day, it isn't so important whether I can convince you of my own positions. What matters is nothing but the truth. And since it's not so easy to ascertain the truth purely through the self-exploration of human thought, there will always be differences of philosophical opinion. Believing that we could somehow answer our questions once and for all would therefore amount to a fundamental error. Instead, the crucial thing is to set our thinking in motion, so that we can open up new forms and fields of thought.

As we'll see in due course, I take it to be a decisive criterion of reality that we can get it wrong. And because thought itself is something real, we're not somehow immune from error when we tackle the question of what exactly it is. Thinking about thinking is no easier or less likely to lead to mistakes than thinking about any other part of reality. Though, needless to say, I'm fairly convinced that my own answer is correct, else I would hardly bother to set it out here.

To unravel the meaning of thought, I will introduce you to the notion that there is an actual *sense* of thought. The key thesis of the book says that our thought is a sense, just like sight, taste, hearing, feeling or touch. Through thinking, we touch a reality accessible only to thought, just as colours are usually accessible only to sight and sounds to hearing. At the same time, I argue the case for giving our thought a new meaning, in the sense of a new direction. I want to provide orientation in an age in which – as in all ages before it – we find our thinking thrown into confusion by a multitude of ideological currents and their propagandists. Just think of the thoughts you've recently had about Donald Trump! Was it really sensible to have had *all* of these? Isn't it precisely one of the traps laid by Trump's savvy media strategy that we spend so much time talking about the ever-swelling tide of scandals that engulf him?

As inhabitants of the infosphere – our digital environment – we are exposed to a relentless flood of information. This presents philosophy with new challenges. This book represents an attempt at sustained reflection on what thought really is, so that we might regain some form of control over the terrain currently occupied by the dubious magicians of Silicon Valley and their technophile adepts, who ostentatiously insist that they have created genuine artificial intelligence. We need to demystify and disenchant our gadgets and do away with the belief in their omnipotence.

Otherwise, we condemn ourselves to a future as mere victims of digital transformation, hopeless info-junkies or brain-dead techno-zombies.

Introduction

The human being is the animal that doesn't want to be one. This is because, at some point or other, it began to wonder who or what it really is. Insofar as we have an implicit or explicit image of ourselves as human beings, we also make claims about the nature of the good life. **Ethics*** is the discipline that asks what a good life looks like. It is therefore based upon **anthropology**, the discipline tasked with figuring out what precisely distinguishes the human both from other animals and from the lifeless expanses of the inanimate universe.[1]

Our image of the human being is closely intertwined with our values. A **moral value** is a yardstick for human behaviour. It distinguishes between actions that ought to be performed – the good ones – and those that ought not to be carried out – the bad, morally deficient ones. Every value system should also have room for actions that, at least in most cases, are neither good nor bad (driving on the left-hand side of the road rather than the right-hand side, twiddling your thumbs, taking a deep breath, buttering bread, and so on), as well as for actions that are utterly unacceptable – that is, evil (torturing of children, for example, or poison gas attacks on civilian populations).

Not every morally wrong action is automatically evil, because not all morally wrong action causes far-reaching harm to the value system itself – think of those occasional white lies told to protect a friend or of cheating at a board game. Evil, by contrast, completely undermines the value system in which it arises. Thus, the prototypical sadistic totalitarian dictator, of which the previous century has provided us with all too many examples, subverts his own value system. Unable to trust anyone or anything, he has to create a total surveillance apparatus.

---

* Words appearing in bold type appear in the Glossary at the end of the book.

1

For as long as we remain mired in deep uncertainty as to who or what we are as human beings, we will not be able to calibrate our value systems properly. If the very nature of the human is in question, ethics too is at stake. This doesn't mean, I hasten to point out, that other living beings (including plants) or even lifeless, inanimate matter are morally irrelevant – far from it. But, in order to determine what we owe both to ourselves and to the rest of the reality we affect, we have to ask ourselves the question of who we really are and, in the light of the truth of who we are, who we want to be in the future.[2]

Unfortunately, it is very difficult, impossible even, to determine *who* the human being is from a neutral standpoint. For it is necessarily a matter of self-determination to attempt to determine what the human actually is. This self-determination cannot simply consist in naming natural facts, because the human is a specifically *minded* animal, where human mindedness (or **Geist**, as we say in my neck of the woods) is the capacity to lead a life in the light of a representation of who the human being is. More concretely, this capacity finds expression whenever and wherever we develop stories and images of our lives and of the conditions under which we deem them a success. We thereby aim to be happy, but without being able to give anything like a universally valid account of what happiness is.

From a philosophical point of view, **happiness** designates nothing other than a successful life. There are no universally valid standards for this; neither is there a set of principles of which we might somehow draw up a definitive catalogue. At best, we can state the framework conditions that are valid for any successful pursuit of happiness – namely, human rights. Yet this does not mean that philosophy or any other discipline could come up with a recipe for happiness.

Today, however, the concept of the human being hangs in the balance. The digital age has already brought about a world in which what was previously the privilege of humans – that is, solving problems in an intelligent fashion – is now carried out, in a range of situations at least, with far greater speed and efficiency by the machines that we have built in order to make our life and survival less burdensome.

Ever since the initial flourishing of philosophical thought in Athens, where it developed simultaneously with the first democracy, one of its central tasks has been to point out confusions circulating in the marketplace of ideas. Today's marketplace of ideas is the internet, the central medium of the digital age. The slogan of this book is: *think first, digitalize second*. This is just a version of Kant's famous Enlightenment motto: 'Have courage to use your *own* understanding!', but tailored to our own times. This is an urgent necessity in an age in which global digital propaganda systems, with their continual bombardments of newsflashes and posts, hurl our thinking into turmoil and confusion.

The first **key thesis of this book** states that thought is a sense, just like our sense of hearing, touch and taste, our sense of balance, and everything else that we nowadays count as belonging to the human sensory system. This thesis runs counter to the now widespread idea that thinking is basically a matter of information processing and therefore a procedure which can essentially be re-created in silicon or some other non-living material. In short: computers ultimately think just as little as do the good old ring binders familiar from our analogue bureaucracy. Programs are simply systems of data management, which we can use to solve problems far quicker than we ever could without their help: booking flights, solving equations, translating foreign languages (more or less adequately), writing books or sending emails.

At the same time, I want to argue that our human intelligence is itself a case of artificial intelligence – indeed, the only real one we happen to be acquainted with. Human thought is not a natural process governed by the laws of nature, like the dynamics we find in the sun or in sandstorms. Unlike the moon's orbiting of the Earth or the expansion of the solar system, we cannot understand our thinking if we abandon mentalistic vocabulary – i.e. language designed to articulate the meaning of thought – which typically includes words such as intelligence, thought, belief, hope, desire, intention and the rest.

The human being is the creature who is conscious of this very fact. And, accordingly, it orients its life around its ability to make targeted interventions into the conditions of its own life and survival. This is why humans elaborate sophisticated technologies in the form of systems for improving and simplifying their survival conditions. The human is thus networked with technology in its very self-understanding. In my view, the deep root of this interconnection lies in the various ways in which we are the producers of our own intelligence. The ways in which we think are formed by socio-economic framework conditions that human civilizations have been developing and transforming over millennia. This is how our artificial intelligence comes into being: by way of the self-determination of our human mindedness.[3]

Our mindedness, our self-determination as human beings, was

first set down in written form many millennia ago. Before the development of writing, our ancestors passed on various possibilities for self-determination in other media (such as oral traditions, artworks and rituals). These traditions continue to shape us, because they confront us with the question of who we want to be in the future.

Over the millennia, human life has revolved around the question of who or what the human being really is. One of the oldest known answers is that the human being is a rational animal. It is to Aristotle that we owe the corresponding designation of the human as *zoon logon echon*, the animal that – depending on translation and interpretation – possesses language, thought or reason.

Yet it is precisely this (supposedly) distinguishing characteristic and privilege of us human beings which the digital age brings into question. The Italian philosopher Luciano Floridi (b. 1964) goes so far as to see contemporary developments in AI research as a deep affront to our sense of our humanity, comparable to such seismic revolutions in our self-image as the heliocentric worldview, Darwin's theory of evolution and Freud's discovery of the unconscious.[4]

Of course, it has long been the case that the computers we carry about with us pretty much all the time – such as smartphones, smart watches and tablets – can outsmart most human beings in simulated situations. Programs can play chess better than humans, beat us at Go and at good old Atari games. They are better travel agents, can search the entire internet at lightning speed, immediately report the temperature in every corner of the globe, and find patterns in gigantic data sets which would take humans an age even to notice. As if that weren't enough, they also carry out mathematical proofs that even the very best mathematicians can understand only with considerable effort.

In the light of these advances, scientists, futurologists, philosophers and politicians like to engage in speculation about how long it will be before **the infosphere**, as Floridi calls our digital environment, attains a kind of planetary consciousness and liberates itself from its dependence on us humans. Some fear that a digital worst-case scenario, known as the singularity or superintelligence, will occur in the not too distant future. This position has found a prominent salesman in Raymond Kurzweil (b. 1948), himself inheriting ideas from pioneers of AI research such as Marvin Minsky (1927–2016). Even such famous personalities as Bill Gates (b. 1955) and Stephen Hawking (1942–2018) have warned of a fast approaching intelligence explosion, in which intelligent machines will take control and potentially exterminate humanity.

Others think all of this is only so much humbug, believing that the infosphere is no more intelligent than our shoes. One of the pioneers of the philosophy of artificial intelligence, the American philosopher John Rogers Searle (b. 1932), has long been arguing that the computers manufactured by humans cannot really think and that the likelihood of their ever attaining consciousness has not increased a bit over the last decades, that it continues to lie at exactly 0 per cent.

The truth certainly lies somewhere in the middle. The infosphere and the digital revolution aren't leading us towards a dystopian future, such as the world depicted in the *Terminator* films or in novels such as Michel Houellebecq's *The Possibility of an Island*; nor does the latest leap forward in technological progress lead towards the solution to all of humanity's problems, contrary to the hopes that the German tech entrepreneur Frank Thelen (b. 1975) expressed in a dialogue between the two of us in the German *Philosophie Magazin*.[5] We will not solve the impending crises of food and water shortages through better algorithms and faster computers. Thinking we will is really to get things back to front: it is technological advancement in the digital industries – i.e. attaining higher computing power through more efficient hardware – which contributes to resource scarcity and world hunger – and not only because of the alacrity with which we bin our 'old' smartphones and tablets so that we can buy the latest versions with their ever higher processing power. Computers do not solve our moral problems; they aggravate them. We mine the earth in poorer parts of the world to extract rare metals for our smartphones, use plastics for our hardware, and waste untold quantities of energy in order to keep digital reality running twenty-four hours a day, seven days a week. Every click and every email uses energy. We tend to notice this only indirectly, but that doesn't make things any better.

To be sure, technological progress can mean rapid improvements in medical science and living conditions in industrialized countries. But, at the same time, we are currently experiencing the collateral damage wrought by the digital transformation of our infrastructure, in the form of cyber-warfare, fake news, large-scale cyber-attacks and the rest. And that's not to mention the varieties of social alienation caused by social media's erosion of the distinctions between public and private, between times when we're available and times when we're not. Then there are the obviously very real phenomena of phone-tapping scandals (in the Obama era); Twitter propaganda (in the Trump era); bots that undermine democracy; terror attacks hatched online; a terrifyingly extensive surveillance apparatus in the People's Republic of China, which monitors and sanctions the population's online behaviour; and so on and so on.

In order to untangle the conceptual knot, I will be working in what follows with two anthropological principles, both of which will come up time and again. I mentioned the **first anthropological principle** at the outset: the human being is the animal that doesn't want to be one. This principle explains the presently widespread confusions that go by the names of post-humanism and transhumanism. Both movements are built on bidding farewell to the human being and welcoming the cyborg, a hybrid combining both animal-human and technological components.

Post- and transhumanism, both especially rampant in California, propagate the view that the human being can be overcome, surpassed. The place of the human is to be occupied by the infamous *Übermensch*, first conjured up by Friedrich Nietzsche (1844–1900). In a society in which an ever-expanding collection of superheroes has become a staple of popular culture, in which Hollywood propagates the fantasy that we might shake off the earthly shackles that tie down us normal mortals and propel ourselves into a superior future, it is no accident that technology and scientific research find themselves in thrall to the Nietzschean fantasy of the *Übermensch*.

In this connection, the French sociologist Jean Baudrillard (1929–2007) reminds us of the notorious rumour that Walt Disney tried to have himself cryogenically frozen, hoping to be awakened one day in order to witness the technological wonders of the future.[6] One of the main problems animals have to face is that they are mortal. Everything mortals do revolves around life and death, whereby we find life for the most part good and death for the most part bad. For a long time now, technology has been bound up with the fantasy of overcoming death on Earth. Today, this (pathological) wish finally to discard our animality and to become an **inforg**, a cyborg consisting purely of digital information, affects every level of society.

If we can dissolve ourselves into information, it is seemingly possible to install our minds onto some superior hardware, to upload consciousness and our personality onto digital devices. This idea is brilliantly explored in the American TV series *Westworld*. The series is set in a futuristic theme park called Westworld, in which visitors encounter robots indistinguishable from humans. The humans can use them entirely for their own pleasure. In the second series (spoiler alert . . .) it transpires that the firm operating the theme park extracts behavioural data from the visitors, which they then use to perfect the robots. Behind the entire enterprise is the mind of Westworld's creator, which has been uploaded onto a server and plans to co-opt one of the perfected robot bodies, thus merging inforg and cyborg. But this whole fantasy could never in fact be realized. Let's not forget that the TV series *Westworld* does not show us a single robot. What we actually see are human actors playing robots who at some point begin to play humans! This is the reality displayed by *Westworld*: the human wish to become a robot who becomes human.

To combat this flight from reality, I make the case for an **enlightened humanism**. Enlightened humanism is based on an image of the human that, from the very outset, allows no room for doubt that everyone, whether foreigner, native, friend, neighbour, woman, child, man, coma patient or transsexual, counts as human in the full sense. This is important to emphasize, because the classical humanist positions developed since the Renaissance have usually, implicitly or even explicitly, taken white, European, adult, politically significant and well-to-do men as the standard of being human. Even Kant's writings are unfortunately filled with racist and misogynistic assumptions, which is why in practice he denies people who were deeply foreign to him, such as the inhabitants of the southern hemisphere, their humanity, explaining for example how 'humid warmth is beneficial to the robust growth of animals in general and, in short, this results in the Negro.'[7] Yet Kant is by no means just a racist. He is above all a theorist of the universal dignity of human beings, which raises the question of how he could combine both sets of views in a single personality. The good news is that we enlightened humanists of the twenty-first century need not follow him, as we are the heirs of moral progress and of insights into the disastrous shortcomings of the first-wave enlightenment project – a project that was deeply implicated in other pathologies of modernity (such as colonialism). However, none of this entails that moral universalism is flawed, as one of the verdicts of universalism is precisely that colonialism, violent Eurocentrism, racism, and so on, are morally unacceptable forms of radical evil.

The **second anthropological principle** says that the human is a free, specifically minded animal (*freies geistiges Lebewesen*). This means that we humans can change ourselves by changing our image of what it means to be human. The specific freedom of the human mind lies in how our human life form is self-determining. We define our being human, and on the basis of our self-definitions we discover the moral values around which to orient our actions. Other animals have only a dim understanding of morality, and they certainly do not participate of their own accord in the enlight-enment project of moral progress. There is absolutely no gender equality in most animal societies, and there is not even a hint of the notion that they should cooperate in order to help foster other species. Cooperation in the animal kingdom is typically a matter of symbiosis and not of rule-governed moral thought designed to enhance the living conditions of everyone. Lions do not consider becoming vegetarians, and we do not blame them for their culinary preferences, because we know that they lack a sufficiently explicit grasp of the standing possibility of moral insight and perfectibility.

This is not to say that humans always act as their values dictate, or even that there is a high probability that they will. Freedom means precisely being able to act in this way or that way – morally or immorally. Yet our freedom also means that we cannot do anything at all without regulating and directing our behaviour. In modernity, therefore, the ultimate horizon of our self-determination, the highest value, is given through our *conception* of the human. We no longer seek the highest value beyond the human being, in a divine sphere, but we look within ourselves. This does not mean that we are steered around by the voice of conscience; rather, it means that we can steer and control our-selves, by recognizing that we are all united in being human. In this way, modernity is oriented around humanity as the bearer of reason and, if it is to be consistent, naturally has to recognize the value of non-human life too. Enlightened humanism therefore also demands the recognition of animal rights and the careful cultiva-tion of the environment, to sustain the conditions of human and animal life quite generally on our planet.

Nothing less than this already lies in the expression *Homo sapi-ens*, which was introduced by the Swedish naturalist Linnaeus (1707–1778) in his *Systema naturae*. In Linnaeus's classification, the human differs from all other life forms in being the creature subject to the Delphic oracle's demand: 'Nosce te ipsum, know thyself'.[8] Wisdom (*sapientia*) is the capacity to determine oneself. The problem is that wisdom does not automatically entail that one does the right thing. This is why the Delphic oracle, whose dictum is quoted by Linnaeus, designated Socrates as the wisest of all men.[9] For Socrates understood the structure of the oracle's invoca-tion: to the question of what the human being is, the answer is not fixed by pointing to any norm set by God, the gods or the cosmos; rather, it is determined solely by how we determine ourselves. We are condemned to be free, as Jean-Paul Sartre (1905–1980) put it, somewhat misleadingly.[10]

This book is an act of self-determination. Human self-determination occurs at two levels: at one level, what matters is that humans – whether we like it or not – are animals of a certain kind. It is only thanks to our being the animals we are that we are in a position to know reality in the first place. Cognition is not a process that takes place in some ethereal realm; it is one that is tied to ineliminable biological parameters. We are neither gods, nor angels, nor computer programs run on **wetware**, the slimy matter of our nervous systems. At another level, though, we are not just animals of a certain species. Unlike the 'last pre-human mammals of evolution', as the German poet Durs Grünbein (b. 1962) puts it, we are not 'creatures halfway between humanity and the rest of the zoo'.[11] As minded beings who, thanks to language and reflection, have a particularly developed sense of thought, we humans are in contact with infinitely many immaterial realities.

As the American philosopher Saul Aaron Kripke (b. 1940) rightly notes, reality shouldn't be confused with the 'enormous scattered object that surrounds us'.[12] Reality as we know it is just not identical with the material-energetic system of the universe. The real is what we can be wrong about and what – for that very reason – we can grasp as it truly is. Our thinking belongs to reality. It is itself something real – just like our feelings, unicorns (in films such as *The Last Unicorn*), witches (in Goethe's *Faust*), stomach aches, Napoleon, toilet bowls, Microsoft and the future. This was the idea I set out and defended at length in my book *Why the World Does Not Exist*.

Because of the globalization of commodity production and the digital interconnectedness of our news services, we are currently experiencing a dangerous ideological shift. By an **ideology**, I understand a distorted conception of the human that fulfils a socio-economic function, usually the implicit justification of an ultimately unjust distribution of resources. These days we are continually encouraged to believe that reality could be entirely different from how we believe it to be. And this notion is only nourished further by political sloganizing about a 'post-factual age', fake news and alternative facts, right through to 'post-truth'.

We have thus arrived in an age of a new metaphysics. By **metaphysics**, I here understand a theory of reality as a whole, which distinguishes between a real world (being) and the appearance and deception that supposedly has us humans caught in its snares. Our age is metaphysical through and through. It builds on the illusion that, in its most important facets, our entire life is an illusion, one we can see through only with great difficulty, if at all.

Yet the illusion that reality is an illusion is ultimately a distraction from what's really going on: the digital revolution of the past decade is a consequence of the modern knowledge-based society. In the age of first-wave enlightenment, the combination of all forms of knowledge was still the priority, the aim being the 'education of the human race'.[13] In the second half of the nineteenth century, positivism came to prevail, with its doctrine that all relevant human achievements can and should be sought in the sciences of technology and nature. Today, the metaphysics that sets the tone is **materialism**, where this encompasses both the doctrine that everything that exists consists of matter and the ethical conception that the meaning of human life ultimately consists in the accumulation of goods (cars, houses, sexual partners, smartphones) and their pleasurable annihilation (burning fossil fuels, ostentatious luxury, gourmet restaurants).

From a socio-political perspective, materialism corresponds to the idea that the primary function of a government is to develop and enforce the regulations necessary for material resources to be distributed in such a way that as many citizens as possible can experience the enjoyment of squandering them. This in turn serves to foster the preservation of our materialistic image of the human.

The digital revolution is closely connected with the surveillance apparatuses of modernity. As depicted in the TV series *The Americans*, it famously emerged on the back of military research projects in the Cold War. The major internet companies of our time are advertising platforms whose existence places traditional media under ever more pressure, forcing them to compete for the attention of the reading public with opinionated coverage and titillating scandal.

Yet my aim here is to provide not so much a *sociological* description as a *philosophical* diagnosis of the intellectual mistakes that underlie the materialist ideology of our time. In particular, we will be concerned with our own thinking. An ideology is a kind of intellectual virus circulating through the bloodstream of our thought; at first, it strikes here and there at the foundations of our health, without our so much as noticing, before finally overwhelming us. To take up a formulation of Peter Sloterdijk (b. 1947), I'll be looking to develop a *co-immunism* – that is, to improve our mental immune system.[14] We have to vaccinate ourselves against the false notion that we cannot know the truth and that, in the age of the internet, reality may no longer exist at all.

This means entering (in thought at least) right into the lion's den: into the age of reality shows and the ever-expanding and encroaching online society. The task will be to reclaim a sense for our own thought, which will protect us from the error of believing that we are on the brink of abolishing humanity and stepping into a paradisiac age of total digitalization.

The first key thesis, as I've already said, is that our thought is a sense. Besides the familiar sense modalities – which are hearing, sight, taste, smell and touch, but also the sense of balance and a few more besides – we have a sense of thought. I will expand this thesis into the **nooscope thesis**: our thought is a sense that we can use to scout out the infinite and then represent it in a variety of different ways – mathematically, for example. Our thinking is thus unlike our other senses: it is not restricted to our proximate environment but can – in the form of quantum mechanics, say – even refer to other universes or grasp the foundational mathematical structure of our own universe in the language of theoretical physics. Our nooscope therefore surpasses corporeal reality and connects us with an infinity of immaterial realities.

This thesis is directed against the currently popular idea that our mental apparatus consists merely of perceptions and cognitions, out of states triggered in us by the external world on the one hand and states that arise from the internal linkage of perceptions on the other. But it's simply false to believe that an external consciousness- and mind-independent world first tickles our nervous system, triggering chains of internal processes, at the end of which stands an image that has nothing further to do with the external world. Our mental life is no hallucination arising within our skull. Rather, on account of our sense of thought, we are in contact with far more realities than we'd think at first glance.

This book does away with the foundational error of modern epistemology: **the subject–object divide**. This consists in the false notion that, as thinking subjects, we confront an alien reality, a world into which we don't really fit. Hence the widespread impression in modernity either that we cannot know reality at all or that we can never know it even approximately as it is in itself. However, as thinking, perceiving creatures we do not face a reality that is somehow separated from us. Subject and object are not opposed parts of an overarching whole. Rather, we are part of reality, and our senses are media that act as contact points between the reality that we are and the reality that we are not. These media do not distort a reality that is fully independent of them. Instead, they themselves belong to the real, as interfaces or points of intersection. And thinking, exactly like all the other senses, is just such an interface.

Interfaces enable communication over various fields of sense. Take our visual experiences, for example. I can currently see a Berlusconi voodoo doll, which I bought in the shop of a Portuguese museum. I see the doll from my standpoint. I couldn't take up this standpoint if I didn't possess an intact brain, if I were currently sleeping, or if I no longer recalled the doll. But the fact that I can recognize the doll in the first place is also a component of my standpoint. And the real presence of the voodoo doll is just as essential for my perceptual mental state as my brain.

I perceive in colour. And I have a specific colour palette at my conscious disposal only because I am an animal whose colour receptors were selected over millions of years of evolution. The human sense of sight is an interface enabling communication between physical fields (containing light rays, for example, which can be measured and investigated by physics) and the field of my conscious experience (in which I can purchase and see voodoo dolls). Our visual sense and our subjective standpoint are not one jot less real than the light rays, the voodoo doll, and the elementary particles without which there wouldn't be any voodoo dolls at all.

As we will see, the same goes for our thought. Thought is a real interface connecting us up with countless immaterial realities – numbers, justice, general elections, truth, facts and much more besides. Yet thought also stands in direct contact with material energetic systems, which is why we are able to think about these too.

In this context, a further thesis is that *what* we think (i.e. our thoughts) is not material. The view that there is not only a material energetic system, the physical cosmos, is what I call **immaterialism**. Thinking is the grasping of immaterial thoughts. Thoughts are neither brain states nor any form of information processing that we measure physically. Yet humans cannot have any thoughts without being living creatures who find themselves in certain brain states – or, more generally, in certain physiological states.

Combining these theses, we get to our **second key thesis**: biological externalism. **Biological externalism** maintains that the expressions we use to describe and understand our thought processes are essentially related to something biological (see p. 141). With this thesis in place, I'll argue that there can be no artificial intelligence in the generally accepted sense. Our modern data-processing systems, including of course the omnipresent internet, do not really think, because they lack consciousness. But this doesn't make them any less dangerous or the debate surrounding digital transformation any less urgent.

We have to regain the sense of thought and defend it against the wild notion that our thinking is a computational process taking place within the cranial vault – a process of which we could, in principle, make an exact re-creation or simulation. Simulations of thoughts are just as much real thoughts as a Michelin map of France is identical with the territory it maps (see pp. 57ff.). Yet what we call AI is utterly real. Only it's not intelligent – and that's why it's dangerous.

One of the underestimated sources of danger in our digital age is that our self-understanding as humans is oriented around a misleading model of thought. For, insofar as we believe that advanced data technology must automatically conquer the realm of human thought, we create a false self-image. In indulging this belief, we attack the very core of being human.

In every epoch that has witnessed technological breakthroughs, the idea has taken hold that our artefacts could someday take control. **Animism** is the belief that nature as a whole is ensouled. Today this belief is also called **panpsychism**. AI research, however, is an internal rather than an external attack on the human being: for it's not just that our artefacts might attack us; instead, by propagating a false, essentially animistic picture of them, we attack ourselves.

Since time immemorial, the human has regarded its thought as something that comes to it from outside, be it from the gods, from the one God, or possibly from extra-terrestrials, as in films such as Stanley Kubrik's *2001: A Space Odyssey* (1968) or, more clumsily, Ridley Scott's *Prometheus* (2012), which unambiguously depicts aliens as our creators. Thanks to layer upon layer of our cultural-historical practices, we therefore find it easy to image that our own thought processes might also be found in non-living systems. But this is an unwarranted superstition and we need to overcome it. Many people today would be more willing to ascribe intelligence to a smartphone than to an octopus or a pigeon. But that is a mistake with fatal moral consequences – for humans, for our fellow creatures, and for the environment. It is therefore high time that we let ourselves be guided by realism rather than misguided by science fiction and that we re-establish contact with our human, all-too-human sense of thought. The first step is to recognize it as such.

1

The Truth about Thought

Complexity without end

As a first step towards understanding thought, it's useful to see it as having something or other to do with complexity reduction. When we engage in thinking, we process raw data into information: we take what is given to us and separate out the essential from the inessential. This enables us to grasp patterns in reality. Indeed, it's only thanks to this kind of complexity reduction that we can deploy our powers of thought to orient ourselves in reality.

In fact, thinking is a kind of journey through infinity. It's precisely because we're continually exposed to the infinite that we have to simplify reality through thinking. If you doubt that we really do find ourselves faced with the infinite, consider the following rather mundane scenario.

Cologne Central Station is usually pretty overcrowded by German standards. Imagine that one Monday morning you find yourself heading towards platform 9 to catch your connection. Making your way there, you try to steer clear of other passengers. Perhaps you still have a little spare time, are hungry, and so start to scout out something to eat. Maybe you also decide to buy a small gift for somebody.

As you're dodging passers-by, surveying the gastronomic situation and scanning for potential gifts, certain objects and events catch your attention. If you want to avoid colliding with the passers-by, you have to have them in view and predict their next movements at lightning speed; if you're looking for something to eat, you'll notice the station supermarket and the currywurst stand; if you're keeping an eye out for a present, you'll likely be expecting to find a florist or, depending on the intended recipient, a toy shop. You pay attention to various events as they play out in the station. After all, you'll also have to be wary of pickpockets and swerve out of the way of passengers who are in a particular hurry. All of this presupposes that you recognize the scene as, say, a Monday morning in Cologne Central Station and embed the various individual events within the overall scene.

Scene change 1: Now imagine that a physicist and an engineer have positioned themselves at a suitably safe distance from the station. They want to know how much energy the system 'Cologne Central Station' consumes in a certain amount of time. In setting about their calculations, they take into account the energy balance of the commuters, as they too belong to the system, but they ignore their various interests and experiences. Perhaps the physicist even pieces together a picture of the situation that does without the concept of a human being altogether: for his estimates, he uses only concepts that map the material-energetic reality of the universe. If he's up to speed on his subject, he'll concentrate not only on electromagnetic radiation but also on so-called baryonic matter, the matter composed of atoms. As their names suggest, however, we don't know enough about dark energy and dark matter for them to be included in such calculations. The physicist will therefore take into account neither absolutely everything in the highly complex system called 'the universe' nor absolutely everything that goes on in the observable scene. In short, this scene change involves complexity reduction across a number of dimensions.

Scene change 2: Making use of some (to us) unknown technology, a group of extra-terrestrials surveys the area of planet Earth that *we* know as Cologne Central Station. They don't realize that humans live in the (deluded and even dangerous) belief that everything on Earth revolves around them. Not being humans themselves, however, they don't share our interests or fears. And, consequently, they don't know that the humans at Cologne Central Station attend to and orient themselves primarily in terms of the behaviour of their fellow humans. They investigate neither humans nor the purchasable goods in the station, nor the energy balance as controlled by humans; instead, they focus on objects and events that exist on an entirely different scale.

Perhaps their instruments operate at such high resolution that they're effective on a smaller scale than anything currently accessible to our human researchers. Perhaps these extra-terrestrials are so small (considered relative to our dimensions) that they operate below the Planck scale – that is, on a scale where the laws of physics as we know them no longer apply in any straightforward sense. It's quite possible that the extra-terrestrials go about their business by using completely different units of measurement. Who knows, perhaps the scale on which they operate is that of the reality observable to insects, so that what counts in their eyes is the number of insects per cubic metre?

At this point, we could keep on introducing scene change after scene change; certainly, more than you'd care to read about and more than I've the energy to come up with. For there are infinitely many possible ways of grasping any single scene, such as the scene that plays out at Cologne Central Station on a typical Monday morning. Corresponding to each of these possibilities is a reality with its given laws and sequences of events.

I call each of these infinitely many realities a field of sense.[1] A **field of sense** is an arrangement of objects where these objects hang together in a particular manner. I call the manner in which they hang together a **sense**.

Our senses (for example: sight, taste, hearing, etc.) belong to reality (see **pp. 138ff.**). Our senses (our sense modalities) too are ways for objects to hang together, such as in our subjective visual field. What I see in front of me right now involves my sense modalities, which together constitute my perspective. A seen scene is essentially related to sight. Our sight is the sense of such a scene. The same goes for something that we hear. When I hear that there's a knock at the door, my hearing belongs to reality just as much as the knocking does. Our senses don't peer into reality, as though through a keyhole; they are themselves fully paid up members of reality and thus participants in determining how things really are. Sensing is as real as it gets.

There are, of course, fields of sense that no thinker ever does or can know about. At any rate, we've no reason to rule out such fields. Only if there were an omniscient God would it be the case that all fields of sense are knowable. Yet even an omniscient God would have difficulties with the infinite proliferation of fields of sense: he would have to know not only all the fields of sense located outside of his own field of sense but his own field of sense too – else he wouldn't really know *everything*. This raises a host of difficulties, which, since they're a matter for philosophical theology, will not concern us any further, or not in this book at least.

(But just entertain the following little thought experiment: if God knows everything that is not God, and, moreover, knows himself too, then there is an overall domain that he knows: the domain whose members are God and the world (everything that is not God). But if God continually attends to both God and the world, does he also attend to how he continually attends to both God and the world – and thus to how he attends to how he attends to how he continually attends to both God and the world? Can God reflect on God and the world and, in doing so, reflect simultaneously on his reflection on God and the world? A bottomless barrel.)

The point of this whole exercise and of introducing the possibility of infinite scene changes is to draw your attention to how there is no privileged reality, no field of sense on the basis of which you could have a meaningful grasp and comprehension of all fields of sense. You cannot get totality in view, as getting anything at all in view presupposes some complexity reduction. There is no point of view to which absolutely everything is given. Even if you could solve the theological puzzle I just sketched, this would have little bearing on our human predicament, because we're not God and thus not omniscient. In general, my philosophical approach recommends that we replace the notion that there is *one* world or *one* reality with the idea of an infinity of fields of sense, where these hang together in endlessly many ways. There is no such thing as 'reality' in the singular; rather, what there really is turns out to be an irreducible complexity that can never be captured by any all-encompassing theory. Moreover, we cannot master this complexity by simply deploying a singular term such as *reality* or *complexity*.

This little introductory argument is designed to show how no investigation of even a single scene, however familiar it might be, can grasp everything that belongs to it. Every science contains within itself the possibility of a further scene change. And nobody can grasp a scene like our Monday morning at Cologne Central Station, together with all of its possible scene changes. Reality necessarily escapes our grasp to some extent – but, as I'll be insisting, this in no way means that we cannot grasp true thoughts about a particular scene.

What is thinking?

Meet the protagonist of this book: thought. As a first approximation, we can already say that thought is a journey through fields of sense and that the aim of this journey is to provide us with an orientation within the infinite. This all depends on our capacity to grasp local facts, facts which obtain in a given field of sense concerning some range of objects or other. To unpack this a little: **thinking** is the grasping of thoughts. A **thought** is a content of thinking. It is that which one grasps. A given content of thinking is concerned with what occurs in a field of sense – for example, with what is presented in a scene involving a swimming pool. Thought contents have a form. They see to it that an object – say, someone who's just dived into a pool – appears in a certain manner. Philosophers usually express this by saying that something is grasped *as* something. For example, I grasp someone who has just dived into a pool *as* a swimmer. Hence, I don't try to rescue this person, but observe the scene in a more or less disinterested manner. Thoughts therefore have an object. The **object** of a thought is that which the thought is about. The **content** of a thought, by contrast, is the way in which the thought is about its object (how its object appears to a thinker, or what its object appears to a thinker *as*).

As I'll explain later on (see **pp. 216ff.**), we cannot produce thoughts, but only receive them. Thoughts occur to us. We can only be receivers of thoughts, by tuning our thinking to the right frequency. In a similar vein, the American philosopher Mark Johnston (b. 1954) points out that we are not 'producers of presence' when we think but, rather, 'samplers of presence'.[2] We first of all have to receive data, where this reception is not a process that we control by producing the data before we sample them.

Thought sets signposts for its own orientation. A signpost for orientation through Cologne Central Station is the concept of a passer-by; another is the concept of a platform. A concept fulfils the function of making the unlike alike in some respect. The British philosopher Hilary Lawson (b. 1954) sees this as the nature of thought as such – an idea that is by no means original to Lawson: it shapes the history of philosophy from Plato to Theodor Wiesengrund Adorno (1903–1963), who subjected it to a thorough critique in his 1966 book *Negative Dialectics*.[3]

In order to understand what's at stake, I'd like to offer an illustration of this particular thought about thought. Platform 1 and platform 9 at Cologne Central Station are, considered in all their specificity, rather different. The steps leading up to them are not covered in exactly the same quantity of accumulated dirt, different trains stop at each of them, and their respective tracks are not identical either, being worn down, on closer inspection, to slightly different degrees. Moreover, platform 1 can be found at a different location to platform 9. Expressed philosophically, this means that platforms 1 and 9 differ from each other in virtue of having different properties. A **property** is typically something in virtue of which something differs from something else for which one might otherwise mistake it (with the philosophically remarkable exception of properties shared by all objects in a given field of sense, or maybe even of all objects full stop, such as the property of having properties).

Although platforms 1 and 9 are not identical – because they have different properties – they are nonetheless comparable. Their comparability is established by their function. Trains stop at both platform 1 and platform 9. The timetable states which train departs from which platform at which time – or at least when they're supposed to do so. Platforms 1 and 9 are thus similar in certain respects without being identical. And these similarities between the two platforms are brought together in the concept of a platform – hence the idea that a concept frequently has the function of making the unlike alike. Without concepts, we wouldn't be able to orient ourselves. You can think of them as the signposts thanks to which we are able to recognize anything at all.

Thought is the medium in which we orient ourselves on our journey through infinity. It points out the directions in which we should look out for the objects and events that matter to us in pursuing our different goals – the goal, say, of catching a train or of buying an apple juice on your way through the station. Of course, you might orient yourself in the station in a completely different way if, for example, you're looking to peddle drugs there or, on the other side of the law, if you're a police officer trying to identify a drug dealer. And there's doubtless also some espionage being conducted at Cologne Central Station, but this is noticed by none but a very small number of people; for, in order to recognize such activity, you'd have to acquire concepts that spies and the secret service would, as their name suggests, rather keep secret.

Humans are not the only thinkers

Without thought, we wouldn't be able to orient ourselves within the infinite. It's thanks to your ability to think that you can comprehend what I've written here about Cologne Central Station. You've almost certainly imagined the scenes I've been sketching in some way or other, and you've done so by exercising your imagination, which is a component of your ability to think. Depicting something in imagination is a means of grasping a thought – that is, of thinking.

Thinking is not a privilege of human beings. After all, other living beings also have to orient themselves. They also have concepts at their disposal, which they deploy as signposts in thought. A pig, for example, thinks that it will be fed. When someone runs towards it wielding an axe, it thinks that danger is present. It most certainly thinks a whole host of further thoughts that we're pretty much clueless about, as human life and porcine life have to make use of quite different signposts. So just as pigs cannot even begin to suspect who Super Mario is, let alone why he increases in size whenever he collects a mushroom, we cannot have any inkling of the many vicissitudes of porcine life or of the concepts pigs deploy as they scuttle about in the fields of sense that matter to them but not to us and vice versa.

At this point it's important that we rid ourselves of a terrible prejudice inherited from the philosophy of the previous century. This prejudice is associated with the term 'the linguistic turn'. **The linguistic turn** is the transition from investigating the real to investigating our linguistic tools for investigating the real.

Now if that were all there was to it, the turn would be innocent enough and, as we shall see, could even lead to good philosophical practice. However, this turn traditionally goes together with the view that our thought is linguistically constituted through and through, such that we (supposedly) literally think differently when we speak a different language. In addition, this idea has occasionally been tied to the claim that, in any case, only humans can think, because only they possess a language in which to think. As far as our current actual evidence in linguistics, philosophy, biology, zoology, neuroscience, etc., goes, such a view is false from start to finish. For one thing, other animals also possess language, and it is simply wrong-headed to work on the assumption that thought is a prerogative of human beings. Such an assumption only recommends itself given a prior identification of a particular form of thought with thought as such. So far as we know, only humans engage in higher mathematics and form rational thoughts about, say, games such as chess. So far as I'm aware, no other animals can play chess, though I could be wrong. And, as a code for thought, language is indispensable in human life. In the form of oral and written communication, it stands at the origin of our **civilization** – that is, of the organization of human coexistence via explicitly formulated rules transmitted in linguistic codes.

In order to avoid the pitfalls of the linguistic turn, we should distinguish between concepts and words. **Words** are counters or tokens in a natural language such as German, Hindi, Arabic, and so on. 'Word' is a word, as is 'ouch' and 'and'. In actual fact, the business of precisely distinguishing and classifying the words of a language as individual lexical units is no simple matter; that's why the science of linguistics is still trying to do just this both for various particular languages and for language universally. Linguistics is concerned with linguistic structural formation. Using scientific modelling, it divides linguistic behaviour into units and establishes the specific rules that govern them. This throws up the difficulty that the actual linguistic behaviour of, say, all the Chinese who speak Mandarin is ultimately impossible to survey. Nevertheless, one can identify certain structures without which meaningful communication between speakers of Chinese just wouldn't be possible. Meaningful communication presupposes that speakers can recognize one another's behaviour as conforming to certain rules, rules of which they need not have any explicit grasp. Professional linguists therefore try to discern rules in linguistic behaviour, so that they can distinguish such units as phonemes, words, sentences, texts, and so on.

Unlike a word, a concept is not a counter in a natural language. The concept I have of a platform is exactly the same concept that the Italians have of a *binario*. The words 'platform' and 'binario', that is, have the same meaning. Their meaning is the concept of a platform, which puts various different platforms on a par and distinguishes them from other objects within relevant fields of sense that aren't platforms.

Of course, it's common enough that the meanings of words in different languages overlap only partially, and it's this phenomenon that has led some to think that we think differently in different languages. But it would be more accurate to say that we do not so much *think differently* in different languages as that we *think something different*.

The same goes for sentences within a single language. There's no need here to indulge in wild speculations about the (supposed) otherness of Far Eastern vis-à-vis European thought, for example. As the American philosopher Willard Van Orman Quine (1908–2000) quite rightly insisted, the problem of radical translation – that is, the translation of a language yet to be interpreted by our linguists – begins at home.[4] Even in cases in which we do understand another's language, it's common enough for us to find, when we attempt to work out what they think, that they're not on the same wavelength as us, that what they understand by their words is deeply alien to us, perhaps even incomprehensible.

We therefore need to take stock of the idea that thinking is not the same thing as silently, 'mentally', speaking to oneself. Thinking as the grasping of thoughts is conceptually, not linguistically, coded. We can translate what we think into language, but this does not mean getting a superior or more precise grasp on it. A painting can be the expression of a thought with just as much right as a sentence, as a painting presents something as something – even where this is a colour scheme within a piece of abstract expressionism. When we try to envision a scene, we often think in images. The pictures in which we think can express thoughts (something that can be true or false) just as much as sentences can.

There is of course a feedback loop between conceptual thought and its linguistic expression. When we express determinate thoughts linguistically, we often learn something about what we really think. Yet the code in which we think is not any natural language. A sentence of a natural language is true or false only if it's understood as the expression of a thought. Without an act of understanding that for its part is not linguistically coded, a sentence would be no more true or false than a dab of paint on a canvas. A sentence or a painting expresses thoughts only when there's someone to think thoughts that aren't sentence-like or imagistic in turn.

The scope of the universe

In all likelihood, someone convinced of the merits of a radical version of postmodernism or the linguistic turn, or otherwise infected by doubts about our capacity to know language-independent reality, will either have stopped reading by now or be demanding to hear how I can possibly know all these things I've been claiming to know so far. 'Who knows', they might well ask, 'how pigs think or whether they even think at all?' 'And furthermore', my critic will continue, 'how on Earth has Markus Gabriel made all these discoveries about the infinite complexity of reality? Aren't all these claims simply far too ambitious?'

To address this problem, I'd like to dig a little deeper. For how do we in fact know that there is an independent reality beyond our consciousness? Couldn't our entire life just be a long dream? Or perhaps a radical illusion but where, unlike in a dream or in *The Matrix*, there isn't even an external world?

These questions are the domain of the philosophical subdiscipline called epistemology: **epistemology** primarily addresses the question of what (human) knowledge is and how far it extends. What can we know and how can we justify knowledge claims?

But you don't need to be a professional philosopher to pose epistemological questions. In our digital age, we are all familiar with the increasing difficulty involved in distinguishing reality from fakes, fact from fiction. When it comes to social and political questions, there is the additional issue that we see things mostly through the lenses of our values and prejudices and judge accordingly. We are biased social animals who are often deluded about our own situation. In this respect, we seem to be trapped within the cage of our opinions and unable to grasp objective reality.

In the digital age, we find ourselves bombarded with information without independent authorities telling us where it all comes from and which sources are even reliable. Given the speed at which both genuine and fake news is disseminated and the ease with which we can access an extraordinary amount of information at the click of a mouse, we're at risk of finding the ground slipping beneath our feet. Our present lifeworld, influenced by the infosphere, can easily generate the impression that we inhabit a gigantic meshwork of illusions which nobody can really see through any more.

But this impression is misleading. In truth, things are the other way around: the digital age is an epoch of rapid increases in our knowledge and of multiple replications and reproductions of reality. What is new is not that reality is hidden behind screens and communication media, but that we're now in a position to create new realities and alter old ones by using various media to intervene in the universe. We haven't so much lost our means of establishing contact with reality as made them endlessly more complex. There has, so to speak, never been so much reality, knowledge, facticity and objectivity in human life as there is today. We live in a knowledge society which is so busy spreading the fake news that we can no longer distinguish between fakery and reality.

At this point, I want to draw attention to a widespread error called 'empiricism'. **Empiricism** is the thesis that everything we can ever know about reality boils down to an interpretation of data delivered to us by our senses. In this context, a *sense* is understood as a system that receives stimuli from the world and transforms them in such a way that we can never directly grasp the stimulus itself, but only ever an interpretation of it.

One of many people to have noticed the problem with this conception is the Oxford physicist David Deutsch (b. 1953). In his book *The Beginning of Infinity*, he rightly classifies empiricism as a fundamental error, a misguided philosophy, which is not only false but even impedes scientific progress.[5] He believes that modern physics – as an important expert in the field, he singles out quantum theory in particular – explores the infinite reaches of the cosmos without having to restrict itself to gathering observational data and transforming it into a theory. According to Deutsch, the basis of our knowledge in physics is the reality of abstractions and not inference to the best explanation based on sense perception.[6] Borrowing from the physicist and computer scientist

Douglas Richard Hofstadter (b. 1945), he develops a pioneering argument for this claim. Imagine we wanted to set up a chain of dominos. Each domino is wired to a surface in such a way that we can either make it stand up again if it falls over or fix it so it cannot be knocked over. Now suppose that the wires are controlled by a piece of software that solves simple mathematical puzzles such as the addition of whole numbers. The way it then works is that if you want to calculate 2 + 2, for example, first two and then another two dominos fall over. The fifth domino remains standing. When a domino remains upright, this signals that the calculation has come to an end. You can then count up the fallen dominos, which gives the result of the function $x + y = z$ for any given values that one can calculate using the domino system. Obviously, it's easier to use a pocket calculator, but let's stick with the example.

The point is that someone who sees just the dominos could ask why the fifth one is still standing. He could take a look at the wiring and figure out why it stays upright. But no explanation of the physical processes by themselves would be superior to the explanation that the fifth domino is still standing because 2 + 2 = 4 and that the software of our little set-up has thus calculated correctly. This is why the fifth domino differs from the sixth or seventh. From a physical point of view, they are all still standing because the wire holds them in place. But there is a significant difference between the fifth domino and all the others: it is the first in the series of still-upright dominos. And it's obviously this difference that allows us to use the domino system as a rather poor but, nevertheless, functional calculator.

With the help of this example, Deutsch wants to show that physics is not a reductionist theory; that is, it is not a theory that reduces all events to material-energetic structures. In this context, we can understand **reductionism** as the assumption that physics strives to trace all events and structures of the universe back to a fundamental level – for example, to the distribution of elementary particles at the lowest-level microphysical scale of the universe. In its crudest variant, reductionism boils down to the materialist assertion that all events and structures in the universe are nothing other than tiny material-energetic configurations.

The fundamental laws of arithmetic are not themselves material-energetic objects; they are abstract structures. The number 2, for example, doesn't have any particular location and didn't come into being at any particular point in time. If we have the ability to know about mathematical objects such as numbers, geometrical figures, multidimensional spaces and infinite sets, empiricism must be on the wrong track when it says that our cognition as a whole is grounded in the way we receive and interpret stimuli from the universe. For abstract structures don't always arise through our activity of interpreting sensory evidence; rather, they show us, in many instances at least, what is really the case, which is why we can formulate laws of physics in the form of equations. Indeed, the reality of abstract structures, together with innovations in the technological instruments deployed in experiments, are important elements in the ever surprising and game-changing project of modern science.

On the basis of this line of thought, Deutsch draws the conclusion that our capacity to pursue mathematics puts us in contact with the infinite. What is more, he maintains that this contact is not itself sensory. It's not a matter of our instantiating stimulus–response schemas, as we do in our perception of external environmental stimuli such as colours or sounds. To arrive at mathematical insights, we don't need to interpret data gathered via our sense organs. Rather, without our independently justified grasp of abstract structures, we could not even gather any kind of data to begin with and recognize them as evidence for our theories. In short, Deutsch disputes the truth of empiricism and argues that we understand quantum theory correctly only once we acknowledge that it 'is a claim that something abstract – something non-physical, such as the knowledge in a gene or a theory – is affecting something physical.'[7] Just as we've seen with the fifth domino.

According to Deutsch, **the universe**, the object domain of physics, is reducible neither to tiny component parts nor to the cosmos, the largest structure that encompasses all the others. He therefore thinks physics gives us reasons for holding both reductionism and holism to be false. **Holism** (from the Greek *to holon* = the whole) traces all of the events and structures of the universe back to its maximal overall cosmological structure. Reductionism, by contrast, tends to want to explain all complex structures in terms of the interaction of simpler ones – in the ideal reductionist theory, this will boil down to an explanation of the smallest building blocks of the universe (which, to be sure, we are yet to discover).

Neither reductionism nor holism can be derived from current physics by purely scientific means. We know neither whether there is anything like objectively the smallest building blocks of matter, nor whether the observable universe is the largest physical whole. Regardless of how far physical research progresses, it can never exclude the possibility that there are other universes connected to our own in ways we cannot discover; or that there are yet smaller building blocks that compose the units we currently take to be the smallest. Moreover, there is much that speaks in favour of an interpretation of quantum theory according to which there are in fact many universes besides our own, and this is in any event incompatible with empiricism.

Natural science generally is departing from classical empiricism. This is largely thanks to the increasing exploration of the effects of complexity, which is advancing through the use of computer simulations that can study complex systems with a previously unattainable scientific precision. The modern scientific worldview is itself changing at a rapid pace in the light of the continual breakthroughs whose effects have become familiar features of our everyday lives in the wake of the digital revolution. Technological progress has been accelerating since the discovery of quantum theory, which joins with logic and computer science to make a formidable team. Indeed, it forms the basis of our modern scientific and technological civilization. Empiricism, in short, is thus a terribly antiquated outlook for our advanced knowledge and information society.

Unfortunately, many contemporary philosophically minded scientists like Deutsch are still not totally free of another prejudice. This prejudice places thinking and our senses on either side of a fundamental divide and so fails to revise the equally outdated opposition of sense and thought which this book is designed to overcome. I therefore want to disable both stubborn prejudices in one go and reject the idea that thinking is a matter of processing data given to the senses by rejecting the very idea of a difference between sensing and thinking. We need to go further than just moving beyond outdated empiricism: we also need to develop a new theory of knowledge and perception, which will allow us to understand thought itself as a sense. We can then test this hypothesis with all the tools that the natural and human sciences place at our disposal.

Aristotle's senses

It was Aristotle, the great-grandfather of most of our extant scientific disciplines, who developed the first theory of the senses. His work *On the Soul* has shaped our understanding of the human senses for more than two thousand years. In a highly influential passage, he (hesitatingly) concludes that we are equipped with five sense modalities: sight, hearing, smell, taste and touch.[8] By our present scientific standards, his grounds for this presumption are somewhat adventurous and consist of a series of falsified presuppositions. For example, he invokes considerations about the four elements – water, earth, fire and air – that we know to be false. Yet in spite of this rather questionable prehistory, which has long since been overtaken by modern neurobiology and physics, we still tend to speak of our five senses.

Thanks to modern sensory physiology we know that there are more sense modalities than those postulated by Aristotle. As a first approximation, we can say that a sense modality corresponds to one of our senses, such as sight for example. We can also understand as senses our sense of balance, our heat sensitivity, our proprioception (that is, our sense of our bodily position), and even our sense of time. It is our sense of time which gives us notice that it's time to go or time to wake up.

The individual modalities provide us with information which we experience as qualities: different sensory qualities for different sensory modalities. A single qualitative experience (the smell of the coffee on the fold-down table, the blue of the train seat in front of me) is called a **quale** (plural: **qualia**). Despite many recent discussions in philosophy and cognitive neuroscience, there is nothing mysterious about qualia. They just are the specific contents of a given sense modality, such as sounds, colours, shapes, smells and, as I shall argue, thoughts.

We experience a difference between red and green, between different shades and pitches, but we also experience how our position changes in space. Think of how we tend to believe that we suddenly glance upwards when a plane takes off even though nothing has altered in our line of sight. We look straight ahead, but it feels as if we were looking upwards, because of an interference effect of our sense of our body's spatial position on the sense of sight. We sense with different sense modalities that the plane is taking off or landing. The way in which our sense modalities influence one another is known as **cognitive penetration**. In particular, it seems that what we learn about reality changes our sensory experiences, our qualia. The very same wine tastes different to the wine connoisseur than it does to the layperson, and the same symphony sounds different to the expert musicologist than it does to someone unfamiliar with the relevant context, or to someone who's hearing the symphony for the first time and stumbles across unfamiliar sound sequences.

Aristotle made the very first attempt to distinguish our sense organs via an analysis of sensory modalities and qualities and to locate the various differences between them in our biological constitution. Being a radical pioneer in this enterprise, he of course knew much less than we do today, and his hypotheses were often pretty wide of the mark. Yet we still owe him some highly valuable insights. Indeed, even if we should definitely give up the false idea that there are only five senses, not everything Aristotle has to say about the soul should be confined to the past.

Common sense made sensible

There is an array of standard (and fully justified) criticisms of the empirical details of Aristotle's sensory physiology. Yet what tends to be overlooked is his somewhat obscure but visionary doctrine of common sense. We still talk today of plain and healthy common sense, which corresponds to the Latin expression *sensus communis* and to *aisthêsis koinê* in Aristotle's Greek, which is the origin of our phrase 'common sense'. The Italians speak of *il buon senso*, the French of *bon sens* and the Germans of *Gemeinsinn*. As we use such terms today, they designate something like broadly shared, appropriate beliefs, although it's not really clear how we're meant to ascertain what constitutes common sense. Aristotle himself, however, associated 'common sense' with a quite different idea.

To be sure, in the famous section in which he names the five senses, Aristotle does not unequivocally commit himself one way or the other on the question of whether there is in fact a common sense. Rather, he says that, in the light of his account, one would, at least to begin with, be entitled to work on the assumption that there are five senses. He then raises the objection that there would have to be a further sense modality, which he connects with the 'common' sense, thereby hitting upon a problem that has in no way been solved by contemporary physiology, the so-called **binding problem**. This problem arises from the fact that we do not just perceive isolated qualities but enjoy experiences that form (or at least seem to form) a coherent unity. Our conscious experience is a more or less unified impression with a certain temporal resolution. I am, for example, currently confronted with a train scene, and not with a jumble of sense-data. Things seem different under the influence of drugs; hallucinogens, for example, make our qualia blend into one another in a synesthetic blur. But, even in this case, a more or less stable scene remains in place; it just differs from the structure of my experiential field when not on hallucinogenic drugs.

In this context, another leading theorist of the structure of our minds and conscious experience even goes so far as to understand our consciousness as the very structure of cognitive penetration. In his famous *Critique of Pure Reason*, Immanuel Kant gives the following account:

> There is only one experience, in which all perceptions are represented as in thoroughgoing and lawlike connection, just as there is only one space and time, in which all forms of appearance and all relation of being or non-being take place. If one speaks of different experiences, they are only so many perceptions insofar as they belong to one and the same universal experience. The thoroughgoing and synthetic unity of perceptions is precisely what constitutes the form of experience, and it is nothing other than the synthetic unity of the appearances in accordance with concepts.
>
> Unity of synthesis in accordance with empirical concepts would be entirely contingent, and, were it not grounded on a transcendental ground of unity, it would be possible for a swarm of appearances to fill up our soul without experience ever being able to arise from it. But in that case all relation of cognition to objects would also disappear, since the appearances would lack connection in accordance with universal and necessary laws, and would thus be intuition without thought, but never cognition, and would therefore be as good as nothing for us.[9]

Kant is right that we experience not a sensory turmoil but scenes. A colleague at Bonn, Wolfgang Hogrebe (b. 1945), therefore speaks of 'the scenic existence of human beings'.[10] Because of our perception, we have the impression of standing in contact with a reality containing red chairs, trains, tables, and much more. Such experiences would not be possible without our various qualia forming an interconnected nexus. This nexus is processed scenically, we might say; that is, we expect distinctive plots, narratives and patterns of action, which allow us to experience a sequence of events as a typical scene. Without exercises of the imagination based on memory, repeated confrontation with similar scenes, etc., we would be frozen in a continual state of shock. As conscious animals, we generate an everyday world that leads us to believe that reality is much simpler than it really is. For, in reality, the individual scenes of our lives are fields of sense integrated into infinitely many further fields of sense. In reality, there is no *real* beginning of everything and no *real* end – the infinite awaits us in all dimensions.

Kant formulates his version of the binding problem on an Aristotelian basis. Aristotle talks about how our thinking as a whole is a combination of various impressions. The Greek for combination is syn-thesis (from *syn* = together and *tithenai* = to place/

put). Just like Aristotle, Kant understands thinking as a combination of concepts – that is, as *syn-thesis*.

The contemporary, neurobiological version of the binding problem arises from the fact that physiology has yet to explain how the different sense modalities are bound together neuronally, be it *intra-modally* (e.g. for various shades of red) or *inter-modally* (e.g. for the connection of tactile and colour perception). When it comes to the physiological framing of the issue, we haven't come substantially further than Aristotle, which is why many theorists simply jump to the conclusion that there might be no such thing as the unity of consciousness by dissociating consciousness and self. In my view, this is not very helpful, as it ignores the important fact that we always experience any given scene from a point of view, which *is* the self.

Still more surprising is that Aristotle managed to formulate a further pioneering insight, which we would do well to take up today. This is his actual argument for assuming a common sense. It begins by pointing out that we also 'perceive that we see and hear'.[11] At the present moment, I not only perceive the lid of my water bottle, but – as this very sentence attests – I am also conscious that I perceive the lid of my water bottle. And as I write this paragraph after returning from Paris, I recall my impression of the wine-red seats on the train home.

In having such awareness, I possess a higher-order attitude, which Aristotle characterized as perception of perception. A current term for this is **metacognition**, the traditional philosophical term being **self-consciousness**, i.e. consciousness of consciousness. We can call consciousness of something in our environment or in our organism **object-level** consciousness. By contrast, consciousness of this consciousness, i.e. self-consciousness, is **higher-order**.[12]

So far, so good. Now, if we had only the five senses listed by Aristotle, we would have to be able to grasp our sight, for example, by means of another sense. Yet none of the other standard senses does this. Our sight itself has neither a colour nor a smell. Nor can we touch it. But how come we know that we have sense modalities in the first place? This cannot be settled by a given sense modality or by any combination of the five senses alone (another failure of empiricism).

Aristotle's suggestion, therefore, is that we have a common sense, which he links to thought (*noein*) and imagination (*phantasia*).[13] His decisive thought is that perception is able to become conscious of itself, to perceive itself, because it has an inherent objective structure, a *logos*, as one says in Greek. 'The perceptual capacity is a ratio [*logos*].'[14] In characterizing thinking as common sense here, Aristotle has in mind the capacity for having an insight into the structure – into the *logos* – of perception. Yet he shies away from adding thought and imagination to his list of sense modalities. And this was arguably a mistake.

The meaning of 'sense', or: the many ways of being wrong

Insofar as our sense organs are part of the very nature we perceive, it would be misleading to say that perception merely takes in information: perception *is* itself information. Perception is part of reality; it belongs to the very domain to which it relates. This is because perception has an internal structure and reveals differences, such as the difference between red and blue, or sweet and sour. When we perceive something, we do not peer into a sensory reality from which we're shut out. We do not look into reality from without or briefly listen in on the universe. That is, perception is not a way of gradually grasping our way towards an alien, external world; rather, thanks to perception, we are already in touch with the real. This is what Hubert Dreyfus (1929–2017) and Charles Taylor (b. 1931), in their book *Retrieving Realism*, labelled a **contact theory**. They too echo Aristotle, who connected the sense of touch, the haptic, with thought. We continually touch the real; we are in con-tact with it (from the Latin *con* = with, and *tangere* = to touch).[15] There is no way out of reality – in any event, perception is not an act of transcending the world.

This simple, but often ignored idea runs counter to the widespread habit of opposing sense and cognition (the inheritance of the classical antithesis of perception and thought) from the outset. Unfortunately, it has become standard practice to distinguish internal thought processes (cognitions) from perceptions triggered by distal stimuli – that is, by the influence of the reality external to our organism. But this distinction is ontologically flawed. To be sure, perception is sometimes also understood as a form of cognition, where 'cognition' is used in the most general sense to designate any kind of information processing. Yet the contact theory suggested by Aristotle has a quite different take on the theoretical landscape: it conceives our thought as a form of perception rather than our perception as a form of thought. Perception is the genus and our thought one of its species.

But what do we really mean by 'perception', or by a modality of perception, a 'sense'? Let's define a **sense modality** as a *fallible* *mode of establishing contact with objects, which can recognize objects across gaps in conscious awareness.* This somewhat formulaic definition can be easily understood with reference to our sense of sight: I can still see a red bottle cap on a water bottle. But if you want a more interesting example, simply imagine something that you'd very much *like* to see right now (I'm sure you have a few ideas). I'll do so too. In the meantime, I'd quite forgotten about the bottle cap, even though the bottle remains standing there, right by my computer, and is hard to overlook. I thus re-cognise the cap. But perhaps my colleague Jens, who works in the office next door, switched the bottle when I wasn't looking. If so, I was in error just now when I believed I was once again looking at the same old red bottle cap.

The fact that I can be deceived has as a concomitant that I can also not be deceived. This leads us to the philosophical concept of objectivity. **Objectivity** is that feature of an attitude which means we can get things right or wrong, be correct or incorrect. Bear in mind what objectivity does *not* mean: it does not mean taking up a view from nowhere and grasping reality from a fully neutral standpoint. On the contrary, the essence of objectivity is that it is correlated with subjectivity. **Subjectivity** consists in the way in which we can be deceived and go wrong. When and how I go wrong says something about me. Without subjectivity, there is no objectivity – and vice versa. Since objectivity and susceptibility to error hang together, there is no a-subjective objectivity.

This is by no means to say that we don't know things as they are in themselves. Perception is objective. The notion that we are prisoners of our mind or brains vatted in our skulls, forever at a distance from things in themselves, is simply one of the misguided epistemological concoctions of the (generally misguided) scientific worldview. I currently see my fingers – from a certain angle. And, supposing I do, I can know thanks to my perception that I have fingers. I could also be deceived. This is certainly hard to imagine, but perhaps I'm dreaming right now. Supposing I'd lost my fingers, my dreaming of having fingers right now could be a piece of wish fulfilment (whatever psychoanalytic meaning might lie behind this).

Objectivity does not mean putting one's subjectivity to one side and judging things with the utmost possible neutrality. Rather, we traffic in the objective whenever we possess a faculty – a sense, for example – that can either hit or miss its objects. Our perception is therefore unequivocally objective. But it is just as subjective too, insofar as I, as a complex organism embedded in my surroundings, participate in the perceptual process. Given my biological constitution, I contribute information to the natural environment, which is why you can also see me when you meet me, or hear me when you give me a call. A further aspect of my personal contribution to the environment is that I interact with fields that, in the form of radiation, can be subjected to physical investigation. As an organism, I am physically embedded in causal interactions without which I couldn't establish any contact whatsoever with material-energetic objects such as my red bottle cap. This is why we cannot reduce perception solely to a physical interaction between my nerve endings and the water bottle without leaving subjectivity unexplained.

Many are still seduced by the false belief that our perception is not objective, because they conflate the concept of objectivity with an unattainable chimera. This chimera corresponds to the idea of a **view from nowhere**, an idea which the American philosopher Thomas Nagel (b. 1937) has skilfully refuted.[16] As we've seen, objectivity does not consist in somehow looking in on reality from outside – in any case, this is also physically impossible, as perception is in part (though not exclusively!) an informational, causally effective exchange between environment and organism that can be investigated by physics. Of course, perception is also subjective in respects that are highly individual and autobiographical. The ways in which I can deceive and be deceived reveals something about me – and the same goes for you too. And yet we perceive the same reality (only differently).

The loneliness of cosmic exile

Nagel's critique of the view from nowhere is frequently misunderstood. That there is no view from nowhere, no absolute, standpoint-free objectivity, does not mean that we cannot know reality as it really is in itself. Nagel did not mean that we can never escape from our mental prison, with the paradoxical consequence that we cannot grasp any pure facts (after all, this would itself be a pure, objective fact grasped by Nagel). He merely pointed out that objectivity means that our mental capacities put us in a position where we can either grasp or fall short of reality. But we can only ever do so from a given standpoint. The great American philosopher Willard van Orman Quine expressed this very thought when, at the end of his important book *Word and Object*, he wrote that 'there is no such cosmic exile.'[17]

Yet humanity still clings on to the illusion of just such a cosmic exile. The theme of aliens with perceptual and technological prowess far surpassing our own is central to contemporary science fiction, and we will see in due course how AI is another such fantasy of a cosmic exile, of an ultimately alien form of intelligence. Even God is misused by religious fundamentalists as representing a kind of cosmic exile, insofar they conceive him as an aperspectival, absolute observer, whose thoughts are forever beyond the reach of our poor earthbound reason. We've already seen the shortcomings of this idea (see p. 17).

The bestselling *Trisolaris* trilogy by the Chinese science fiction writer Liu Cixin (b. 1963) depicts our captivation by the spectre of cosmic exile with a dark and sinister accuracy.[18] Liu describes a scenario in which humanity contacts an advanced extra-terrestrial civilization at the time of Mao's cultural revolution. On the hunt for alien life, a Chinese research team receives a message from an extra-terrestrial whistle-blower, warning them that, unless they cease their research activities immediately, the distant civilization will journey to Earth and destroy it in three hundred years' time. The humans unfortunately fail to heed the warning of the well-meaning messenger and provoke an expedition of extra-terrestrials towards Earth. In the meantime, struggles break out between competing parties: while some humans want to form a resistance movement, others celebrate the impending end of humanity and worship the extra-terrestrials like gods.

One of the many interesting details of this prize-winning masterpiece of contemporary science fiction literature is that the aliens aren't able to lie. Guided solely by the facts, and with a wholly neutral intelligence, they devote themselves exclusively to the technological optimization of their own species and its survival. This accounts not only for their strengths but also for their weaknesses, which the resistance fighters seek to exploit. But it's worth noting that it also gives us a vivid representation of a misconceived conception of objectivity.

After this brief cosmological diversion, let us return to the concept of sense. The idea I want to press is that a mental faculty is objective if it enables us to grasp or fall short of an object. Our objectivity is not a matter of refraining from making evaluative claims or from adopting any particular perspective; rather, it consists in how the very way in which we can know reality as it is in itself also contains the possibility of failing to grasp it.

Epistemology studies perception because it is such a rich source of knowledge.[19] In the terms of contemporary epistemology, perception, unlike an error, constitutes a case of success. This is because of the **factivity** of perception: from the fact that someone perceives something it follows that things are as the person perceives them to be. If I see a red bottle cap in front of me, it follows that a red bottle cap is in front of me; when I hear my daughter calling for me because she's woken from a bad dream, it follows that my daughter is calling for me. The lesson, in a nutshell, is as follows: objectivity and factivity belong together. Wherever we're in a position to know how things really are, we can also be deceived.

Not all objects are things

When people talk about sensory physiology, we usually think about specific kinds of objects that we grasp through our senses – that is, that we perceive. Let's call these objects things. A **thing** is a meso- or macroscopic spatiotemporally extended object. Things are those objects with which we make contact through our nerve endings. These objects are the cause of our perceiving them.

At this point, we cannot avoid considering the popular, albeit inadequate, **causal theory of perception**. According to this theory, the external world, the world located outside of our consciousness or of the surface of our bodies, contains things that stimulate our sense organs. These sensory stimulations are processed internally within the organism and formed into impressions via information processing in the brain.

Within the logic of this theory there is no room for common sense. It must therefore assume that the way our thinking functions is by taking hold of the information we receive from outside via causal connections and subjecting it to further processing. But this means splitting off perception from thought (cognition) in a highly problematic way. And it is this error which, for all that it conceals a kernel of truth, condemns the causal theory to failure. Yet the causal theory, in one form or another, represents the ideological foundation of our contemporary sensory physiology.

Let's return to the red bottle cap. It is quite correct that I could not perceive that thing standing on the table in front of me were it not the cause of my perceiving it. We need only consider that, if someone put something else in the place of the bottle, I'd perceive that instead. If I switch the bottle for my green coffee cup, then the latter will be the cause of my seeing it rather than the red cap. This means: no red cap, no perception of a red cap, and no green coffee cup, no perception of the green coffee cup.

The red cap, of course, is not sufficient all by itself for me to see a red cap. I need to open my eyes and direct them at the object.

And, further, I wouldn't see the red cap if I had no concept of a red cap. For my perception of the red cap is conscious, indeed self-conscious, perception. At this very moment, I know that there is a red cap in front of me, which is the cause of my seeing it. If another creature, who had no concept of red caps (and who was perhaps unable to perceive any colours within the red spectrum), were now placed in front of the bottle, it would also perceive what, using the expressive resources of my language, I would describe as the red cap. But perhaps their perception would be qualitatively different from mine, in ways that cannot be captured in my language, just as the way I perceive the object cannot be captured in theirs.

We need to formulate this thought with the utmost care, else we're just out of the frying pan and into the fire. We most definitely want to steer clear of the idea that we impose our concepts of red bottle caps and green coffee cups onto the reality that we perceive. That would get us into deep trouble.

It is important to distinguish between things and objects. Things, as we've seen, are something like palpable items, items which we can consciously identify as spatiotemporal realities such as tables or pineapples or the moon. Our experience has one of its main sources of nourishment in the sense modality that allows us to see things. But if we overrate the sense of sight, we run the risk of confusing reality with a pure thing-world, in which all the various kinds of item that fill the inventory of reality literally stand around waiting to be seen or bumped into.

In a seminar that I ran in Bonn in 2017–18 together with the American-Portuguese philosopher Charles Travis (b. 1943), one of the most significant contemporary theorists of perception, he help-fully referred to things as 'obstacles to free passage'. Travis points out that things in this sense do not give us the paradigm of reality. Not everything real is an obstacle – just think of the invisible radia-tion that surrounds us, which is hardly a thing in this sense.

The distinguishing feature of **objects**, unlike things, is that we can formulate truth-apt thoughts about them. A thought is **truth-apt** if it can be true or false. Following Ludwig Wittgenstein (1889–1951), we can also distinguish between meaningful and senseless thoughts. **Meaningful** (sense-bearing/informative) thoughts are those that are neither necessarily true nor necessarily false. The **senseless** ones, by contrast, are those that are necessarily true, so-called **tautologies** (such as: a cat is a cat), or thoughts that are necessarily false, so-called **contradictions** (such as: this cat is not a cat). If a thought is truth-apt, it is about something. What a mean-ingful thought is about is its object; the *way* in which it's about what it's about is its content (see p. 18). Thus, we can replace the idea that reality consists of objects, obstacles to free passage, and more ethereal things by the more neutral notion that objects are the kinds of things we can think about.

Since we can think about a great deal that is not any kind of obstacle, our thought stretches far beyond the horizon of the straightforwardly material world. We can think about numbers, pains and justice, but also about elementary particles or dark matter. And, likewise, we can think about future events which are yet to take place in the universe. Simply put, our thought stretches far beyond the material-energetic universe. In fact, from the perspective of thought, that universe is remarkably tiny (just compare it, for example, with the infinite dimensions of mathematical reality).

Are there (really) any red bottle caps?

An object is lying right before my eyes. I perceive it. If you ask me what it is, I can offer you a description or specification of the object. This description selects from everything I can consciously perceive at a certain location. In order to make this selection, I need to have various concepts at my disposal. For example, I possess the concept of a red bottle cap. Hence, I can consciously perceive red bottle caps and am not restricted to perceiving something round and red, without recognizing it as a cap. The selection of descriptions and specifications I can offer you depends upon which concepts I possess. Yet, this doesn't mean that I *construct* the red cap by means of my concepts or that I *project* a red cap into the external world. I did not somehow make it up or conjure it out of some strange material forever inaccessible to my consciousness.

Allow me to repeat the mantra of New Realism: constructivism is false.[20] **New Realism** asserts that we can know reality as it is, without this meaning that there is exactly one world or reality that encompasses all existing objects or facts. This means that realism is opposed especially to constructivism. For realists generally subscribe to the view that we *discover* reality and do not *produce* it through our attempts to cognise it, whereas constructivists believe that we construct the real, so that we can never grasp it as it is in itself. They instead believe that we grasp reality through a medium or media that somehow always distort it.

In the case we're concerned with here, **modest perceptual constructivism** teaches that our concepts alter our perception. I currently perceive a red cap thanks to my possession of the concept of a red cap – else I'd have perceived something else. **Radical perceptual constructivism** goes still further and maintains that the concepts we have at our disposal not only alter our perceptions, but affect the things themselves. Where I currently see a red cap, there is really, according to the radical constructivist, neither a cap nor even something round and something red.

Radical perceptual constructivism comes in two varieties. On the one hand, there is **radical scientific constructivism**. This says that there aren't *really* colours and geometrical forms; all there really is is what physics tells us about the objects of the external world. According to this view, there are not really different shades of red, only a spectrum of wavelengths which appear to us as red. More precisely, we're meant to believe that what in reality is a spectrum of wavelengths is experienced as red by us humans in virtue of our particular physiological endowment. But reality itself does not correspond to our colour impressions; considered from the point of view of physics, a surface that we experience as uniformly red can be a mixture of different processes, whose distribution is anything but apparent to the naked eye.

On the other hand, there is **hyper-radical constructivism**. This variant goes the whole hog, arguing that reality itself is not as described either by physics or by the natural sciences as an ensemble, because these disciplines too are merely a construction of the human mind or brain, or – as one sometimes reads – of a certain social system (viz. science).[21] The only virtue of hyper-radical constructivism is its honesty, because it actually follows from the background assumptions of scientific radical constructivism that we need to go all the way – a fact which is usually covered up or simply missed by the scientists who propose these kinds of views, as it would (rightly!) undermine their epistemological credibility.

The problems that afflict constructivism in all its varieties ultimately spring from the same source. But this is easier to identify than to dislodge. At bottom, constructivism conflates *selection* with *construction*. Of course, at any given point in time I can perceive something only via the exclusion of something else. What I can perceive allows of conceptual representation, which we humans can codify in the form of language. I can communicate to you in writing, for example, what I can currently see and hear (the noise of the street, whistling pedestrians, a helicopter overhead, the passing tram, an approaching car, the late summer whirring of my fan, and so on). I can do this because I know how to communicate such concepts in English, German and a few other languages.

Presumably, Goethe could do a better job of communicating what he perceived (at least in German, Latin, French and certain of the other languages that he had mastered to an impressive degree) because he had a much more finely attuned linguistic sensitivity to the concepts he possessed – though he would need to acquire those of a car and an electric fan, something he could likely achieve without too much difficulty.

We can therefore distinguish (false) constructivism from (true) selectionism. **Perceptual selectionism** is the view that, thanks to our acquired conceptual capacities and other modes of registration (which include our sensory and physiological endowment as higher primates), we can only ever perceive some things at the expense of others.

Given both our biological endowment and our general socio-historical situation, certain aspects of reality are accessible to us that remain hidden from non-human creatures and certain other humans. This does not mean that we falsify or distort reality via our concepts and modes of registration. On the contrary: it means that we grasp reality as it is, only partially.

Thinking is not an irritation of the nervous system

There's still a way to travel before we get to the sense of thought. We need to navigate our way around the prejudice that all we can perceive are those things that stimulate our nerve endings. Yet our thought does not consist merely of irritations of the nervous system and their further processing by the brain.

It's vital to bear in mind that we mature members of the human race only rarely (if ever) take in simple objects. It's not as though we take in only red caps, edges, or other forms and movements that could be processed just as well by some facial recognition software. Our actual perception does not resemble the highly simplified models we know from sensory physiology, which admit of scientific and psychological investigation. The way in which we perceive reality differs in kind from the modes of registration of video cameras and other modern technological artefacts of human industry.

Another simple example should suffice here. I currently perceive a tram. While writing the previous sentence, I could only hear the tram approaching, but I've now moved over to the window so that I can see it too and thus confirm that I haven't written anything false. There is of course no simple geometrical form of a tram. They look different in different cities. Moreover, they're means of transport. Means of transport are objects subject to certain rules (such as road traffic regulations). I by no means perceive the traffic regulations in exactly the same way in which I see the corners and edges of my computer screen, or as a new-born child perceives a friendly face, namely by means of simplified patterns and models. We can simulate a smile to small children by drawing a moon face on a balloon, because they perceive their environment much more akin to the way we like to imagine we do when conducting simplified psychological experiments. At first, all they have at their disposal is a capacity for simple pattern recognition, something with which they're equipped thanks to the evolutionary prehistory of their species. New-born babies do not perceive any trams *as such*.

Here we have to take on board the basic insight of New Realism: there is not only one single reality – *the* world, *the* universe, *the* real – but infinitely many. This is why you can perceive a tram on the one hand and something else (edges, corners and colours, for example) on the other. There is no need either somehow to understand the tram in terms of the edges, corners and colours that we process visually or to reduce it to these. So we can also say that, where we perceive a tram, bats, say, perceive something quite different that has not the slightest to do with a tram.

This does not mean that, where I see a tram, there is either a tram or something else. Precisely because not all perceptions can be housed in a single reality, it's possible to allow for a host of realities, which are perceived by various creatures and by various individuals of the same species. When I walk around a foreign city, for example, I perceive things quite differently than do the locals.

This is something with which we're all familiar from the reality of taste. You have to learn (insofar as you care to do so) to distinguish different wines from one another. The difference between red and white is a first step, albeit one that won't get you very far. To become a sommelier takes years of experience and some considerable training. When we train up our senses, we learn to recognize something that was previously hidden. We're then able to concentrate on something to which we simply had no access previously. Each of our various senses, through training and their coordination with other senses, allows us direct access to the real.

I'm here putting forward a version of what's known as 'direct realism'. Generally speaking, **direct realism** means that our senses have direct access to reality. In other words, the thesis is that our senses are the way in which we have access to reality. Usually, they are not themselves what we have access to: we hear a voice, but we do not hear that we hear a voice. Our access to the real is usually undistorted but always has a particular form (a sense modality) through which the real appears to us. Many confuse the fact that we process reality in different media (different sense modalities) with the false idea that we distort it, and then go on to infer that we have no real access to how it really is.

In contemporary epistemology, direct realism is a standard view, although outside the circles of academic philosophy it tends to have the reputation of being naïve in the pejorative sense of the term. Yet direct and naïve realism are two very different animals. **Naïve realism** is the view that we simply take in reality as it is, without any mediation. This is 'naïve' in that it rejects any theoretical elaboration and refuses to have any truck with the manoeuvres that have led many to constructivism.

A naïve realist kicks a stone and, in order to support her realism, appeals to how the fact that it hurts means there must be a stone there. But such an appeal is insufficient. Ultimately, it's an empty assertion, as the constructivist doesn't want to dispute that we have stone-impressions. He merely asserts that reality is (or could be) entirely other that it seems to us when we think that there are stones and that kicking them causes us pain.

Like constructivism, realism too is a theory. Both theories share certain data – for example, that it hurts when we kick a stone – but explain these data differently. While naïve realism is an insufficiently grounded theory, constructivism is aware of its own status as a theory, but it's a theory that commits certain key errors. What we need, therefore, is a better theory – direct realism, for example.

Nothing but the truth

Every form of realism is a theoretical proposal – though, in my view, a far better one than constructivism. A variation on what the American philosopher Donald Davidson (1917–2003) called the 'principle of charity' gives us a compelling argument for its superiority.[22] This principle is often associated with Hans-Georg Gadamer's hermeneutics (from the Greek *hermeneia* = understanding), but this is rather too hasty. Gadamer (1900–2002) was interested in providing a theory for understanding cultural-historical productions (especially texts) and not in giving a theory of perception or of the interpretation of other people's articulations of their sensory states. We will meet Gadamer's hermeneutics again. For now, let us keep him separate from Davidson.

We can call the argument I have in mind the **truth argument**. Its starting point is the observation that we can use sentences to express what we take to be real. Let's call sentences with which we claim to establish what is actually the case **statements**. Statements are usually either true or false (setting the senseless ones aside for the moment). They are, in any case, something that fundamentally raises a question as to their truth. Here's a small selection of statements that most people almost certainly take to be true:

- There are human beings in China.
- Many Indian women have been to New Delhi.
- If someone has ten healthy fingers, they generally also have ten fingernails.
- There are many galaxies.
- Many people lived before I was born.
- Cats are animals.
- Donald Trump is (alas) the president of the United States of America.

It wouldn't be difficult to extend this list by adding infinitely many statements. Logically, this wouldn't be much of a feat to pull off: after all, to know that a disjunction is true you have only to know that one of its disjuncts is true. A **disjunction** is a statement of the form that something or something else is the case. If something is true, you can preserve the truth by adding some disjunct, regardless of whether or not what you add is true. The truth of a statement ensures the truth of the disjunction to which it belongs. From 'A', it follows that 'A or B'.

From a logical standpoint, if it's true that there are human beings in China, it's true that there are human beings in China or that Cologne Cathedral is made of sausages. So long as I take something to be true and recognize a few simple logical principles, I can then take an infinite number of statements to be true: from any minimal statement – from any that asserts that something is the case – infinitely many further statements follow that I also take to be true. If I take it to be true that there are human beings in China, I should not, of course, infer from this that Cologne Cathedral is made of sausages, but merely that the former does not exclude the latter.

There's obviously nothing spectacular about this. But it's important to bear it in mind when pondering the significant philosophical question of whether we humans can enjoy knowledge of reality. For given how it requires little effort to see that we can know infinitely many things, we should conclude that we can know reality.

Given how we demonstrably know infinitely many things, we must in fact be rather good at knowing reality.

The truth of statements ultimately consists in nothing more than a connection between statements and what they're about. Let's call that which statements are about, when what they are about is not itself a statement, **object-level reality** (notice that this statement, which states something about object-level reality and statements about it, is not itself part of object-level reality). The statements in my short list above (see p. 42) all concern object-level reality. If the statements are true, then things are as they say they are. Otherwise the statements are false.

This is the view that Aristotle expresses in the very first definition of truth in Western philosophy. **Aristotle's definition of truth** reads as follows:

> For to say of what is that it is not, or of what is not that it is, is false, whereas to say of what is that it is, or of what is not that it is not, is true. So he who says of anything that it is, or that it is not, will say either what is true or what is false.[23]

In the landscape of contemporary theories of truth, this definition usually goes by the name of minimalism. **Minimalism** is the view that a few easily comprehensible principles hold good for truth and establish what propositional truth consists in. In particular, what is known as the 'disquotational principle' (DQ) holds for truth. For decades now, philosophy students have learnt this principle in connection with the slogan:

> The statement 'snow is white' is true if and only if snow is white.

Given a more general formulation:

> (DQ) 'p' is true if and only if p.

This means that a statement with the content 'p' (a placeholder for every statement that can be true or false) is true if things are as it states. The statement 'people live in China' is true if people live in China. Otherwise, it would be false. Moreover, while true right now, it will one day be false that people live on what today counts as the territory of the People's Republic, because at some point or other all humans will have died out. A statement can be true today and false tomorrow.

Of course, the theory of truth contains a host of subtleties that

we cannot go into here.[24] For our purposes, we need only hold on
to the insight that propositional truth is nothing spectacular. This
fact is easy to overlook if you believe that the media or our senses
impede our access to reality. But, really, nothing is easier than the
truth.

Sometimes it's difficult to find out what the truth is ('Who ordered
the last chemical weapons attack in Syria?'). But this doesn't mean
that the truth is difficult. It was either the Assad regime or another
of the all-too-numerous warring factions. Whoever it was will certainly lie about it, meaning it takes some detective work to find out
what the truth is. But we can be sure that someone knows what the
truth is – whoever it was that ordered the attack.

Constructivism fails on account of its inability to acknowledge
the conditions under which quite ordinary, everyday statements
are true. It conflates truth with its recognition by man-made institutions. Let's again take the proposition:

> Some human beings live in China.

One of the most famous constructivists, who would likely register
his doubts here, was the French philosopher, historian and sociologist Michel Foucault (1926–1988). His epoch-making book *The
Order of Things* was first published in French in 1966 and rapidly
became a worldwide bestseller. In this work, he maintained that
the human being is a construction based on assumptions made in
the human sciences (mostly in France) from the seventeenth to the
nineteenth century. In this period, he claims, 'man enters in his
turn, and for the first time, the field of Western knowledge.'[25]

We might well ask what could possibly be meant by this claim,
which, at first glance, seems simply absurd. First and foremost, we
might wonder what 'Western knowledge' is. Foucault doesn't tell
us. If we understand this term to designate the kinds of reflection
that arose in the advanced civilizations of the Mediterranean Basin
(which, rather one-sidedly, are generally associated with ancient
Greece and Rome), then people reflected on the human being long
before the seventeenth century. The question of what the human
being is is pretty much the central theme of Greek philosophy,
mythology and tragedy. Foucault is obviously aware that we're
not likely just to buy his surprising historical claim outright, and
he immediately offers the following retort:

> Strangely enough, man – the study of whom is supposed by the naïve
> to be the oldest investigation since Socrates – is probably no more

than a rift in the order of things, or, in any case, a configuration whose outlines are determined by the new position he has so recently taken up in the field of knowledge. Whence all chimeras of the new humanisms, all the facile solutions of an 'anthropology' understood as a universal reflection on man, half-empirical, half-philosophical. It is comforting however, and a source of profound relief to think that man is only a recent invention, a figure not yet two centuries old, a new wrinkle in our knowledge, and that he will disappear again as soon as that knowledge has discovered a new form.[26]

Notice that Foucault doesn't tell us why it is naïve to see the question of the nature of the human being as 'the oldest investigation since Socrates' or even as the oldest investigation full stop. In this passage he makes a series of assertions that he neglects to back up with either empirical evidence or philosophical argument. And these assertions shouldn't be taken as self-evident, especially as Foucault writes in a way that by no means guards against radical constructivist interpretations of his highly ambivalent position. Indeed, he is frequently interpreted as a constructivist who holds that, in reality, the 'human being' does not exist. Instead, there is supposed to be a constellation of discursive practices, of ways and means of dealing with the human, which first brought the human being into existence. But even while Foucault is certainly a thoroughgoing constructivist (albeit not a radical one), this passage in fact aims to convey something rather different.

According to Foucault, the term 'human' begins to assume a special meaning in the seventeenth century, leading to the development of a certain notion of normality oriented around that of 'humanity'. If he is right, we began to represent ourselves as humans by creating a norm of humanity which, far from having existed at all times, is historically contingent. For Foucault, this representation has ethical consequences, i.e. consequences at the level of our action coordination: a historically contingent image of the human comes to be central to our mode of self-understanding and, among other things, displaces the idea that we ought to coordinate our actions in the light of the concept of God. Foucault does not point to any discovery as the ground for this fundamental reorientation but, instead, discusses various restructurings of classification systems. The permeation of humanism into our social systems, he thinks, has a contingent prehistory. According to his own historical investigations, modern humanism was thus more or less an accident. At any rate, it was not the result of an intentional or teleological implementation of an ideal of humanity. It could all have happened otherwise.

Still, Foucault exaggerates the philosophical consequences of his historical investigations. These do not in fact support the strong thesis that the human being was first thematized as such in the seventeenth century. To refute this idea, one merely needs to read pre-seventeenth-century texts that deal with the human being. These could be the Greek tragedies, the Koran or the Old Testament, which (rather famously) takes up the issue of the origins of man right at the beginning and considers which role human beings are to play within the overall order of non-human things. Moreover, classical Greek philosophy – paradigmatically represented by Plato and Aristotle – expressly addresses, both scientifically and philosophically, the question of who or what the human is. We therefore need to place serious caveats on Foucault's strong thesis.

Foucault himself was later to acknowledge the limitations of his earlier views, and this realization led him to extend his historical research back to antiquity. In particular, he went on to investigate the constellation that constituted the transition from pagan forms of self-examination to those of early Christianity. This transition is at the heart of his large-scale study on *The History of Sexuality*, the last volume of which was recently published posthumously.[27] In addition, his late lectures were devoted to the themes of enlightenment and its origins within the milieu of ancient democracy. He wanted to explain why scientific discourse, even today, has to be focused on speaking the truth and how exactly this hangs together with processes of social emancipation.

Foucault himself thus revised the historical thesis of *The Order of Things*, in part by finding the origins of the modern image of the human being within antiquity. Nevertheless, it is unfortunate that he had an exclusive orientation to Athens and Rome without tracing the many other influences (such as from Egypt, China, India, Japan, Israel and, later, Islam) on the development of the West.

Besides the dubious historical thesis that the human being is a spontaneous invention of (French) modernity, which could just as easily vanish as endure, Foucault has a further, philosophical, thesis up his sleeve in *The Order of Things*. The thesis is somewhat elusive, but let's try to see what he had in mind. Foucault presumably wanted to advance the following claim: from the seventeenth to the nineteenth century, humans thought about themselves in a specific way. Following his general methodology, which he called an 'archaeology of knowledge', Foucault sees this self-understanding as a 'discursive practice', that is, as a socio-politically powerful classification by means of which humans generate and justify institutions such as prisons, mental asylums or sexual practices.[28]

Lurking in the background of this thesis is the warranted suspicion that one cannot simply appeal to 'humanity' or to 'the nature of the human being' in order either to bring into being a certain institutional order – be it a nation state, left- or right-wing politics, universities, healthcare systems or what have you – or to justify it after the fact. The appeal to 'the human being' is usually hollow and not infrequently serves quite other purposes than the improvement of our condition. Foucault's historical investigations help to make precisely this point, insofar as they alert us both to the deep contingencies that led to the modern view of humanity and to the conceptual difficulties which it has brought in its wake.

In this respect, Foucault's historical studies are an important contribution to helping us realize that there is nothing self-evident about how we are to understand ourselves as human beings, that there is a large spectrum of possibilities when it comes to filling in the abstract ideal of humanity. Who or what the human is is not something we can simply read off from nature. This is why the human does not have any obvious position in any of the classification systems Foucault discusses. So much was acknowledged by Linnaeus when he admitted that we can understand the human being only in terms of its capacity for self-knowledge.

Nevertheless, none of this necessarily implies that 'the human' is an invention of the historical period spanning the seventeenth to the nineteenth century. At best, it tells us that a certain image of humanity was predominant at that time.

Anthropological constructivism is the view that the human being is entirely a product of itself, such that there are no truths about us independent of our self-constitution. Yet, such a strong claim does not follow from the realization that a certain image of humanity is bound up with the contingent conditions of its origination. The problems of interpreting Foucault's dubious historical findings as a justification for anthropological constructivism are clear enough when we consider the consequences of his bold and provocative claim. If there were no truths about the human being independent of our respective self-images, the statement 'some human beings live in China' would not, just as such, be true, if we couldn't say what human beings are in a universally valid sense. Foucault therefore has to reinterpret the meaning of the true statement that some human beings live in China. Maybe he thinks what this statement really expresses is something like:

> Given the historically conditioned and ultimately arbitrary border between the territory of China and its neighbours in

Asia, and given the scientific construction of our image of the
human being in the seventeenth century, from the standpoint of
someone like Michel Foucault, it looks as though some human
beings live in China.

The statement 'some human beings live in China' would be either
false or, at best, true under entirely different conditions from those
we usually assume. Such is the consequence of buying into anthropological constructivism, i.e. into the idea that humans don't
simply exist but are produced through discursive practices.

Constructivism tends to alter our discourses. It doesn't leave our
established linguistic practice unaffected. Let's take two examples,
each of which illustrates the general spirit of constructivist manoeuvres. A widespread doctrine is **colour constructivism**, which says
that colours do not really exist. Rather, colours are supposedly
generated by animals with certain neuronal equipment in order to
facilitate their conscious dealings with an in-itself colourless world.
According to colour constructivism the proposition:

Grass is green

is true not by dint of grass being green but because light rays with
determinate physical properties hit our nervous system, which then
constructs a mental image in which it looks as though grass is
green. In reality, grass itself is not green, but colourless.

Today constructivist theories are depressingly common, especially in ethics, a field where they are liable to do particular damage.
Many believe that the statement:

You ought not to cause gratuitous suffering to any
sentient creature

or the statement:

All persons ought to be equal before the law irrespective of their
gender, race or heritage

are in fact true only in virtue of expressing the implicit values of
some given community. The idea would then be that there are, say,
'Chinese' values in contrast to, say, 'European' ones. There would
thus be no natural rights valid for all human beings, but only con-
structions of value systems, each recognized by a specific group of
humans. One might think that a theory of this kind resonates with

the quasi-anti-imperialist idea that we shouldn't foist our so-called Western values on other cultures. Yet, universal human rights are absolutely not a 'Western' invention; they belong to human beings as such. Nobody in their right mind – be they in Germany, Japan, Russia, China or the Congo – believes that one should torture children just for the fun of it. Nobody wants to be tortured themselves. Universal human rights stem from such basic reflections as these and not from any kind of European perspective. Further, it follows from an appreciation of universal human rights that both the colonization of other cultures and imperialism contravene them – a fact that makes it easy enough to understand that they are not by themselves instruments of imperialism.

All constructivist manoeuvres have a common denominator: they don't take generally accepted statements at face value. Instead of just recognizing that some human beings live in China or that all human beings (ought to) count as equals before the law, they construe the truth of these statements differently. Constructivism's answer is an uncomfortable alternative: *either we have to assume from now on that an infinite amount of what we hold true is really false, or at the very least we have to understand it in a completely different way from how we have done until now.*

At this point, we can point to a relevant point of contact between the philosophy of Davidson and Gadamer's hermeneutics. What I have in mind is the following: say we get to know somebody and ask ourselves what they really mean by their words. After all, we regularly talk to people whom we don't know, even if our conversations with them might be utterly fleeting. If I want to understand what somebody means by a statement, I have to assume that they accept as true most of what I accept as true if I'm to have any chance of having a successful conversation with them.

A simple example: say I ask someone what they do for a living and this person tells me they're a management consultant. It would be extremely bizarre if this person were using the words 'management consultant' in order to tell me that they are currently studying forest management. Now take this idea a step further: could I even understand someone who told me that they are a management consultant, although they're actually a student of forest management who also believes that nobody lives in China, that they have seventeen fingers, that Britney Spears is the wife of Angela Merkel and that we all actually live in the Matrix? If we didn't all have a fundamentally similar conception of what reality is like, we would have no common basis for linguistic communication. Truth matters because it underlies the possibility of communication.

The world as a wish list

Our very ability to converse with one another is built on the widely confirmed (and true!) assumption that we share a common basis of true beliefs. The number of assumptions we share with our conversation partners is actually infinite. Otherwise literally no communication would take place. Every difference of opinion over any matter of any importance whatsoever presupposes that we have a shared system of mostly true beliefs.

If constructivism were true, though, all of our beliefs that fall within its scope would either not be true at all or would have completely different meanings from those we usually ascribe to them. In a nutshell, a radical constructivist does not speak English but invents an alternative language. We might call it 'Constructivist Newspeak'.

We have not yet fully explored the logical problem inherent to constructivism. If the statement 'some human beings live in China' is true, then, as the constructivist should agree, this is not true in virtue of the fact that somebody holds it to be true. And, conversely, the constructivist will hopefully not want to tell us that no statement not held to be true by anybody can be true.

Let's assume that all humans thought the following statement true:

There is an extremely large, but finite number of suns.

The contrary of this statement is:

There are infinitely many suns.

If all humans hold the first statement true, then from a constructivist standpoint the second statement could not be true. We humans couldn't be mistaken if we all took the first statement to be true. If we create the truth through our discourses, because (almost) all of us believe it, nothing can stop us from making the Earth into a flat disc by creating the truth that it is a flat disc. This would certainly have the advantage of letting us make the world however we please. We would just have to agree to describe whatever pleases us with statements that we take to be true. But this questionable conception of 'truth' does nothing whatsoever to alter the fact that our statements about reality are, in most cases, not true because we take them to be.

The conclusion of the truth argument, we can now see, is that constructivism is ultimately a more or less well-disguised bundle of absurdities. The constructivist alters the sense of every statement. Yet, in doing so, he alters the sense of his own assertions, and that just means that we cannot really engage in conversation with the constructivist at all. We don't normally believe that our statements alter reality: instead, we believe they refer to a reality containing a vast number of facts and objects that are not themselves statements. And we're quite right to do so.

Frege's thoughts

Our question is what thought really is. And we're now ready to consider one of the great attempts to answer this question: that of the mathematician Gottlob Frege (1848–1925), who made a series of decisive contributions to philosophy. I think Frege's answer contains vital insights, and so it sets the stage nicely for the answer I'd like to offer you myself. Frege understands thinking as a matter of grasping thoughts. In his highly influential essay of 1918, 'The Thought: A Logical Inquiry', as well as in other writings, Frege's primary concern is to explain what a thought is.[29] In offering his explanation, he also indirectly determines the concept of thinking, of having a thought.

According to Frege, a thought is something that can be true or false. Thoughts are truth-apt. In this respect, they resemble statements. Thanks to our capacity to think, we're able to entertain truths and falsehoods. Thinking is the interface between us and the real. Just like Plato before him, Frege speaks of how we *grasp* thoughts. He thus uses a haptic metaphor in order to convey how we are literally in touch with a world of thought (a world of ideas).

An important part of Frege's insight is that we can entertain thoughts independently of holding them to be true. I can, say, wonder why people are racist, while holding that their views – their thoughts – about those they consider to be 'other' are simply false. To think a thought does not mean to hold it true.

The characteristic feature of a thought is that it is either true or false regardless of our opinion on the matter. Frege therefore consistently distinguishes between truth and holding-true, a distinction I like to label the **contrast of objectivity**.[30] We find this contrast wherever we can make a distinction between the truth, and so the facts, and our opinions about it.

Another thing we owe to Frege is a reminder about the original meaning of the expression 'sense'. A sense is a direction, as you may know from travelling in Italy, where a one-way street is called a *senso unico*. The meaning of the Latin *sensus* is also easily recognizable in other Romance languages. A sense points in a direction. A sense holds out the prospect of there being certain objects in a designated area, and when that area really does contain those objects, we're dealing with truth.

Wittgenstein also advocates this fundamental Fregean idea in his *Tractatus*, which we've already had cause to mention above. In proposition 3.144 he notes with characteristic brevity:

> Situations can be described but not given names.
> (Names are like points; propositions like arrows – they have sense.)[31]

Objects we can think about can be encountered. The way in which we encounter them is a sense. With our thoughts, we point to what is real. This is neither because of the psychological constitution of human beings nor merely due to our complex neurophysiological makeup. Rather, we are in contact with a reality that is independent of our contact with it, because our senses grasp information that they're not themselves responsible for producing.

Information and fake news

Information in the modern sense of the word – the topic of computer science and, therefore, the concept which led us into the digital age – corresponds to what philosophy since Frege has understood as the sense of thoughts.[32] Computer science builds on the achievements of modern logic and mathematics, including Frege's seminal work on logic's foundations. Without Frege and the thinkers who followed him, especially Bertrand Russell (1872–1970) and Alfred North Whitehead (1861–1947), the digital revolution would never have occurred. Together with certain other thinkers, these philosophers revolutionized logic by understanding thinking as the processing of objectively existing information (facts). Frege, Russell and – in their wake – Wittgenstein think of facts in terms of structures of really existing information, which we grasp in our thinking and express in our statements.

The senses make contact with something real and thus belong to the facts. There is no metaphysical gap between mind and world or thought and being – which does not mean, of course, that they are one and the same. We might even say that, when we think about facts, the facts refer to themselves. Information derives from the fact that we can take in facts and turn them into the content of thought. In the domain of our thinking, this means: a legible and cognizable fact structure. This is why we can encode our thoughts in a material-energetic form, allowing me to write this book, for example. The book contains information insofar as it's an expression of my thoughts. It is therefore not some meaningless arrangement of black print on white paper but an expression of meaning. Neither you nor I project the meaning of my words onto meaningless material; rather, we detect the information that is really there, right now, in front of your eyes.

This insight has a significant consequence, which Luciano Floridi is currently developing into a grand conceptual edifice: a universal philosophy of information. The consequence is that there can ultimately be no false information, only false uses of information.[33] There can be false information just as much as there can be 'alternative facts' or 'fake news'. Both expressions are themselves already fake and serve only to sow confusion. There are facts, but they're often poorly or inadequately reported, as in the depressingly common opinion pieces that plague contemporary journalism and do more to unsettle than to enlighten the public. Fake news is not the reporting of supposed alternative facts but, rather, bad reporting littered with evaluative commentary that distorts the facts.

Reporting needs to be distinguished from spin. And the two need to be kept apart much more clearly than they are today, in an environment in which traditional media outlets compete for clicks and likes in order to charge higher fees for their advertising slots. The result is an obfuscation of information, a situation in which it is no longer so easy to extract genuine information from empty opinion in the massive jumble of information.

Frege proposed that we understand a fact as a true thought.[34] Reality, he thought, is just as true thoughts present it to be. There is thus no insurmountable difference in principle between reality and thoughts about the reality. Thought and being are not separated by a metaphysical chasm. So, the assertion that it is true that Angela Merkel was chancellor in August 2018 has no content besides: that Angela Merkel was chancellor in August 2018. We can label this insight **alethic transparency** (from Greek *alêtheia* = truth). To say that something is true is merely to underline an assertion, not to alter its content.

The inspired gambit behind what has been a basic assumption of logic from the time of the ancient Greeks onwards is that true thoughts directly disclose to us the world as it is. The real is no different from how we know it to be. Frege took up this assumption and radically modernized it: he developed a new presentation of logic that, thanks to its pure, formal mathematical structure, goes further than Aristotle, to whom we owe the first fully elaborated logic in the West.

Whoever thinks truth claims amount to naïvety, or to a naïve realism, commits an error that's easy enough to spot: that of confusing truth with holding-true. Whether a thought I think is true or false does not, as a rule, depend on whether I think it is true or false. When I claim to know something, I make a move beyond mere thinking: I claim that my thoughts are true. I can of course be wrong. Although a thought cannot be wrong, I certainly can be. A thought is objectively true or false while only thinkers can be in error; namely, by holding something true to be false or something false to be true.

Our sixth sense

Frege's contributions to the theory of thought cannot be overstated. But we have to go further than he realized. For if we follow Frege in opposing thinking, the grasping of thoughts, to our senses in the usual sense of 'senses', we'll end up going astray. Rather, our sense modalities are themselves so many different ways of grasping thoughts. To see that it's raining is a kind of thinking. In seeing that it's raining, I grasp the thought that it's raining.

To get this point clearly in view, we have to distinguish between two different ways in which we talk about perception, each of which tends to obscure the other. On the one hand, we understand a perception as an achievement and treat 'perception' as a success term. On this understanding, I can see that Jenny is crossing the street only if that's what she is currently in fact doing. On the other hand, we also describe false perceptions (such as hallucinations) as perceptions and say, for example, that someone has seen Mary in a vision, even though his psychiatrist doesn't believe him. A perception therefore grasps a thought encoded in a specific sense modality. If the thought is true, then we're dealing with a successful case. Otherwise we're dealing with an illusion.

It's important to steer clear of conflating these two cases. For the sake of simplicity, let's call them the *good case* and the *bad case*. Conflating them leads to what John Searle, in his book *Seeing Things as They Are*, simply calls 'the bad argument'.[35] The bad argument is the motor of constructivism, and it goes roughly as follows. The good case resembles the bad case. Therefore, we can confuse them with each other. That is, we cannot unerringly distinguish between the good and the bad case and, consequently, we cannot prove that there is ever a good case. Life as a whole could thus be a long series of illusions. *Life is a Dream* – so reads the title of a seventeenth-century Spanish play (penned by Pedro Calderón de la Barca), of which the arch-constructivist Arthur Schopenhauer (1788–1860) was especially fond.[36]

However, from the fact that in any given individual case we can, in principle, be mistaken as to whether we're in the good or the bad case, it does not follow that all cases at once could be bad. At most, one might express a doubt here, but that's not yet to offer a rational justification. Every character in a detective story might be the murderer, but it hardly follows that all of them committed the murder together. They might have; it's a possibility. But it would be a curious special case, one we've generally little reason to entertain.[37] Hence we usually try to look for the murderer without simply suspecting everyone at once.

Our perceptions in the usual sense modalities are indeed objectively liable to error; but that does not render them all false. It is thanks to our capacity for thought that all of our sense modalities are objective. Thinking itself is objective and stands alongside the other sense modalities as the sense that, thanks to various accidents of history, has found expression in us human beings. As Aristotle pointed out, the human being is the *zoon logon echon*, the living being that has a logos. We possess a logos because we are continually in fallible contact with a reality about which we can communicate in language. To be sure, a pig also possesses a logos. Pigs also think, and fallibly so. So we need to make a slight addition to the classic definition and instead say that the human being is the creature that orients its life in the light of the fact that it has a logos. Pigs, presumably, do not ponder the meaning of their lives. They live and, while they live, they also think. Yet this connection is hardly the foundation of their life and community.

It is therefore an essential part of our rational endowment that we make the very fact of our humanity an issue, a problem, a question. We can think about our thinking. Thought distinguishes itself from the other senses insofar as it is self-directed and can know itself as a medium within the medium of thought. Thinking of thinking is a form of self-understanding or self-mediation. It is, I should stress, as fallible as any other instance of thinking. Just consider how many mutually incompatible theories of thought there are, only some of which can be true. Some people's views about thought must be wrong.

Thinking about thinking satisfies the criteria of being a sense. It stands in fallible contact with its object: thought. Let's sum this up in the claim that, besides the classic senses, we have a sense of thought. It is our sixth sense, a sense complemented and supplemented by the sensory systems that we know ever more about thanks to modern sensory physiology – but very much a sense in its own right.

2

Thought Engineering

The map and the territory

In the Prix Goncourt-winning novel *The Map and the Territory* by Michel Houellebecq (b. 1956), we learn of a painter called Jed Martin. Martin becomes world famous by photographing Michelin maps, which he uses to construct an indirect portrait of France. Instead of painting landscapes, Martin creates maps of the landscape. A map, we read, 'transform[s] the objects of the world into pictorial ones'.[1] In this respect, they resemble artworks:

> Jed devoted his life (or at least his professional life, which quite quickly became *the whole of his life*) to *art*, to the production of representations of the world, in which people were never meant to live.[2]

His career peaks with an exhibition provocatively entitled 'The Map is More Interesting than the Territory'. The narrator tells us how Patrick Kéchichian, an art critic at *Le Monde*, equates Jed Martin's art with the standpoint of God, who looks down at the Earth from the far reaches of the universe.[3]

This comparison is worth dwelling on, providing us as it does with a nice illustration of our **basic principle** concerning the relation between so-called artificial intelligence (AI) and **human intelligence** (**HI**): AI relates to HI like the map to the territory. With AI, we are not really dealing with *thought*, we are concerned with a *model of thought*. For a model to be a model, it has to resemble what it models (its *target system*) in some way or other. Further, it is not a mere copy; a model can have entirely different properties from that which we (try to) use to understand and explain it – in short, from that which it models. A model of thought need not think in order to achieve the goal defined by its engineer. Given that we have no real evidence that AIs are thinking (although we have recently acquired a manner of speaking about them in this way), it is more

57

rational to think of AIs as unintelligent, unthinking devices used in human contexts than as truly autonomous agents who compete with us in cognitive tasks.

I'll be coming back to the question of what exactly we understand by 'intelligence'. For HI at least, the intelligence with which we are intimately acquainted, we can keep things simple for the time being and follow Floridi in understanding **intelligence** as the capacity to think.[4] Of course, this doesn't get us very far. Everything then depends on how we understand 'thought' – the topic of this book.

The basic principle follows once we see how computer science has its origins in logic. **Logic** studies the laws of thought and thereby the principles of thinking, insofar as thinking consists in grasping thoughts. Thoughts, that is, hang together, and we can use models to articulate the connections between thoughts by means of logical laws. Frege called these laws 'laws of truth'.[5] My young daughter, for example, recently discovered such a law. She'd noticed that, if I were no longer to exist (were to go away) and, in addition, her mother were no longer to exist (were to go away too), then she would be all that remained of our little nuclear family. She then wondered – and demanded to know – whether our family would still exist at all if she too were to leave. She had thus recognized a logical connection between the overall composition of her family as father, mother, child and its individual members. The family-whole consists of parts. If all the parts disappear, so too does the whole family.

Our everyday language is full of logical connections. If I am the father of a daughter, I am thereby the father of somebody. From this, it follows in turn that I could also be the father of somebody else; it can hardly be excluded logically that I might still become the father of further children. Reality, that is, is quite obviously logically structured. Fathers are *really* fathers of children; and families *really* consist of members. These days, we have a more diverse picture of the family, and a nuclear family can also consist of partners of the same gender, for example. This represents an example of logical progress, as we now know that the composition of a family is not a *biological* but a *logical* structure. Within the context of a family, 'father' and 'mother' designate roles, not biological kinds. The biological father of a child need not be identical with the father of a family. To contest this is just to commit a gross logical error. Being a father is not identical with a biological kind.

This is not merely a change of convention, but a discovery. That is, it is a fact about human families that they are composed of roles that can be filled in different ways. That we *need* a division of roles may well also be a biological fact about humans as a certain kind of animal. But these facts do not prescribe how exactly the various roles have to be filled. A change of convention does not consist merely in the fact that many of us today think about the family differently from, say, how our parents and grandparents did in the 1950s; it also consists in the fact that we now simply know more about the human being, from both a biological and a socio-cultural perspective. We haven't simply adapted our conventions on a whim. Rather, under the weight of the facts, we have managed to arrive at a new insight – namely, that our previous conventions were not sufficiently compatible with the facts.

Each of us continually engages in logically structured reflection. Just think about how we plan our day-to-day lives: even this most basic of tasks (sheer survival) succeeds only because reality itself is logically formatted. Now, this brings us closer to the **broad concept of information**, which goes back to the famous mathematician and engineer Claude Shannon (1916–2001) and contributed to the great successes of computer science. According to this broad concept, wherever a question can be answered with a 'yes' or a 'no', we are dealing with information. In certain relevant respects at least, information therefore resembles the concept of sense in philosophy, developed primarily by Frege and Wittgenstein (see p. 51). It is no accident, by the way, that Wittgenstein is cited towards the end of Houellebecq's novel.[6]

We all know the unit of measurement called a 'bit'. We owe this to information theory. Bits measure information by breaking down thoughts into simple questions and answers. A bit is a binary digit, a binary unit. A code is binary provided we can imagine two settings, corresponding to a switch being 'on' (1) or 'off' (0). The answer to the question 'Is the light on?' is given by whether the single light switch allocated to the question is on or off. The position of the switch is the answer to the question, and thus a bit.

Given this set-up, we can use electrical impulses to encode information. Computer chips function by implementing simple logical laws in a way that allows them to process an input internally, which in turn leads to an output. Computers are pure logic, installed on a piece of hardware in accordance with the laws of physics. These laws are expressed in mathematical relations (equations), which divide the universe into logical structures in order to render it calculable and theoretically comprehensible.

This all functions as smoothly as it does because reality itself is an information provider. Physical reality (the universe) is at any rate knowable to the extent to which we have acquired knowledge about it. But, from the fact that we know the universe in part, it hardly follows that we know it as a whole. And, to be sure, one of the things we don't know about the universe is exactly what we do not (yet) know about it.

At this point, it is important not to blur the boundary between the fact that the light is on and the fact that the light switch is in the 'on' position. There is a graspable logical connection between the two facts. But the light's being on is not identical with the light switch being in a certain position (for example, there can always be a problem with the electrical circuitry). The logical structure of a physical theory, or of computer science, is not identical with the logical structure of reality itself. Rather, they overlap only partially. When theory and reality overlap, there is often enough of an isomorphism between them – i.e. the theory and the reality have the same structural properties, but realized in different ways. The standard model of particle physics describes properties of elementary particles and the laws of their interaction. Yet it doesn't itself consist of elementary particles. A theory is not a series of direct mappings of reality but is subject to its own laws and principles, which determine how the different elements of the theory are linked together. Elementary particles don't discover themselves: we discover them within the framework of whichever methods have a track record of success.

We might say that what physics investigates is the connection between the position of the light switch and the light's being on. This is how it can discover law-like regularities and go on to express them in a formal language. Yet this doesn't mean that, whenever the light switch is in the 'on' position, the light will also be on. Physical reality, that is, is always more complicated than its theoretical simplification in models might suggest. Our scientific methods are never going to deliver us secure, infallible knowledge of the universe as a whole, knowledge that can never be subject to revision. It is in the nature of scientific theories that the models we deploy need not resemble the target systems they model. Yet, we know that the reality of target systems has to have some structure or other if we want to retrieve the information that is already 'out there', as we tend to put it. But this doesn't mean that we are entitled to infer the structure of the universe as a whole even from the best physics of the day. More importantly, the software underlying a given AI application should not mislead us into thinking that it thinks. For it to function in the way it does, it is quite sufficient for an AI to be a model of thought (rather than itself an act of thinking). Again, we have no reason to believe that the actual physical architecture of our everyday digital reality is to any extent intelligent, conscious or whatever it takes for a system to be genuinely knowledgeable.

Can computers speak Chinese?

In the information age, it is often difficult to separate out random communications from the facts. Not everything that's sold to us as information corresponds to reality. The *infosphere* is structurally different from the *solid ground of facts*. To be sure, both are real. The infosphere – which you are navigating as you read these very lines and which I at some point emailed as a document to my editor – is a totally legitimate reality – a reality, of course, which also leaves physical traces. An email is not some kind of mental or spiritual entity zooming around the fibre-optic network, but a code, which can accordingly be realized in a variety of material-energetic forms. This is what allows it to be delivered from one device to the next.

The common confusion of random information with facts was criticized forcefully, if not fully adequately, by a prominent critic of AI. In one of the most widely discussed contributions to the philosophy of AI, John Searle attempted to prove that computers cannot think.[7] Among his targets was a line of argument that we owe to the AI pioneer Alan Turing (1912–1954). Although the discussion surrounding Searle's thought experiment is not exactly the most recent, it still retains a great deal of relevance. At several points in his argument, Searle recognized something absolutely foundational, and so it's worth introducing his reasoning here.

Let's imagine that John Searle, who, as I can attest, speaks no Chinese (though he knows one or two characters), is locked in a room. This room has two small openings, one in each of two of its facing walls. In the middle of the room is a desk, on top of which is a book containing English-language instructions. These instructions describe how certain Chinese characters (which are also displayed in the book) should be placed beside one another and stuck onto pieces of paper. Paper and glue are also provided.

Some pieces of paper are now handed through one of the openings. Written on each piece of paper is a Chinese character. John gathers up the pieces of paper until he sees that he has enough of them to follow one of the instructions in the rule book. He glues the pieces of paper in the prescribed order and passes them through the other opening. He then hears someone outside the room pick up the piece of paper. It turns out that two Chinese people are using him to communicate with each other: one stands on one side of the room and feeds in characters, which John – without knowing this and without understanding what he's doing in there – joins into sentences, which the other then reads as messages.

The first point of this famous thought experiment, known as the **Chinese room argument**, is that John neither understands nor speaks Chinese. Sticking together characters according to a rule book does not amount to understanding Chinese sentences. According to Searle, AI is analogous to John's role in the Chinese room (needless to say, many of his critics dispute this – in part with good reasons, as we shall see). An algorithm installed as software on a given piece of hardware does not understand the information it is being used to process. No computer processes information in an intelligent manner because no computer understands anything. Nor can it possess a capacity to think.

By and large, Searle simply presupposes all of these points as premises of his argument, and so I would like to try to justify them (albeit rather differently than Searle likely would). The difference between a computer, on the one hand, and John sitting in the room and gluing characters together, on the other, is ultimately the difference between an animal with the ability to speak – a human being called John Searle – and a formal system. According to Searle's argumentation, a computer is a formal system insofar as every combination of (non-biological) hardware and software manages structures and transforms them according to rules. Searle thus touches on the decisive point, even if he doesn't manage to back it up with a completely decisive argument. The case he develops with his thought experiment is flawed, even if he advances it to defend the right position.

The point Searle is ultimately homing in on is that one can construct syntactically correct (well-formulated) chains of characters by following prescribed rules without having the slightest inkling of what they mean. Syntax (the rule-government arrangement of words or, rather, word-symbols) is not semantics (which deals with the meaning of words, sentences and texts). According to Searle, AIs are purely syntactical machines without the slightest access to semantics.

We can copy hieroglyphs in a museum without thereby being able to read them. If we do this, we get hold of the syntax without understanding a word of what those Egyptians actually wrote. For Searle, AI is a formal system for constructing and reconstructing chains of characters. *We* can then read these chains. The programme *Word*, by contrast, is not currently reading what I'm typing, even if it's installed on my computer in a way that allows me to save this particular chain of characters and transfer it onto a USB stick. My computer doesn't tell the USB stick all about how this text is devoted to investigating the boundaries of understanding and the meaning of thought. They won't hold a conversation with each other.

Whoever believes that computers are literally intelligent and, like Skynet in the *Terminator* films or some other fictional entity in the modish AI genre, could possibly take over the planet might as well also believe, so far as Searle is concerned, that our shoes could take over the world in revenge for our millennia-long habit of treading them into the ground. Information processing in non-biological computing machines runs without consciousness, and this fundamentally distinguishes them from human understanding. In our day-to-day lives, we humans make intelligent use of chains of characters in order to convey information and with a view to both investigating and altering the facts. The infosphere is parasitically embedded in our form of life. But, Searle thinks, unlike a biological parasite, it doesn't lead any kind of life of its own.

Unfortunately, this line of argument is somewhat loose. At the decisive point, it really boils down to a stalemate.[8] Searle does not *prove* that we have to understand an AI as analogous to a certain kind of system – namely one that has external information fed into a central unit and merely processes it according to syntactic rules without any understanding whatsoever. For there is no more a homunculus, busy processing data into information, sitting in the AI than there is in John Searle. Moreover, it is not even clear whether we could even rig up an AI syntactically if it didn't have any take on semantic structures. Searle imputes to computers a kind of deficient understanding of signs, even though what he really wants to show is that they don't have any understanding of signs at all, and so no access to syntax either. So, while he is certainly on the right track, his famous thought experiment does not quite justify his underlying insight. Indeed, he realized this himself, which is why he went on to supplement his strategy with a further line of attack.

Photos don't remember Crete

Searle puts forward a version of biological naturalism that gets very close to what we're after.[9] His **biological naturalism** identifies all the mental states of human beings (which include the ability to learn, speak and understand Chinese) with processes produced by neuronal events – that is, through parts of the brain. Mental states, on this view, are generally emergent states of particular organizational units of the brain. According to Searle, then, the brain (or, rather, some relevant, as yet unknown subsystem of it) produces consciousness in virtue of some biological principles no one has yet fully figured out.

While there is plenty that is problematic with this thesis, what tends to be underappreciated is that it enjoys a certain theoretical advantage over many of its competitors. For it does explain why there is a difference between John and the Chinese speakers in the Chinese room thought experiment. If we were to peer into the Chinese speakers, we wouldn't find any little people sitting there who understand Chinese. There is no control centre in the brains of the Chinese speakers, where linguistic codes are applied without being understood. Rather, Chinese speakers are those biologically adapted systems (living beings) who – as reality attests – are capable of speaking Chinese. The difference between John and Chinese speakers is that the latter are adapted to a linguistic environment thanks to processes that include brain plasticity and, more generally, the formation of connections in the nervous system via complex transformations in the human organism, none of which anyone yet fully understands. Yet, we know that it works and that there is a serious difference between learning one's mother tongue and learning a second language, a difference that is doubtless due to some biological principles or other.

Rooms, by contrast, lack the relevant properties, which is why neither John nor the overall system comprising the room, the characters, the rule book, the openings in the walls, etc., can speak Chinese. Searle reminds us that there needs to be at least a sufficiently healthy and trained-up brain in a sufficiently healthy and trained-up living being for there to be someone who so much as understands anything at all. The Chinese room is not a living being which could learn anything but, rather, a box containing a person who puts together chains of characters without understanding them. To be sure, John could figure out Chinese by adapting to his linguistic environment – something which would be very hard, but not impossible. But that again presupposes exercises of his biological capacities which any non-living system lacks.

There is therefore an unbridgeable chasm between a piece of speech recognition software and your capacity to understand this sentence and determine whether it is true or false. Searle's explanation for this chasm consists in the assumption that all intentionality is a property of the brain. By **intentionality** (from the Latin *intendere* = to hold out, to stretch out) philosophers understand the way in which mental states are directed at something that is not necessarily itself a mental state. On this understanding of the word, intentions do not in the first instance have anything to do with expressions of the will, merely with the directedness of our thought towards its objects. Contemporary philosophers call this feature of intentions their 'aboutness'. Right now, for example, I can think about Barack Obama without much difficulty and express my thought via the medium of this sentence. If you know who Barack Obama is, then you too direct your thought at him when you understand this sentence and the previous one. You think of him as the very object that my sentences are about. Intentionality is the property thoughts and sentences have of being about something that figures in reality.

Searle's basic idea is that sentences are about Obama only because we lend them our human intentionality. This is the **thesis of derived intentionality**.[10] A website that you scan for possible holiday destinations is about, say, hotels in Crete, only because humans have already thought about that island and deposited this fact in non-human storage media: in holiday photos, travel brochures, ancient European epic poems and, more recently, cyberspace. Holiday photos do not themselves think about Crete. Nor do they recall their last Mediterranean holiday. They are aids to memory without being memories themselves. Frankly, they could not care less about your holiday.

An ant is crawling on a patch of sand, and why this has nothing to do with Winston Churchill

In order to get a better grip on the thesis of derived intentionality, it is useful to reflect on another thought experiment, which in certain decisive respects moves us beyond Searle's biological naturalism. Thanks to the *Matrix* trilogy, this experiment has even found its way into popular culture. I'm thinking of the first chapter of Hilary Putnam's book *Reason, Truth and History*, which bears the title 'Brains in a Vat'.[11]

In this chapter, Putnam (1926–2016) discusses the question of whether our entire conscious life could be a simulation generated by the stimulation of our brains. Further, in the scenario he sketches, our brains aren't in fact anywhere on planet Earth but are floating somewhere in a vat and wired up to an advanced piece of technology that generates hallucinations. We'll have to come back to this (see pp. 170ff.). Yet, before we decide what to make of this scenario, we need to have a look at the idea with which Putnam begins his chapter. It may well be something you've wondered about yourself in one form or another:

> An ant is crawling on a patch of sand. As it crawls, it traces a line in the sand. By pure chance the line that it traces curves and recrosses itself in such a way that it ends up looking like a recognizable carica-ture of Winston Churchill. Has the ant traced a picture of Winston Churchill, a picture that *depicts* Winston Churchill?[12]

Consider now for a moment whether you believe that the ant has really produced a drawing of Churchill. To give you a moment to think about it, I'll leave some space before the next sentence . . .

So, what do you think? If you're still unsure, ask yourself the following question, which ultimately has the same structure: Are there really constellations? That is, is there really a huge wagon or plough up in the night sky, waiting to be seen?

If you're still hesitant, then think of cloud formations that look like cows, or think of the face of the moon.

What all these cases have in common is that none of them con-cern intentionally produced images. We *see* a picture of Winston Churchill because *we* know Churchill. We believe that we see a large plough because we know about ploughs. And there are plenty more examples we could give. The ant doesn't know Churchill, which is why it cannot produce a drawing of him; and, likewise, the night sky doesn't know about any ploughs. It doesn't know about anything at all.

Putnam calls the view that ants might by chance produce a Churchill drawing, or that clouds might by chance arrange them-selves into cow formations, a **magical theory of reference**. It would be something like a miracle if clouds could be images of cows with-out any interpretation on our part. Which purely meteorological process could possibly explain such a thing?

Putnam brings a vital insight to bear against the magical theory of reference, one which can help bring us a further step forward. This insight is known as semantic externalism. **Semantics** is the discipline dealing with (linguistic) meaning. **Semantic externalism** is based on the idea that many elements in the expressions we use to direct our thoughts at things that aren't themselves expressions are given their direction from outside, so to speak. That is, the *objects* of expressions determine what the expressions are about. The specific things we then have to say about them, however, do not determine the objects. For example, if I express a false opinion about Barack Obama – and, like many a misled American, believe that he wasn't born in the USA and isn't even a real American – then my statement is false, because it is about Obama, and he is both an American and someone who was born in the USA. This is why we can make false statements about something: the objects of our statements are not exhausted by the fact that we make statements about them, and they are not always exactly as our statements represent them to be. They co-determine what our statements mean from outside (hence externalism), to some extent regardless of whether they are true or false.

In a still more general sense, Charles Travis talks about how truth is a *two-party enterprise*.[13] If a thought is true, this is both because there is a given thought and because reality is as the thought depicts it. Thoughts can be true or false, because it is not only the thought but also reality that has to say its piece in deciding questions of truth.

But these are all the relevant players. There is not, in addition, some third party, as constructivism would have it – say, the construction of reality by our sense organs or our membership in a social group. Nothing can be true for Trump that isn't true for Barack Obama. Accordingly, there can be no alternative facts. To be sure, many things are true only because Trump exists (including that he is the forty-fifth president of the United States). But that is not true because he wants it to be.

The god of the internet

So, ants can't think about Winston Churchill. When we look at the results of the ant's labours and think we are seeing a picture of Churchill, we are lending our intentionality to the lines in the sand. We are endowing reality with a meaning it would not have without our own mental endowment.

We can call this a **projection thesis**. Such theses are known from the critic of religion Ludwig Feuerbach (1804–1872), who, in his epoch-making book *The Spirit of Christianity* (1841), put forward the thesis that Christianity first projects God's properties into the heavens and then believes that there is a God. According to Feuerbach, the Christian God has so many human properties

because we made him according to our own image before projecting him into the external world. This criticism of religion follows a
pattern that we first find in the sixth century BC in the pre-Socratic
philosopher Xenophanes:

> But if horses or oxen or lions had hands or could draw with their
> hands and accomplish such works as men, horses would draw the
> figures of the gods as similar to horses, and the oxen as similar to
> oxen, and they would make the bodies of the sort which each had
> of them.
>   Ethiopians say that their gods are snub-nosed and black; Thracians
> that theirs are blue-eyed and red-haired.[14]

The main characteristic of the human being is its distinctive sense
of thought. In an episode of the series *Episodes* (5: 4), a (fictional)
British comedian accidentally shoots a wild boar. He and his wife
Beverly want to rescue it against the wishes of Matt LeBlanc, who
plays himself. This triggers a discussion about whether wild boars
have a right to sojourn on Matt's ranch, something that Matt
denies on the basis that he, unlike the boar, has forked out 8 mil-
lion dollars for it. Sean and Beverly counter that the boar can claim
rights because it is intelligent, provoking Matt LeBlanc to ask why
it is, then, that he's the one with the gun.

Of course, my aim here is not to say anything against animal
rights. On the contrary! From the fact that human intelligence is
in multiple respects superior to that of a wild boar, it by no means
follows that we are entitled to treat them badly. We do not treat
small children badly just because we adults possess a more fully
developed intelligence. Living creatures merit moral respect not
on the basis of their intelligence but because of their capacity for
suffering.[15] Hence we have moral obligations towards wild boar,
but not towards smartphones. Smartphones possess more computing power than all the pigs and all the new-born humans who ever
lived put together. Yet we can chuck away smartphones and not
new-born children.

Humans are not the only living creatures with a sense of thought
but, so far as we know, we are the ones whose sense of thought is
the most elaborate and sophisticated. This is obviously connected
to our capacity for translation, which allows us to encode thoughts
in the form of pictures, symphonies, theories, tools and sentences
of natural language.

The relevance of the projection thesis to our current concerns
is that we tend to transfer human properties on to our technology. Just as, for thousands of years, humanity has decked out the

universe with a panoply of meanings it does not really possess, but which are instead tailored to our own purposes, we today conceive of technological progress as a superior force lying outside our control. For many people nowadays, machines have taken the place once occupied by God, but only because we have installed in them our own logic.

One of the foremost achievements of human beings lies in discovering the laws of thought through the power of reflection and expressing them in scientific form. This achievement represents both the blessing and the curse of technology, and thus of civilization as we know it from the time of the first advanced human cultures onwards. But it is important not to think of logic as simply falling down from heaven. It is not a divine revelation but a structure that we can discover only within the framework of the human life form.

What we can take from Searle and Putnam is the lesson that not everything that seems to be a thought or an instance of thinking is in fact a thought or an instance of thinking. We regularly project our own thought processes onto our natural and social environment. Everyone is familiar with at least some variation of the situation where, after a gap of several years, you suddenly see an old friend in a foreign city at the very moment you happened to be thinking of them. But this obviously doesn't mean that the friend is hanging around in the foreign city in order for the two of you to meet up again 'accidentally'. It would be somewhat odd if the poor soul had spent years trying to bring about a chance encounter that, moreover, should occur at the very moment you happen to be thinking about them. It would be just as odd if some superior being, a god say, were to direct 'fate' so that you meet each other, and also to give you a little hint beforehand about the happy coincidence. The happy coincidences of life are just that: happy coincidences. And the unhappy contingencies, the accidents, are likewise nothing other than *contingencies*.

Civilization and its discontents

Infinitely many factors feed into human life. We find ourselves confronted with a vast interplay of occurrences that are anything but intentional through and through. Our civilization is not a rational set of arrangements planned out at the drawing board. All amelioration of socio-economic conditions depends upon a complex set of circumstances that is never fully surveyable.

There's a simple enough reason for this. As animals, we find ourselves confronted with an environment that is to a large extent non-intentional. The **non-intentional environment of our lives** comprises those facts that obtain without anyone having planned that for them to do so. The work of human enculturation from which our modern, technologically upgraded civilization emerged consists in the ongoing attempt to reduce the oppressiveness of contingency and to create ever more structures for keeping a dangerous and unpredictable nature at bay. The problem, though, is that, as living beings, we are ourselves parts of an unpredictable nature. To some people, this suggests that the next logical goal is to overcome our own biological nature – but this is a mistake.

We reduce environmental pressures by producing niches of derived intentionality. We nest in our own culture, so to speak. Floridi describes this as the 'semantization of Being'.[16] His idea is that, in our capacity as thinking beings, we react to the absence of meaning in our environing reality by constructing an infosphere, where this functions as something like our mental or spiritual atmosphere.

Traditionally, we often speak of 'culture' in this connection. Floridi's diagnosis of the information age runs as follows: we have extended our networks of meaning to such an extent that we have now inhabited the world of information for a greater period of time than we have a nature untouched by that world. While I write this paragraph during a flight to Naples, a couple of tourists to my left are planning a walking route through Ischia using maps and information that they have assembled from online searches or from a classic, printed travel guide. Everything they will experience on Ischia (besides an earthquake, such as there was recently) will be through the lenses of the information with which they have already equipped themselves. They will be wandering along mental paths already marked out beforehand rather than having an original experience putting them in contact with an inhuman nature.

We (rightly) avoid such contact. For, inhuman nature is neither our friend nor our enemy. It is the sheer presence of matter and natural laws, phenomena that arose entirely independently of our expectations of meaning. Building on this idea, Floridi understands the sense of our mental lives as a flight from our primal anxiety before the meaninglessness of things:

> Mental life is thus the result of a successful reaction to a primary *horror vacui semantici*: meaningless (in the non-existentialist sense of 'not-yet-meaningful') chaos threatens to tear the Self asunder, to drown it in an alienating otherness perceived by the Self as nothing-

ness, and this primordial dread of annihilation urges the Self to go on filling any semantically empty space with whatever meaning the Self can muster, as successfully as the cluster of contextual constraints, affordances, and the development of culture permit.[17]

Today, information bubbles and echo chambers are the subjects of lively discussion and causes of grave concern. But they have existed for as long as human beings have exploited a division of labour in order to defend themselves against a nature that confronts them with the ultimately irresolvable task of survival. Regardless of how much progress we make in this regard, the very structure of the universe guarantees that, sooner or later, all human life will vanish. This fact is unsettling because it is a cosmic mirror of our own mortality. We experience reality essentially through the prism of our continually imminent death, which is why Martin Heidegger (1889–1976) went so far as to call the human being a 'being-towards-death'.[18]

Day in, day out, we modern humans encounter signs that signify something only because we have lent them a significance. Among these are the road signs, election campaign posters and advertising boards in our towns and cities and, for the last few decades, the sign labyrinth of cyberspace, which we lug around on our smartphones and now even take to bed with us. The shimmering reality of our smartphones bombards us with derived intentionality. The difference between a cloud formation and a website, of course, is that a website requires the participation of several individuals, each of whom deposits their intentionality. Every website is a communication, a vehicle for conveying thoughts. A cloud formation, by contrast, communicates nothing.

Human culture consists in reducing the impression that we are at the mercy of factors lying beyond our control. We are relentless in repressing the fact of our own ethical degeneracy and of all the pain and suffering for which we ourselves bear direct or indirect responsibility. Uncontrollable accidents occur at every moment, and these are provoked in part by our cultural activities.

Ruben Östlund's Palme d'Or-winning film *The Square* (2017) provides us with a masterful aesthetic depiction of this process. The protagonist, the director of a museum for contemporary art in Stockholm, is plagued by one unfortunate event after another. The film shows us his continual attempts to domesticate the uncontrollable through art, and we witness how his efforts end in failure. But it also explores the ethical abyss opened up by the mass media's tendency to suppress genuine moral problems by creating a situation in which we continually talk about refugees, the homeless, child poverty, etc., without really doing anything that significantly contributes to alleviating these ills.

At some point or other, all human life on planet Earth will come to an end. Depending on the precise effects of increasing entropy in the universe, it may come to the cold death of the universe as a whole, to a state in which there simply are no more structures capable of encoding information.[19] In any case, we should get used to the fact that every human, like humanity as a whole, has to die sooner or later, and that every one of us will face intolerable misfortunes, at the latest in the shape of our own demise.

Our culture works to force this reality to the outer edges of our attention (with certain exceptions, of course, such as the chapter you're currently reading). In our contemporary culture, it is common to find the topic of death's inevitability banished from the public realm. When it does make an appearance, it mainly does so in the form of news items, which have an overwhelming focus on fatal calamities. They detail terrorist attacks and plane crashes but neglect to report how people get to know one another in planes, fall in love, or attempt to alleviate the world's suffering by adopting an orphaned child. Our news channels are outbursts of a return of the repressed: they confront us with our fear of death by projecting it elsewhere and by pretending that we can keep ourselves safe from the misfortune of having to die by erecting more borders and by engaging in more foreign wars.

An important function of the contemporary news media resides in its contribution to providing an indirect symbolic justification of our modes of cultural activity. In the light of the horrors that are always unfolding elsewhere, we feel entitled to hold fast to the everyday structures of the status quo. Many find it secretly reassuring if a civil war is taking place somewhere else, since at least it's not taking place over here. A concomitant problem is that it becomes ever more difficult to see how the causes of others' sufferings are closer to home than we'd like to believe. We are all, in some form or another, links in causal chains that culminate in the suffering of human beings; it suffices to own a smartphone, drive a car or buy goods that are neither sustainable nor manufactured under ethical or just conditions. Besides, our daily (and, for the most part, utterly senseless) use of plastics harms both human beings and other species and is therefore neither sustainable nor morally justifiable. The sign labyrinth of the infosphere, which always and everywhere accompanies us, is a symbolic order that we generate at least in part so as to delude ourselves that we are somehow immortal, or at any rate considerably less dependent on the vicissitudes of the material-energetic universe than is really the case. Silicon Valley's vision of attaining eternal life through overcoming our biological nature is nothing other than wishful thinking. It is an attempt to fulfil the understandable function of unburdening ourselves from our being-towards-death.

These fantasies of immortality are sources of harm, facilitating as they do the technological advances that are massive contributing factors to our present ecological and social crises. The price we pay for the glossy ideology of Silicon Valley is all too well known both to the wage slaves in the factories that manufacture our smartphones and to all the other human beings whose daily lives are devoted to producing the material foundations of this fantasy of immortality.

We modern consumers at the global apex of the capitalist pyramid are in this respect like latter-day pharaohs: instead of immortalizing ourselves in pyramids built by slaves (which are of no use to anyone), we immortalize ourselves in the infosphere (which is ultimately of just as little use). Hence the precariousness of our intellectual and spiritual lives. Human beings can always fail in their adaptation to reality and in managing their needs and expectations. Indeed, we experience this on a daily basis, when we make plans for the coming days, weeks, years or life stage – plans that we continually (have to) adapt in the light of ever-shifting circumstances that transcend our control.

In *Civilization and its Discontents*, Sigmund Freud (1856–1939) therefore diagnosed a general instinctive repugnance in human beings towards the very fact of their having a niche in reality.[20] We can never be rid of this discontent. An important task of philosophy as a critique of the ideological distortions of the zeitgeist is to keep an eye out for the damaging models and influences that feed into humanity's cultural self-image. In our own time, these include the idea that we can realize a form of immortality here on Earth through ongoing progress in computer science and the permanent expansion of digitalization. Technology will not make us immortal. Rather, it simply prolongs the lives of some at the expense of the lives of others.

Emotional intelligence and hidden values in the digital labyrinth

Thanks to our senses, we stand cheek by jowl with reality at every moment of our conscious lives (including in our dreams). Our sensations, our contact with that which really exists, fortunately confront us with more than just the more resistant and repulsive aspects of life. Humans are social animals to such an extent that members of our species don't even have a hope of surviving the initial months and years of their lives unless they have the fortune of experiencing love, in the form of other members of their species taking them into their protective care. In his *Principles of the Philosophy of the Future* (1843), Ludwig Feuerbach summarizes this point as follows:

> Thus, love is the true ontological proof of the existence of an object apart from our mind; there is no other proof of being but love and feeling in general. That object whose being affords you pleasure and whose nonbeing affords you pain – that alone exists. The distinction between object and subject, between being and nonbeing, is a distinction just as pleasing as it is painful.[21]

Depth psychology was developed in the nineteenth century on the basis of similar considerations. But we don't here need to reconstruct the entire history of psychoanalysis and its origins in German idealism and romanticism. For our purposes, what's important in this tradition is a central idea, which might be put as follows: as thinking beings, we have an attitude towards ourselves. We always experience our acts of thinking and their contents (that is: our thoughts) in a determinate manner – and thus, so to speak, as emotionally colourful.

There is no intentional consciousness without phenomenal consciousness. This means that we cannot think about anything without at the same time feeling something or other.[22] At any given moment, our overall mental state is composed of thoughts and feelings, without our experienced feelings and moods themselves referring to reality. And phenomenal consciousness, the way it feels to be yourself, never exists without intentional consciousness either. This doesn't mean that all our thoughts about things that are not thoughts themselves are somehow governed or controlled by our feelings; but we could not think anything in particular if we did not also feel a certain way. Our emotional states co-determine what we think about and how we think about it. There simply is no pure rationality which is not to some extent inspired by emotions.

Not every thought feels some particular way or other. Strictly speaking, our **phenomenal consciousness**, what it is like to be who you are at any given moment, is the background noise of our entire organism. Countless factors contribute to this, including what is colloquially known as our abdominal or 'second' brain, the enteric nervous system located in our gastrointestinal tract.

Subjective, phenomenal experience is a kind of echo chamber of our organism, whose states are processed internally and intentionally accessible. If I have a headache, this tells me something about the state of my organism; thanks to my intentional consciousness I can then react to this and, say, take a painkiller. As we all know only too well, though, the intentional information that we would need to determine what exactly is going on within our organism is not something we can simply read off from our feelings. Feelings are not linguistically encoded thoughts, and they lose some of their qualities if we translate them into linguistic code.

At the same time, however, phenomenal and intentional consciousness interact with each other in the phenomenon we know as gut feeling. Frege recognizes this too and speaks of the 'colouring and shading'[23] of a thought. Our language contains emotion words (interjections such as 'ah!' and 'oh!', and so on), which express how we feel in the light of a particular thought.

We cannot escape from the structures of our personalities, even in thinking about thinking. When we reflect on thinking itself, we also express attitudes as to who we take ourselves to be and how we would like to be seen. The thoughts that we think do not occur to us merely because we are interested in their truth. There are just too many true and false thoughts (transfinitely, i.e. infinitely times infinitely many) for truth to be the sole factor determining our thought processes. In the background of conscious experience, our human life form and our individual lives select which thoughts occur to us.

This process is commonly known as emotional intelligence. Yet it is important to see that this doesn't originate purely within our organism, as a kind of self-observation of the nervous system; rather, it emerges in the context of our ecological and social niche. Our organic states are literally shaped by education during early childhood, and our nervous system is formed in reaction to environmental experiences (beginning in our mother's womb). There is a feedback loop from our surroundings, through our motor experience, to our inner states.

In this context, Freud postulated an inner conflict between the reality principle and the pleasure principle. He linked the reality principle to perception in particular: thanks to our senses, we stand in intimate contact with a reality we have not ourselves produced. Yet this reality is hardly tailored to our needs. In a stable psychic economy, the pleasure principle therefore relies on reality being adapted to our needs to such an extent that we can still, in principle, distinguish between the two.

The emotional colouring of experience simply cannot be separated from our general human intelligence. There's a philosophical argument for this. Let's run another simple thought experiment and once again put ourselves in a familiar situation. We want to go travelling with friends. We've packed our bags and currently find ourselves at the airport. We're looking out for the desk where we can check in our luggage.

This typical travel scenario, which most of us know in one version or another, functions only because there are virtually infinitely many things that we *don't* notice at the airport. For example, travellers tend not to observe the precise speed of the baggage conveyor belts. They ignore the dark matter all around them, which not even physics can determine with any precision. Moreover, they don't bother to study the complex system of trade and exchange which means that there are newspapers and croissants to buy at the airport.

When we consider it more closely, the situation in such a scene is once again infinitely complex. Where exactly does the airport begin? And how does it look at some random point on the (by our lights) extremely small scales investigated by quantum mechanics? Even the attempt to effect a precise demarcation between the airport and the rest of the universe should make it clear just how multi-layered and unique the situation really is.

Furthermore, reality does not contain any typical 'travel' scenario. Each journey ultimately plays out differently, which is why we presuppose patterns to use by way of orientation. That's why travel is so stressful: it never pans out precisely according to the patterns we would like and which we had in mind when we handed over considerable sums of our hard-earned money to the travel agent. There would clearly be no airports and no travellers either if it weren't for the fact that we can grasp reality at levels far less complex than infinity.

Now add into the mix that, as animals, humans can only ever live under time pressure. We never have enough time to take on board all the information we would need in order to make our way through the travel scenario in an optimal fashion. Hence so-called emotional intelligence is a central factor of human intelligence. Intuition, gut feeling, is so decisive for every exercise of our intelligence that we would never be able to recognize anything without it. Without emotional intelligence, without our specific ways of experiencing the multiple scenes of our lives, it wouldn't be possible for us to stand in the face of infinity and select out particular objects of thought and reflection from the overwhelming repertoire of reality. Our emotional intelligence systems pre-select information on our behalf, which we process in the form of the consciously available data that then goes on to play a role in our problem-solving activities.

Human intelligence is fundamentally emotional. Our experience is qualitatively coloured through and through. We could never account for the (more or less manageable) emotional complexity of our everyday lives without a trained capacity for pattern recognition. Training in pattern recognition takes place in the womb and in the first years of life leading up to language acquisition. It does so largely within the framework of evolutionarily acquired systems, which interact within the human organism in a way that allows our body to learn to distinguish itself from its environment. In all living beings, the foundational distinction between I and not-I has its original basis in biology. As organisms, we distinguish ourselves from our environment by creating a niche for ourselves within which we can survive. In this way, thanks to evolutionary adaptive mechanisms, the basic structure of a distinction between I and not-I emerges.

As the famous Chilean biologists Francisco Varela (1946–2001) and Humberto Maturana (b. 1928) have shown in their classic *The Tree of Knowledge*, the basis of all higher-order intentionality is autopoiesis, the self-organisation of the living.[24] A similar position had already been developed by Hans Jonas (1903–1993) in his book *The Phenomenon of Life* (1966).[25] Living beings exist only because, over millions of years, they have formed systems that spare them from having continually to deal with the infinite.

Our adaptation is only ever geared to a highly restricted segment of reality. It is misleading to think that our cognitive apparatus is directed at some gigantic complexity, which bombards our nerve endings with information that we then have to build up into a manageable world of objects with the help of evolutionarily adapted nerve endings in the brain. When we're online, we are not bombarded with Big Data but are connected with physical reality. Our emotional intelligence means that we experience this contact in a determinate manner, and this allows us to subject the selected part of reality to further intentional – i.e. logically formatted – processing.

As living beings, we manoeuvre our way between different scenes from the very moment of our birth. This means that we never simply grasp individual objects, but only ever objects that hang together in different contexts. It's on this basis that we develop the ability to pay attention to particular items and investigate them more closely. The idea that there is a complex reality 'out there', which we process 'in here' (within our brain or our consciousness), is for its part only one scene among many, albeit one that does not necessarily correspond to reality.

The contemporary discussion about the nature and extent of AI betrays a misconceived underlying wish to construct a form of intelligence free from emotional attachments, something like a perfect Mr Spock who doesn't even consist of biological material. Yet such an intelligence would no longer be genuinely intelligent in the first place. It couldn't grasp anything at all. This is why there are in fact value assumptions built into every algorithm. No algorithm simply scans through a heap of data and recognizes patterns at lightning speed. Rather, as models of thought, algorithms already possess a structure geared towards re-creating the qualitative experience of humans in a quantitative manner.

Our qualitative experience is so fine-grained and individual that it is interconnected with infinitely many conditions at any given moment. We'll never be able to figure these out completely, which is why we cannot possibly re-create our experience directly. In the best case, we can take advantage of technological progress to improve our thought models and put them to useful work. To believe that our artefacts could consciously think in the sense that living beings do (or even in a similar sense) is just to repeat the mistake of Goethe's sorcerer's apprentice (see pp. 147ff.).

This is why AI systems are in fact a danger to humanity: they implicitly recommend to us the value systems of their human creators without making these recommendations transparent. Silicon Valley pursues an ethics, a picture of how we ought to live. In this sense, it programs an artificial reality, which merely assumes the appearance of the value-neutral computation of patterns that are supposedly recognizable in large data sets. Patterns lurk in even the very largest data sets, even if nobody notices them. But this doesn't remotely mean that all patterns are equally ethical.

A religion called 'functionalism'

Over recent decades, a strange idea has managed to take hold: human thought, we often hear, is somehow like a piece of immaterial software that, for more or less contingent reasons, has been installed in the body of a primate. To understand better how this idea maintains its grip, we need to break down the emotional components of all real intelligence still further. In the discussion around AI, and in large swathes of the cognitive sciences, thinking is understood as a rule-governed process which can, in principle, be detached from the hardware of a human (or other) organism and installed on non-biological hardware.

This basic idea is known as functionalism. **Functionalism** generally presupposes that human intelligence is a rule-governed system that processes data with a view to solving certain specific problems. In the current jargon, this system is supposed to be **multiply realizable,** meaning it can be installed on different pieces of hardware. As evidence for this thesis, its advocates point to how sentences, considered as physical items, are generated in widely different ways across different individuals: my voice sounds different to yours and, if you take a closer look, our brains are also rather different. It's not as though the language modules located in the brains of two different people consist of exactly the same number and arrangement of neurons. After all, these are continually changing. And so we arrive at the idea that what matters is not the precise structure of the hardware but the function it fulfils.

Everything a human being does exhibits a structure for us. So too does everything of which they or someone else can become conscious. In language, we describe this structure with expressions such as 'thinking', 'driving a car', 'being surprised' – that is, by deploying a vocabulary of action terms. This vocabulary presupposes that there are typical scenarios, that there are various common patterns of action. The physical, biological and social reality that we find whenever some pattern is realized varies from individual case to individual case.

To vary a *bon mot* of the pre-Socratic Heraclitus: you can't get on the same bus twice. The 609 bus continually changes its physical structure: its tyres get worn out, it becomes rusty in places, sometimes it has a full tank and sometimes it doesn't, and so on and so on. Also, the 609 bus can, on occasion, be replaced with another bus that fulfils the same function, namely serving the route of the 609 bus. A functionalist will therefore identify the 609 bus with its functional role and not with any specific physical structure. The role 'the 609' can be fulfilled by various items provided they are an appropriate mode of transport. The 609 is thus multiply realizable.

Yet while this thesis is perfectly correct, it is vital not to see it as a motivation for the rather less well-grounded thesis of **substrate-independence.** This is the assumption that a function such as 'the 609' can potentially be fulfilled by things that have completely different material foundations – in other words: different substrates. Accordingly, you may well be able to replace 'the 609' with vehicles built in a completely different way to our contemporary buses. However, you can hardly build a bus out of chocolate and expect it to serve the 609 route. And water, earth, air or fire won't do either. The bus function can be fulfilled only by something consisting of certain materials: materials suitable to the function. Which materials these are can of course change according to the current state of technology. But there are boundaries.

The difference between multiple realizability and substrate-independence is an important one. The view that artefacts such as standard computers, for example, think or play chess is guilty of conflating the two. Firstly, the idea that computers play chess reduces playing chess to a functional role and prevents us from understanding it as a human activity. Not all chess players are striving to play the perfect game; some just want to get up to a basic beginner's or hobbyist's level. Not to mention that the activity of playing chess is also embedded in a range of social contexts, such as in chess societies, in the conversations that accompany games, and so on. Secondly, people invoke substrate-independence because our standard computers are composed of non-biological material, and certainly not of cells like normal chess players. Precisely because chess computers are not animals, they have nothing like the interests that standardly lead to the desire to play chess. In humans, the ability to play chess is multiply realized insofar as each of us is very different indeed at the cellular level and thus at the level of the brain. Yet, this fact of multiple realizability does not entail the substrate-independence of the activity of playing chess.

Functionalism seems so obvious to so many people because it seems to provide us with a comprehensible image of the relation between 'body' and 'soul'. It revises these classical categories by adapting them to our contemporary technological and natural-scientific self-image. This has helped it become a component of what is now the common religion of atheists, namely **naturalism**. Naturalism is at bottom a fig-leaf materialism, and in its standard form it maintains that human beings, and thus our thinking, are fully describable in the terms of natural science. And it would therefore follow that, in principle, we can re-create that thinking in non-biological matter.

But naturalism is really only a half-hearted kind of materialism. The prospect of supplying a better understanding of our mental states and processes by figuring out the material states of our organism remains a distant one. Our organism is far too complex for us to understand it as anything like a classical 'machine', in which each part is tightly connected to another. Even with the availability of data sets so vast they exceed our comprehension, naturalism can never be sure of grasping the world in its full complexity. On the contrary, there are plenty of indications that there still remains unfathomably much to be discovered. To put it simply: we cannot delegate the task of knowing reality to our computers. We can use them to improve our performance, but not to replace us as knowers.

Notice that, in the final analysis, naturalism is not a scientifically confirmed thesis – it is not even confirm*able*. I'd wager that this is the reason why functionalism is so widespread these days: it allows people to believe indirectly in naturalism and materialism without having to supply any real empirical proof or philosophical argument. Functionalism can then be presented as a working hypothesis, with the help of which we might, in the long term, possibly inch our way closer to naturalism.

In my view, functionalism, just like materialism, bears many of the hallmarks of a religion, at least insofar as it can never be confirmed or disconfirmed by empirical evidence. On no account are materialism, naturalism or functionalism scientifically provable assumptions; they are metaphysical interpretations of reality. By all means, we could use them as working hypotheses, but it's important to bear in mind that a metaphysical insight into the nature of reality does not follow from a well-functioning working hypothesis.

Bare-knuckle functionalists such as the American philosopher Daniel Dennett (b. 1942) and his emulators like to criticize religion and metaphysics as unscientific. But this is just a ruse to distract us from their own metaphysical agenda and the value system that they want to pass off as a model of scientific neutrality.[26]

Thought is not a vending machine . . .

Functionalism only functions if we accept an additional tacit assumption, which allows it to hold off giving the actual details of a properly naturalistic account. This assumption is almost correct – but only almost. Functionalism assumes that we can model mental processes, including perception and thought. We can understand them *as though* they involve an input, the internal processing of that input by means of a specified procedure, and a resulting external output. The simplest model for illustrating this assumption is a vending machine. You insert money into the machine and push a button. Then, something happens inside the machine. If the vending machine functions, it releases a drink, a chocolate bar, a packet of cigarettes or whatever. If it does not function properly, then we lodge a complaint, because we're entitled to expect the machine to realize internal mechanisms that have a clearly defined aim: exchanging money for goods.

Now, every particular existing vending machine is different. No vending machine is physically identical with any other. If you zoom in closely enough, any two machines will begin to look very different. And, in any case, no two machines can occupy the same position in spacetime. Considered in high resolution (on scales far below those we can consciously see), it is probably downright impossible to discern any extensive similarities at all between two vending machines. Yet both are exemplars of the same kind. The reason why two physically distinct vending machines are both vending machines is that they realize the same function.

As we have seen, this is called multiple realizability. The physicist Max Tegmark (b. 1967) mistakes this for substrate-independence[27] and pushes the thought as far as it will go, even taking life itself to be substrate-independent. Two physically different things can exercise the same function and thus be things of the same kind. Yet it is easy to find examples of this simple idea everywhere and inflate it into a full-blown metaphysics – i.e. a theory of absolutely everything. Thus, two people will be rather different when considered on physical scales unperceivable without the aid of microscopes; but they will still both be humans. The unity of two people, their being human, consists in the function or functions they fulfil. Of course, how to fix the functional description of humans is a matter of debate: are we gene copying machines, rational animals, or are we in fact banished souls, condemned to inhabit terrestrial bodies under the continual surveillance of God? Functionalism does not address these metaphysical issues but sidesteps them in an effort to justify a given practice of modelling the behaviour of a target system.

The question of what or who the human animal is doesn't need to be answered at this stage. Vending machines and smartphones are easier to understand in this respect. When we think about these artefacts, we are dealing with objects that are created in the light of an idea. Two physically distinct smartphones can be things of the same type because of their operating systems. The same goes for modern vending machines.

But here we hit upon a very important difference between humans and vending machines: we humans, along with our intelligence, have not been fitted out with an operating system. The evolution of species follows no plan. Nor is it due to intelligent design. Animals are not generally artefacts of other living beings. Of course, we have long intervened in the evolutionary process by rearing other animals. But we do not program any operating system for any given kind of biological intelligence. In the future, this might change as a result of advances in biology and medicine. But, so far at least, the best updates for our human intelligence are a combination of a good night's sleep, the right diet, and a few cups of coffee.

Again, we have no actual reason to believe that we could ever literally build an operating system for our intelligence, complete with inputs, control circuits and outputs that we could predict and control with as much precision as we can a vending machine. No chess program (not even AlphaZero) is even approximately as complex and multi-layered as a single human organism. This is bound up with the way in which the human organism is deeply implicated in its environment and with the fact that this fundamental embeddedness is essential to our intelligence. And there is another reason why our thinking cannot be re-created: it will always be more complex than any model we produce of it consisting of a binary numerical code. This has to be so, for the simple reason that our thinking is not digital through and through.

. . . and the soul is not a pile of beer cans

There is a series of arguments against functionalism. To my mind, the problem of weird realizations, which the American philosopher Ned Block (b. 1942) has spelled out using various thought experiments, is particularly convincing.[28] At first, one can well imagine that a computer might at some point become conscious. Silicon chips, for example, could be arranged in the same way as a thoroughly studied human brain. Functionalism even predicts that it would be possible in principle to re-create a human consciousness using a completely different hardware.

But prima facie imaginability is no guarantee of real possibility. With a few simple considerations, Block undermines the impression that it would really be possible to re-create a human consciousness, a soul. He imagines a huge pocket of land somewhere in the middle of nowhere (in Arizona, say) covered with beer cans. The beer cans are electronically wired up to one another in a way that replicates the functional architecture of a brain. You could now send electronic impulses through the huge pile of cans so as to copy the stimulatory patterns of my brain, for example, and simultaneously map this in a brain scan (using, of course, a very advanced scanner). The functionalist would have to assume that, whenever you implement a given neuronal pattern of mine on this complicated hardware, the pile of beer cans then thinks my thoughts.[29]

Or imagine that the galaxies of our galaxy cluster were so arranged that they functionally realize the very same stimulation pattern that my brain does while it is coming up with this sentence. Would this mean that a part of the universe thinks about itself?

And what if the elementary particles converging on the location where I currently perceive my office door were organized in such a way that they simulated the functional architecture of my consciousness of sitting on a chair? Would my office door then have the feeling of sitting on a chair?

Whoever clings on to functionalism in the face of such problems is immune to any rational objection. For such people, any argument will come up short. Against this, it only remains to insist that beer cans and doors are utterly mindless things lacking in feeling, intelligence and any other state in which an actual animal subject can find itself. And if you think this means we have just reached a stalemate, then it is still probably best not to go along with the functionalist, at least if you believe that sentient creatures are entitled to greater protections than inanimate objects. For functionalism makes it difficult to legitimate ethical values with reference to the fact that some entity is an animal: for the functionalist, animality is just a contingent implementation basis of abstract patterns.

Pacemakers for the brain?

Needless to say, Block's argument has faced a host of rejoinders. In 1996, a colleague of his at New York University, David Chalmers (b. 1966), published *The Conscious Mind*. In this much discussed book, Chalmers, while not himself a functionalist, puts forward a series of considerations which seem to speak in the position's favour.[30]

Chalmers reflects on the fact that we have long been able to make technical interventions in the brain in order to steer certain mental processes. Let's imagine that we could replace a single neuron with a non-biological silicon control centre. This would probably alter nothing about our consciousness. But if we can do this with *one* neuron, why not with *two*? Pursuing this thought, it seems plausible enough to conclude that we could, step by step, replace the brain of a human being with another piece of hardware, so that we would have tested a genuine case of multiple realizability. The beer can argument seems not to refute such a scenario.

But several details of this argument are problematic. In particular, while we can indeed steer conscious processes through medical interventions in the brain (there's no need to appeal to science fiction here: coffee, Ritalin and wine are good enough examples), we have no empirical evidence about what would occur were we to replace a brain step by step with a non-biological structure. For one thing, it would be morally reprehensible actually to replace neuron after neuron in a given (human) animal. Chalmers's reflections on the case are a piece of fantasy, a pure thought experiment, which we could never test empirically, if only because it would be utterly immoral to replace a healthy human brain, neuron for neuron, with silicon chips in order to see whether it ends up with or without a conscious inner life. Even if we could run a version of the experiment on another animal, my own guess is that the animal simply wouldn't survive the procedure after a certain number of neurons had been replaced, meaning we would never get any actual test results.

Like Block's beer can scenario, Chalmers's counter-argument is based on a pure thought experiment. Neither allows of empirical proof. Chalmers uses his example to increase the plausibility of functionalism, but at the level of a priori reflection – of pure thought experiments – this doesn't bring us much further. We already know that there is something of a stalemate between the functionalist and his adversaries at this level. So Chalmers's considerations don't speak in favour of the real possibility of a brain pacemaker; they merely serve to illuminate whatever conceptions of functionalism we might already have for independent reasons.

Yet even if we could install a thought prosthesis in the human organism, this wouldn't begin to prove that non-biological intelligence exists. Nobody thinks that there are non-biological hands and legs that lead lives of their own, just because we can replace amputated limbs with prostheses. Prostheses work because organisms don't reject them. You cannot replace an entire human being with a human prosthesis. Of course, a prosthetic leg can take over the function of a biological leg in the life of the affected person; but it doesn't follow that a prosthetic leg is a leg. If I find a prosthetic leg lying in the street (say it fell out the boot of somebody's car), I don't rush to call the police, suspecting a hideously violent crime. If, by contrast, I find a leg on the street, the situation takes on an entirely different complexion. Think of the famous ear found lying in the grass at the start of David Lynch's *Blue Velvet* (1986). If someone finds an ear in the grass, what they find is an indication that someone somewhere has been involved in a rather gruesome incident. If someone finds a prosthetic ear in the grass, by contrast, it could simply be because someone delivering prostheses has been somewhat careless.

All these considerations lead us to an argument for the following thesis: the functions of organisms can indeed be supported (think of pacemakers, coffee, food, GPS) or even replaced (think of prostheses, pocket calculators) by inanimate products of industrial design. But it hardly follows that organisms are *identical* with their functions. The functions of organs are subordinate to the life and survival of the biological systems to which they belong as parts or limbs.

The idea of technology, or: how do I build a house?

Functionalism is an unfortunate inheritance of the ancient Greek idea of technology, which goes all the way back to Plato and Aristotle themselves. Plato and Aristotle called the functions that make two physically different things of the same kind 'ideas' (using the Greek word *idea*, or, in most cases, *eidos*). What we today call a function corresponds to a slimmed-down version of the Platonic–Aristotelian idea.

Aristotle made the notion more concrete by developing the concept of a function, of a *telos*. The substance of this concept comes from his doctrine of the four causes, which can be nicely illustrated with the standard example of building a house. Interestingly, Humberto Maturana casually remarks that physics is

> an extension of housebuilding, and philosophy . . . an extension of the task of responding to the question of children. . . . I assume that the same intelligence is required to take care of a house as to run a lab or an industry, and just as much intelligence is necessary to solve the problems of a household as is necessary to solve those that arise in scientific research. Under these circumstances, I would submit that what needs to be explained is daily life as the source of all our experiences, however technical and specialized they may be.[31]

With Aristotle – the founder of physics as a science and one of the greatest philosophers who ever lived – we can pose the child's question: How do you build a house?

When building a house, a whole series of factors have to come together. An architect draws up plans, which have to be submitted to and authorized by the planning authority. The ground plan shows us the future form of the house. Aristotle talks about the form or the model or paradigm (*eidos* and *paradigma*).[32] A paradigm is something that one shows (from *para* = besides and *deiknymi* = show).

In order to build a house, you need a plot of land and materials. Aristotle calls this the matter, or that from which something arises (*hylê* or *to hou ginetai*). A plot of earth becomes a space for a cellar, styrofoam, steel and concrete are turned into a wall, wood becomes floorboards, and so on.

For the architect's plans and materials to be transformed into a house, the two have to be brought together by contractors. This is where we find the usual notion of causality. On the usual understanding, causal processes are transformations of physically measurable reality – in our case, the transformation of a plot of land, for example, and the piecing together of building components that have to satisfy the laws of statics. Aristotle talks of 'that from which the change or rest from change first starts' (*hothen hê archê tês metabolês*). This is the famous efficient cause, to which people nowadays tend to reduce causality as such. But as we'll see, reduction here is a doomed enterprise.

The final kind of cause is the notorious *telos*, the goal, from which we get the expression 'teleology'. All that's meant by this is the function of a thing. The function of a house consists primarily in being habitable. Component goals are subordinated to this habitability. In our part of the world these would be, say, a functioning heating system, running water, windows, lighting and the rest.

In textbooks, this kind of account is often summarized using the four Latin terms:

1 formal cause (*causa formalis*)
2 material cause (*causa materialis*)
3 efficient cause (*causa efficiens*)
4 final cause (*causa finalis*).

There's nothing antiquarian about this. In the contemporary natural sciences, social sciences and humanities, the concept of causality is no longer restricted to the narrow notion of natural laws and forces that set the things of the universe in motion. Teleological explanations and causal relations obtaining between non-physical objects have long been parts of our standard scientific explanatory repertoire.[33] The mechanistic worldview, especially dominant in the eighteenth century, has long since become passé, even if it still does the rounds, wreaking all kinds of ideological damage. In short: reality is not a deterministic machine shoved from one state to the next like a giant piece of clockwork or a row of dominos that falls over once you push the first one.

Technology is the actualization or implementation of ideas, the process by which we produce things that were not already there as parts of the natural order. It ought to be distinguished from our technological imaginary. A **technological imaginary** is an attitude to the production of technological artefacts. So if technology is the process of manufacturing tools for the sake of improving our living conditions, a technological imaginary, by contrast, comprises more than the sum of the tools in use at a particular point in time. Rather, it designates our *logos* – that is, our idea of what technology is.

Digitalization doesn't only generate new products; it generates new attitudes towards them at the same time. It provides us not only with new things but with notions of how our different products hang together. Many instances of technological progress consist not just in realizing an idea within a pre-existing space of possibilities but in taking a step forward. Disruptive platforms of the so-called *sharing economy*, such as Airbnb and Uber, throw prior structures into question. They traffic in ideas. They are second-order technologies, technologies that embrace a certain understanding of technologies and exploit a given technological imaginary for their marketing. They don't just make our lives easier, they add new ways of living. People who rent Airbnbs are not just looking for inexpensive shelter; else they would seek out a cave, which would be cheaper still. Rather, people are booking the idea of an authentic life as an additional service to a mere overnight stay.

The revolutionary breakthrough of the digital age consists precisely in generating a technology that implements technological imaginaries. We have therefore taken a decisive step beyond the previous order of things. Technology today provides us with ideas of what we should do and who we want to be. It develops its own technological imaginaries. Facebook is an arrangement of self-portraits, which are trawled through by algorithms and organized into patterns. In turn, we receive recommendations: of friends, events, products, and so on. In this way, our tech products take on a seeming life of their own, which then seduces us to speculations about a coming superintelligence. In reality, however, software engineers are busily managing the algorithms that not only 'intelligently' learn the value systems of users but also predetermine their space of possible actions – and thus their value systems. In most cases, all this goes unnoticed by the end user, which only helps to shroud the contemporary tech world in an aura of mystery.

Total mobilization

In his article (and later book) 'Total Mobilization',[34] the Italian philosopher Maurizio Ferraris (b. 1956) sets out to explain the digital revolution. To do so, he explores the thesis that the internet has taken over an ultimately military function. In his view, digitalization emerged from and continues to be driven by the military-industrial complex. For us end users, what characterizes digitalization is a gigantic accumulation of documents that chronicle a vast mass of social transactions (communications, purchases, preferences, bank accounts, addresses, news reports and much more). On account of its technological constitution, this structure can be fully surveyed and monitored.

Digital reality differs from good old *analogue reality* in being mathematical through and through. It is not only that it consists in information – which is in fact stored at analogue locations (on servers): it is not itself physical. We are to think of digital reality as a dissemination of mental objects – of thoughts, images, memes and the rest – which recognizes no limits or boundaries. Everything that's available online can be hacked; hence the need for continual software updates, which are reactions to developments in the hacker community. Yet there is no unbreakable firewall.

The internet proves that functionalism possesses a core truth: truth-apt thoughts are in fact both multiply realizable and substrate-independent. I can write down the truth without thereby changing it. The truth can be preserved in a photograph, a video, an unconscious, troubling memory, or as graffiti. The internet certainly contains thoughts (information); it is just that this is no reason for the idea that it must therefore also think.

In the course of his analysis, Ferraris reminds us that the digital revolution (especially the computer and the internet) ultimately developed from the arms race that took place both before and during the two world wars, as well as during the Cold War. Cryptography – i.e. the theory of encryption – at first served essentially military ends, and it provided the framework within which massive technological advances could occur – advances without which we would not now be living in the information age.

According to Ferraris, this has the consequence that the internet is necessarily an arena of relentless cyber-warfare. This warfare is not conducted somewhere *beyond* the internet: the internet as such is nothing other than a battlefield. This battlefield is by no means purely virtual. Because it contains information about reality, which does not itself consist purely of information, it is utterly entwined with the analogue reality we all inhabit. You can only book hotels online provided there are hotels in the offline world.

As we all know, online social transactions can have horrible consequences in people's lives. Just think of the violence committed in internet forums, which on occasion can even lead to cases of suicide. Political upheavals are also generated within this new public space. The internet is not a distant world like the world of *World of Warcraft*. It is a real war game, so to speak, since all the moves we make in it have consequences beyond the internet (and that's without even mentioning drones). We should not forget that every email we send is a trace in the universe. The online technological transfer of information consumes energy, and the internet is not to be underestimated as a contributing factor to the ecological crisis.

Ferraris sees the internet as a call to the total mobilization of humanity as a whole. It is a struggle of all against all, which even threatens states, forcing them to respond with new legal systems and surveillance strategies. Yet Ferraris overestimates the role played by digital reality. He thinks this reality has long since taken control and that we are already living in the age of the singularity. Popularized by the inventor and Google employee Ray Kurzweil (b. 1948) among others, the idea of the **singularity** is that we will arrive at a point at which our AI systems will have become so advanced that they are able to develop themselves automatically, without any involvement on our part.[35] Ferraris argues that we reached this point some time ago: the internet already has a social dynamic of its own, which nobody and nothing can control.

Society is not a video game

Ferraris has his reasons for this thesis – but fortunately ones we can refute. In the background of the theory of the information age that I'm developing here is a certain social ontology. The philosophical subdiscipline of **social ontology** has had a prominent advocate in John Searle, who has done much to enhance its respectability. The task of social ontology is to address the question of why many objects and facts count as 'social'. What differentiates a lunar crater from a banknote or a sentence? Money and sentences exist only within the context of group dynamics, whereas lunar craters simply exist, at least without the help of human group dynamics. But what is it that lunar craters lack and which makes money something social?

Ferraris's answer to this question is ultimately insufficient, but illuminating nonetheless.[36] His claim is that something is social if and only if it exists thanks to a document. Documents here are traces that institutions leave in reality. While they are certainly connected with the intentions of agents, their reach easily outstrips them. Take the German constitution, which provides a nice illustration of Ferraris's theory. When this document was first drafted and implemented, nobody could know that the equality of all people before the law would one day acquire a meaning that enabled the German parliament to support same-sex marriage or quotas for women. Our general experience of judicial systems teaches us how a legal text creates facts that reach far beyond the intentions of their authors.

Take a familiar problem: we often sign contracts that, however cautious we might be, contain clauses that could someday come back to bite us. Just try cancelling your internet contract when you move house and you'll realize soon enough that the document you signed has consequences of which you were previously unaware. With a little luck, consumer protection has sufficiently progressed such that the other contractual party, which is loath to release you from the contract cost-free, can also be surprised by documents, at least on occasion.

In Ferraris's view, society as a whole revolves around documentation. In our everyday lives, we experience this through the receipts piling up in our wallets and the countless documented transactions we conclude on a daily basis. These form the glue of society, so to speak. Documents make society what it is, and they can only be counteracted effectively by means of yet further documents.

This theory has a series of advantages over the original version developed by Searle. Searle connects the social to what he calls 'collective intentionality', which is really a circular definition: 'collective' is merely another world for 'social'.[37] Searle is of the view that money exists only because we all somehow continually agree not to abolish it. By the same token, then, he believes that we would put an end to financial crises if everyone simply agreed that they should stop.

A nice idea. But the reason this won't work is that money is not merely conventional. Money documents transactions and the availability of items that for their part are precisely not already social. Thus, a £50 note I carry about in my wallet documents all the goods I can buy with it. To be sure, many goods today are also documents of social transactions, but that's another story. Our market economy is not a pure service provider.

In the end, for all their commitment to a kind of realism, and for all that their contributions have helped provoke the global debate around new realism, both Searle's and Ferraris's theories fail due to their residual loyalty to an outmoded constructivist idea.[38] Both believe, that is, that all social facts would disappear once and for all were nobody to believe in them any longer, or were all documents to be eradicated.

This constructivist residue has the following consequence (as Ferraris has publicly conceded on several occasions): if we expunged all the documents recording the existence of ancient Egyptian culture, then this culture would never have existed. This means that its very existence is dependent on the documents that record it. So in the absence of records, its past existence vanishes too. For similar reasons, Searle accepts the equally absurd assumption that no ancient Greek ever sexually harassed another ancient Greek; after all, they had not yet developed any views about sexual harassment.[39] But that's like saying that slavery was not a form of violence before the thought that slavery is immoral had occurred to anyone and come to enjoy social recognition.

The basic problem with these positions in social ontology is that they conflate the criteria of our being able to recognize social facts with these facts themselves. The problem is the very 'transcendental fallacy' that Ferraris otherwise laments: they both draw conclusions in ontology (the mode of something's existence) from theses in epistemology (our modes of knowing about something).[40] We may well record and prove social facts with the help of documents. But it does not follow that the documents have the magical ability to generate social facts or, in the case of their destruction, to erase facts from the past.

Society is not a video game. It has real consequences. Documents, like thoughts expressed in sentences, also have effects at the level of non-virtual reality, because the two are very much bound up with each other. The internet is not a virtual realm unto itself but part of the same domain of reality inhabited by us animals.

The virtual dimension bears on our ways and means of processing information. But the information itself is not only about further information. Documents don't just attest to further documents, and social facts are not restricted to mirroring (already social!) acts of collective intentionality.

For there to be social reciprocity in the first place, structures lying beneath the threshold of our conscious attention already have to be in place. Social cohesion does not result from human beings getting together at some point and drawing up plans to establish a social collective. Rather, sociality emerges from the unconscious patterns of action undertaken by beings with a distinctive biological prehistory. This, however, is largely unknown; it reaches too deeply into the past of our planet, and it is simply impossible to gather the data on the precise organic constitution of the human being and the human brain that we would need to shed light on the relevant phenomena.[41]

The Achilles heel of functionalism

We can now return to functionalism. For all the legitimate criticism we have levelled against it, it seems to be on the right track. In particular, it explains why an AI can do some things at least as well as we can, and some things even better. A pocket calculator can perform arithmetic better and quicker than practically all human beings, because it performs the same function (calculating) as a human thinker and, on account of its hardware, is better able to apply the rules of mathematics that have been programmed into it. Pocket calculators are more focused than we are because they can do one thing and one thing only: calculate.

The strength of functionalism, and the key to its technological utility, lies in not tying thought to the specific internal processes of living beings (to bits of neural circuitry, for example, or to signal transmission and coordination in the brain). How the function is realized plays no essential role. So long as it's realized somehow, we seem to be dealing with an act of thought of the relevant kind.

Yet functionalism in its pure form has countless weaknesses. The **main problem of functionalism** is that it doesn't give us any description of what human thinking really is. It deals not with *thinking* itself but with a *model of thinking*. Above, we borrowed an initial answer to the question of what 'thinking' means from Hilary Lawson (see pp. 18f.). He develops a theory of reflexivity – that is, of thought's reference to itself – which he explicitly situates in the tradition of German idealism (above all Hegel) and its continuation in the twentieth century.[42] By 'thinking', Lawson understands the way in which we regard the non-identical as identical.

In other words, thinking is the construction of models of reality. For example, I can currently hear seagulls making a racket outside the window of my hotel room in Ischia. The thought that it is seagulls making the noise identifies two different seagulls in respect of their being seagulls. Lawson thereby draws upon a philosophical tradition stretching back to antiquity, since philosophy from time immemorial has understood thinking as the activity thanks to which we recognize similarities within difference. Lawson goes a step further insofar as he also takes account both of how we alter our conceptual apparatus over time and of how our concepts are sometimes utterly ill-formed. Greek philosophy, by contrast, tended to assume that our conceptual apparatus as a whole is essentially fit for purpose, coherent and eternal.

A further problem is that functionalism leaves the door wide open to radical dualism. This has been noted by the French computer scientist and AI specialist Jean-Gabriel Ganascia (b. 1955), who makes this point in his book *The Myth of Singularity: Do We Have Anything to Fear from Artificial Intelligence?*[43] The gap between hardware and software is so fundamental for functionalism that it becomes hard to see how the two can be accommodated within the idea of a closed material universe. Ganascia comes to the correct conclusion that the kind of functionalism so beloved of cognitive scientists is incompatible with materialism.

> The consequence is that mind could exist independently and fully detached from matter. In short, if one pursues the thought through to the end, the traditional monism of contemporary science [i.e. materialism], which the advocates of the technological singularity like to claim for themselves, leads it to recognize a dualism that is as radical as it is absurd.[44]

To get at the underlying logic of this argument, we need to go into the details a little more closely and introduce a few supplementary concepts. A **condition of individuation** is a set of rules that determines when something is identical with something else, and therefore with itself. For example, it is (or still is at any rate) a condition of the individuation of human beings that they are produced by parents, in the sense that an ovum (of the biological mother) fuses with a male sperm (of the biological father). This usually comes about via sexual intercourse, but this is of secondary importance so far as procreation is concerned – so says the functionalist at least, and not entirely without reason; after all, there is of course artificial insemination. This highly simplified mini-theory already faces a problem with twins. Closer research teaches us that the individuation conditions for creatures of a certain species are by no means always easy to determine. Reality tends to be more complex than its functional characterization.

Be that as it may, functionalism as a theory assumes that it has at its disposal a sufficient number of unequivocal conditions of individuation for the biological hardware of thinkers, as distinct from their software. The individuation conditions of the software of thinkers are given in the form of algorithms. Generally speaking, an **algorithm** is a rule that prescribes how a process is to be carried out in well-defined steps in order to arrive at a certain result, a solution to some given problem.

Algorithms are defined in terms of their logical properties. Logic is concerned with the laws of being true; that is, it describes the conditions under which thoughts can be connected with and translated into one another. From the point of view of logic, the thought that Anna loves Sofia is identical with the thought that Sofia is loved by Anna. Moreover, it follows that there is somebody whom Anna loves (namely Sofia). And we could keep going. The important point is that laws of logic describe the control conditions for algorithms. Logic is one of the foundations of mathematics, which means of course that it is one of the foundations of the digital age as well. Yet what tends to be overlooked is that logic for its part has a further foundation, a foundation beyond which we can dig no further: thought. Thought is the foundation of logic, which is why philosophy, the business of thinking about thinking, is still more basic than logic.

Digitalization is the realization of the logical insights of the late nineteenth and early twentieth century on a newly developed technological basis. Unlike analogue signals, digital signals are based on different forms of signal transmission. We needn't get into the technical details involved here, but there is one aspect on which we need to focus. To do so, it helps to think about the distinction between the continuous and the discrete.

Discrete differences sort things into clearly demarcated domains. If you're in London, you cannot at the same time be in Berlin. As statements of location, London and Berlin express a discrete difference. By contrast, there are also **continuous differences**, which are also known as intensive differences. For example, the red covers of two books can each feature a differently intensive red. Our red experience is continuous: there are various grades or intensities of being red, just as a tone can be louder or softer without there being two clear classifications (the loud and the soft).

Now, it is possible to establish certain relations between the continuous (or analogue) and the discrete (or digital). We can think of these as a form of translation. Under certain conditions, analogue information can be transformed into discrete information, and vice versa. We can scan documents and digitalize old photos because we can take the continuous information consciously absorbed in the form of perception and break it up into discrete units. Behind the translation rules that we package up in the form of software are algorithms, basic steps for transforming information, and these translation rules are ultimately grounded in logic. Yet this in no way means that analogue, continuous reality is logical. Logic gives us translation manuals, or, in other words, it determines under what conditions we can produce meaningful translations. If it thereby tells us something about the pre- or non-logical, it does so at best indirectly – specifically, it tells us that it can be partly digitalized. But it doesn't tell us anything about reality as a whole.

The Achilles heel of functionalism therefore consists, on the one hand, in its mostly implicit but nonetheless radical dualism of hardware and software. On the other hand, there is its conflation of logic with the reality of thought. It overlooks how, while our thought is indeed oriented around logical norms, it is under no compulsion to obey them. The reality of thought has a different *form* to the model of thinking that is (mathematical) logic, and thus has a different form to computer science too.

3

The Digital Transformation of Society

It's perfectly logical, isn't it?

Logic studies inferential relationships between thoughts. The meaning of the ancient Greek word *logos* is broad enough to encompass our concepts of relation, measure, proposition, language, thought, speech, word and reason. Ever since Plato and Aristotle established it as a discipline, logic had addressed a fundamental question: supposing we want to acquire knowledge purely by linking one thought with another, *how exactly* do these thoughts have to be connected? Logic has therefore traditionally been occupied with three topics: concepts, judgements and inferences.

A **concept** is something that we can separate out from a thought in order to go on to use it in further thoughts. Let's take a simple thought, call it (A), which we can express as follows:

(A) Angela Merkel lives in Berlin.

We can extract at least two concepts from this thought. First, the concept *Angela Merkel* and, second, the concept *lives in Berlin*. Of course, you could also pick out the concept *Berlin* or the concept *lives in*, as well as the concepts *Angela*, *Merkel* and *in*. But I want to draw attention to the following point: using *Angela Merkel* and *lives in Berlin*, we can arrive at new thoughts. If Angela Merkel lives in Berlin, it follows that other people could live in Berlin as well, unless we have additional information to the effect that only one person lives in that city at the moment. If Angela Merkel lives in Berlin, we also know that Angela Merkel could do other things too. She doesn't just live in Berlin but might on occasion visit Paris, or call Emmanuel Macron. Angela Merkel can do many things, and many people can live in Berlin.

We can grasp such simple truths because, from the thought that

97

(A) Angela Merkel lives in Berlin,

we can derive further thoughts. The most general rules of derivation of new thoughts from given thoughts are logical laws. In this context, so-called **existential generalization**, for example, is a logical law: if Oscar (or Yitzhak, Cem, Mariya or whoever) buys a burger, it follows that someone exists who buys a burger. More generally: if something (call it: a) has a property (P), then it follows that something (x) has the property P. From 'a is P', we can infer 'some x is P'. If the apple is red, something is red. This is hardly a deep insight, but it's often worth making logical laws explicit and studying the ways they fit together. If it were not for the intellectual and technical skills we have acquired through making logical laws explicit, we would still be living in the Stone Age.

The laws of logic determine the relations between concepts and thoughts that we can form on the basis of other given thoughts, such as (A), for example. Logic tries to work out logical laws from the available material of human thought. In doing so, however, it asks not how humans actually or empirically think but how they *ought* to think if they want to behave rationally – i.e. if they want to avoid false inferences and derive true thoughts from other true thoughts according to universally acceptable laws. Logic is not a description of actual human thought processes but an account of ideal, rational thought.

While logic answers the question of how humans should think if they want to derive newly articulated true thoughts from given thoughts in a reliable manner, psychology looks at how humans *in fact* think. Logic and psychology are therefore two essentially different sciences. As such, they cannot be in conflict. This was a point emphasized not just by Frege but also by the mathematician and founder of the philosophical school of phenomenology, Edmund Husserl (1859–1938). Like Frege, Husserl was also both a philosopher and a mathematician, and he too contributed to the foundations of modern mathematical logic.

A similar distinction applies in the case of ethics and behavioural economics: ethics investigates how we ought to act; behavioural economics investigates how we do in fact act. So, just as psychology doesn't refute logic (and vice versa), behavioural economics doesn't refute ethics (and vice versa). The fact that most patterns of actual human behaviour do not consist in carrying out rationally preconceived and ideal plans does not entail that humans never act rationally or that there is no such thing as universal moral laws.

Psychology, logic, ethics and behavioural economics each have a different topic.

The domain of logic extends beyond human thought. Indeed, in the age of big data, we are experiencing just such an extension. By means of simple operations, which we can model mathematically and program as software, an AI arrives at further information via inference patterns implemented in hard- and software. *On this level, AI deploys pure logic decoupled from the noise of actual human thought.* For this reason, a good old pocket calculator is much better at transforming the expression of one thought into the expression of another. This does not mean that a pocket calculator actually calculates in the way in which humans actually think. Absolutely not – otherwise it wouldn't be as reliable as it is.

This is why an AI cannot make mistakes. It can certainly break down, be attacked by viruses and, because no software can ever be perfect, require continual software updates. But when my computer crashes, it doesn't make a mistake. The operations of my computer are, as it were, pure logic. There is no computer psychology. Notice that this notion of logic is compatible with there being different logical systems. Contemporary AI, to be sure, is not just an engine running on the kind of formal systems known to nineteenth- and twentieth-century logic. Machine learning deploys different kinds of logical formal systems, which are designed to function in a context where a task (a problem space) is sufficiently well defined to be the target system of a formal model.

In our digital age, logic dominates over human thought. While our actual human thought is oriented to logic as an objective, this does not mean that we in fact think logically, that we extract concepts from our thoughts and logically connect them up to make new ones in a series of small, definite steps that can be captured in an algorithm. As living beings, we work under time pressures and often prefer to pay the price of committing a logical error over the hassles of engaging in lengthy chains of reasoning. Besides, since we are emotional beings who, given our greater or lesser adaption to complex environments, have widely varying character traits, we don't always resort to logic in order to achieve our goals. Outside of rigorous scientific contexts, human communication tends to be logically undisciplined (and even scientific contexts are not entirely organised in terms of the optimisation of rational procedures, as everyone who works in academia knows only too well).

In everyday life, we exchange fragmentary, half-formed ideas and talk a lot of nonsense while we're at it. The nonsense we share with each other mostly serves the function of greasing the wheels of our social interactions, from small talk to board meetings (and scientific conferences). This is why so many people, privately at least, get so het up about the nonsense people talk day in day out: for beings who discovered logic, it's something of an impertinence to be confronted with so many fallacies and false opinions on pretty much a daily basis.

The psychology of everyday life is a tangle of nonsense, which we have to submit to social structuring if our civilization is not to collapse under the weight of unrelenting mental chaos.[1] Humans simply do not have logically optimized rationality as their sole concern but instead act under highly various influences. There is nothing wrong with this: we are not a bunch of Mr Spocks. And it is precisely because we can draw on different modules of thinking in different circumstances that we are fallible subjects, and thus subjects equipped with objectivity.

AI is not a copy of human thought. Rather, it is a model of thought. It is a logical map of our thinking which abstracts away from the time pressures and needs that characterize our lives as finite beings – beings, moreover, who could not think at all were we not in possession of a mortal organism that plays a decisive role in shaping our interests.

Yet the boundaries of logic are the boundaries of AI. Nothing and nobody is more intelligent than logic. Logic sets the framework of the thinkable because it prescribes how we are to think if our thoughts are to form a coherent whole. To step beyond logic is to step beyond the domain of any recognizably intelligent operation. Logic, in short, marks out the unsurpassable boundaries of thought. There is no thought outside of logic, just pure nonsense. In this respect, the discipline of logic affords us a grasp of the upper bound of rationality. Yet this grasp, of course, is itself fallible and imperfect. We are, after all, indefinitely far away from having discovered all possible logical formal systems. Arguably, it is not even possible to exhaust the space of possible logical formal systems – but that's another topic.

Some set-theoretical ping-pong

The classical ideals of logic are consistency and coherence. A system of thoughts (a theory) is **consistent** provided it neither contains an explicit contradiction nor allows one to be derived from it by its own lights (by deploying its operations). A system of thoughts (a theory) is **coherent** if its parts hang together in a

rational manner. Both ideals have been circumscribed or modified through developments in modern logic. Most important for
our discussion, however, is the following key insight, which has
been well known in logic ever since the eighteenth century (at least
since Leibniz): there can be no completely consistent and coherent total system of all thoughts. Every system of thoughts has to
exclude certain thoughts in order to establish stability. Although
it was known long before him, the insight was canonized by the
mathematician Kurt Friedrich Gödel (1906–1978), who proved his
famous incompleteness theorems for every formal (mathematical)
system of thoughts.

Behind his argumentation lies an ancient logical observation,
one which even found its way into the Bible via Paul's Letter to
Titus:

> There are also many rebellious people, idle talkers and deceivers,
> especially those of the circumcision; they must be silenced, since they
> are upsetting whole families by teaching for sordid gain what it is not
> right to teach. It was one of them, their very own prophet, who said,
> 'Cretans are always liars, vicious brutes, lazy gluttons.'
> That testimony is true. For this reason rebuke them sharply, so
> that they may become sound in the faith, not paying attention to
> Jewish myths or to commandments of those who reject the truth.[2]

Here we find the following famous sentence which, in a revised
form, has become known as the liar paradox:

(B) Cretan: All Cretans always lie.

The paradox is attributed to the Cretan philosopher Epimenides,
who lives several centuries before Paul and is counted among the
pre-Socratics. When a Cretan such as Epimenides says that Cretans
always lie, the paradox becomes clear.

The usual (though not necessarily self-evident) account of lies
has it that someone lies when they utter a false sentence and passes
it off as a truth with the intention of deceiving someone else. So, if
a Cretan utters the sentence that all Cretans always lie, it follows
that the sentence is false. If it is true that all Cretans always lie,
then a Cretan who asserts precisely this must also be lying. Then
the sentence has to be false, else it wouldn't be a lie. If a Cretan,
however surprisingly, ever told a truth in telling us that all Cretans
always lie, then the sentence would be true. But the Cretan would
have expressed a falsehood in this case too. We thus get the paradox that the utterance

(B) All Cretans always lie

is automatically false on the lips of a Cretan if it's true, and true if it's false.

Strictly speaking, (B) is still some way off being the liar paradox proper. The latter is expressed, for example, by the following sentence:

(C) Sentence (C) is false.

For (C) is true if it's false and false if it's true. We therefore need to outlaw sentences of this type when formulating formal theories of truth. Historically, though, this fairly recent problem of formal theories of truth harks back to the passage from Paul and to the difficulty of how we can ever trust someone who belongs to a group of people that are (allegedly) known never to tell the truth.

Modern logic proceeds on the assumption that we have to construct our thought systems in a way that rules out paradoxes from the start. This is in large part due to Bertrand Russell, who managed to develop a paradox that plunged Frege and modern mathematics into a deep crisis. It's important to have a brief look at Russell's insight because it has consequences for our own social reality, which, in the information age, rests on mathematical processes of signal transmission. We can never fully shield digital civilization from logical paradoxes.

Russell points out a problem in what is known today as 'naïve set theory'. The problem is that naïve set theory does not exclude there being a set of all sets. A set can be any assortment of objects that we find and simply gather together. A set is a collection of given items. Any collection of given items constitutes a set. The set of objects on my desk is the pile of stuff that's lying right in front of me: spectacles, cup, computer screen, letters, books, Post-it notes, pens. You can build this set by applying brackets: {spectacles, cup, computer screen, letters, books, Post-it notes, pens}. In this set, we don't find the set itself. The set of things lying on my desk isn't something lying on my desk in addition to the things themselves.

Let's introduce another set. No one has ever thought of all sets. There is therefore a set of thoughts no one has thought of. Maybe no one has thought about the set of opinions that Swedes have about Sweden, about the set of galaxies in a distant, hitherto unobserved region of the universe, and so on and so on. It is also quite probable that many readers of this paragraph haven't bothered to develop any views about the set of everything they haven't yet developed any views about. Therefore, the set of all sets about which some such reader of this paragraph has not yet developed any views belongs to itself: it is itself a set they haven't thought about (before thinking the thoughts expressed in this paragraph).

So, it seems that we have, on the one hand, a set of all sets that do not belong to themselves and, on the other hand, a set of all sets that do belong to themselves.

You might at this point ask Russell's infamous question: Does the set of all sets that do not belong to themselves belong to itself or not? Let's begin by assuming that the set of all sets that do not belong to themselves does belong to itself. It then follows that it does not belong to itself. After all, the set ought to contain only sets that do not belong to themselves. If it belongs to itself then it doesn't. In order to avoid this contradiction, let's assume that the set of all sets that do not belong to themselves does not in fact belong to itself. But, in that case, as it doesn't belong to itself, it is itself one of the sets that doesn't belong to itself. Consequently, it does belong to itself after all – another contradiction.

The awkward upshot is that the set of all sets that do not belong to themselves belongs to itself if it does not, and it does not belong to itself if it does – a miserable, unending game of logical ping-pong.

Everything crashes eventually

This sorry game of ping-pong isn't just a means of passing time in the ivory tower or an exercise in a beginner's course in mathematical logic. You are all familiar with it already from an everyday experience: that of a computer program crashing. If I suddenly see the rainbow wheel of death on my screen, I'll get pretty annoyed if I haven't yet saved my manuscript. All programs crash at some point or other, and this is connected to the fact that it's impossible to write a program that cannot possibly run in an endless loop. This is another version of the problem that leads into Russell's paradox. Theoretical computer science investigates it within the framework of computability theory under the heading of the **halting problem**.[3]

This problem has many technical and theoretical ramifications. But the crux of the matter is that, for any given program, we cannot definitively decide by means of a further program whether it will come to a halt – i.e. crash.

A **program** (from the Greek *pro* = pre-, and *graphein* = write), translated literally, is a pre-scription. At this point, we once again need to bring in the most famous computer scientist of all time, Alan Turing. Non-computer scientists might know him from the (unfortunately rather kitsch) film *The Imitation Game* (2014). So-called Turing machines are named after Turing and, thanks to him, today they're known as computers. Originally, 'computer' simply meant 'someone who computes', primarily a human being. Since Turing, the expression has been applied to machines that share certain features with human computers.

We might think of a **Turing machine** as follows: let's suppose that we had an endlessly long strip of paper consisting of a series of long sections of equal length, separated from one another by lines. We also need a read/write head (as in an old typewriter), which can move along the strip (also known as a Central Processing Unit or CPU). Let's also suppose that on each strip there can be written a 1, a 0, or nothing at all. Now we can develop a series of programs. For example, on one field we can write a 0, on the field to the right of it a 1, and the one beside that one we can leave as a blank space. We can establish the rule that the read/write head moves to the right whenever it encounters a 1 and that whenever it encounters a 0 it overwrites it with a 1, before accordingly moving a further place to the right. Whenever it encounters a blank space it terminates. This program will then halt in the third field if we begin at the 0: the program terminates, as we say.

Now let's take another program, which says that the read/write head should always move one field to the right when it hits a field. This (pretty boring) program doesn't come to an end. It never terminates. It just keeps moving monotonously onwards. Of course, this program cannot actually be realized, because at some point or other every strip of paper will be completely written over and every read/write head destroyed. Moreover, the entire universe does not have enough energy to keep this process going forever, which is connected to the possible increase of entropy, the deterioration of structure in the universe. But let's put this to one side.

We therefore know that there are programs that terminate and programs that do not. Now we have to pose the question whether we can write a program that, for every single program, can determine whether *it* does or doesn't terminate. Let's call this super-program GOD. **GOD** would be the program that can find out whether any given program does or doesn't terminate.

You can probably see where this is going: the problem clearly arises when GOD encounters itself. At some point GOD has to decide whether GOD terminates or not. If the only semantic units at our disposal are 1, 0 and an empty space, we could stipulate that we are to understand 1 as the expression that terminates a program and 0 as the expression that doesn't terminate it. The blank space doesn't contain any expression. For every program, GOD finds out whether it terminates, including itself. It has to deliver a result as to whether it terminates or not. If you feed a program into GOD, it will write a 1 if it terminates, and move a field to the right, and 0 if it doesn't terminate, and likewise move to the right. If GOD doesn't terminate, and just keeps on endlessly investigating programs to determine whether or not they terminate, then it cannot state that it doesn't terminate. If it ever does make such a statement, then it hasn't yet investigated all other programs. But it cannot state this either, as the assumption was that it never terminates! So, GOD cannot make the statement that it doesn't terminate. But, if GOD terminates, that means that every program crashes eventually.

In short, for a program such as GOD to be possible, it has to make an unequivocal statement as to whether every program that's presented to it – including GOD itself! – terminates. In order to state that GOD does not itself terminate, GOD has to terminate.

The halting problem, it should be noted, is considerably more involved than this simplified version suggests. But our little sketch has a considerable advantage: it points in a philosophical direction and to an insight that is much more general than the logical paradoxes of modern mathematics and theoretical computer science. For, arguably, we will ultimately always hit upon paradoxes if we philosophize right up to the limits of thought and ask ourselves how we actually function as thinkers of thoughts. If thinking thinks about itself, it eventually arrives at the insight that paradoxes can never be avoided entirely. This has been shown, for example, by the Australian philosopher and logician Graham Priest (b. 1948) and the Heidelberg philosopher Anton Friedrich Koch (b. 1952).[4]

That mathematical paradoxes can be generalized beyond mathematics was something suspected by both Kurt Gödel and the founder of set theory, Georg Cantor (1845–1918). Both these men sought refuge from their logical difficulties in God: believing that they had discovered the boundaries of logic, they imagined that the logically inaccessible mysteries of the divine must lie on the other side. Gödel even set out his own proof of the existence of God.[5]

Regardless of the tendency of certain logicians to escape from paradox by supplementing logic with mysticism, the key result we need for present purposes is that it is impossible to build a computer that runs all programs. Every new operating system necessarily has its unpredictable pitfalls. Yet this is not simply a consequence of the snares of theoretical computer science: it simply follows from how, for any program we write that recognizably processes information, we cannot guarantee in advance that it will be able to process *any* information that's fed into it. There is no absolutely secure operating system. Everything crashes eventually.

Do computers really know anything?

But why can't we somehow transcend this logical limitation? Why can't we construct some absolutely stable rational order, an operating system that digitally solves all problems (by breaking them down into small steps), and then exploit technological progress to realize it in a piece of hardware?

On the one hand, there is a simple physical reason for this: the universe does not contain sufficient matter or energy to implement every logically possible computation. Plus, not everything that exists in the universe can be simulated by means of a computer. If it could, there would always have to be still another computer, or rather another program, that simulates the computation of all computations. It's not just that this would mean having a screen on which we could run all possible programs, showing all possible processes in the universe. (That would be quite something! We could surf through a potentially endless internet and immediately place ourselves – virtually at least – in any situation we like and take a look at it.) The problem is that our screen, on which all other programs run, would also have to appear on our screen. Yet before we could see our screen on our screen, we would also have to see our screen on our screen on our screen . . .

So, we'd firstly need an infinitely large screen and an infinite amount of memory space in order truly to simulate everything that happens in the universe. Yet even this wouldn't be enough, because this infinite screen would, in turn, have to appear on itself. This means that we would need a transfinitely large screen on which multiple infinities could run simultaneously. But we now know that this story itself wouldn't come to an end, which is arguably a consequence of the transfinite set theory developed by Cantor. More precisely, we know that questions such as 'How would a simulation of the whole universe look on a computer?' are essentially unanswerable. It exceeds both our powers of comprehension and those of every computer.[6] Thus, for both logical and physical reasons, there cannot be a program like GOD. Omniscience is impossible in the universe (which is why God, in contradistinction to GOD, is usually thought to be outside of the universe!).

After these exercises in transcendence, let's return to the familiar terrain of ordinary life. Since the publication of an influential work by Husserl, this terrain has often been known as the lifeworld (*Lebenswelt* in German). In his late work *The Crisis of European Sciences and Transcendental Phenomenology* of 1936, Husserl uncovered a blind spot in the modern understanding of science, which remains unremedied to this day. This is what he called the lifeworld. The **lifeworld** is our everyday understanding of the things that surround us, of the persons and cultural relations that we negotiate as soon as we have undergone even minimal education. It is what allows us to avoid running to our deaths the second we cross the road, to learn to feed ourselves, and few other things besides (such as driving, ordering a meal in a restaurant, having small talk, climbing ladders, etc.).

Among its inhabitants, the lifeworld counts our natural languages, such as English, German, French, Arabic, Finnish, or whichever language you learnt as your mother tongue.

Natural languages are not formal systems. The meaning of most expressions (most likely of all expressions) is not precisely defined. In the philosophy of language, this is known as **vagueness**, and, thanks to Ludwig Wittgenstein's *Philosophical Investigations*, we know that natural language is vague through and through and that it only functions in the first place thanks to this fuzziness. Far from undermining meaning, vagueness is in fact its enabling condition. The *Philosophical Investigations* were published only after Wittgenstein's death in 1953 and, with respect to the development of computer science, has taken on a life of its own, as Wittgenstein was not at all in agreement with Turing, whom he knew personally from Cambridge. In a certain sense, modern computer science is based on Turing's defiant response to Wittgenstein's insight that human intelligence and understanding rests on vagueness, which cannot be reduced to binary digits.

The lifeworld is full of vagueness and would fail to function if we tried to articulate its structure in completely 'clear' terms. In a quite banal situation, Petra says to Walid that Heiko will turn up soon. But when exactly is 'soon'? In five minutes? In two? In seven minutes and thirty-three seconds, or in two hours? And things aren't any more precise when the tour guide in Dallas tells us: 'This is where Kennedy was shot.' Nobody can draw an exact circle around the place at which Kennedy was shot. The precise location doesn't even exist. Or, rather, there can be only a necessarily vague indication, such as 'here', accompanied by the guide's pointing their finger so as to designate an approximate region. This does not mean that Kennedy was shot nowhere in particular (he was), but the location (and time) of his death are vague states of affairs. Reality is not a bunch of binary digits; it is not made up of mathematically rigorous information. Of course, digital systems are part of reality too, but they do not exhaust the meaning of 'reality'. It is therefore a simple mistake when physicists such as Max Tegmark speculate that the universe might essentially be an objectively existing bundle of mathematics.

We might try to make all our concepts utterly determinate by giving our words precise definitions. But this attempt to squeeze our words into semantic straitjackets just won't get us very far. It's easy to show why. Suppose we order Wiener schnitzel in a restaurant. Much to our surprise, the waiter brings us an exemplar straight out of the deep freeze. Disappointed and annoyed, we send it back, because we didn't want a frozen schnitzel. 'Well you could have said so', counters the waiter, and walks off. When he returns with a new Wiener schnitzel, it is burnt to a cinder and scorching hot. We decline this specimen too. In order to be sure and to avoid any unpleasant surprises, we now order a schnitzel that is neither deep-frozen nor charred, but one with the normal temperature, which we can even specify to a precise enough degree. Then the waiter comes back with a schnitzel as large as my thumb. Needless to say, we don't want this either. We want a schnitzel that's neither frozen nor burnt nor too small. But how are we meant to define 'Wiener schnitzel' in a way that compels the waiter to bring us the right one?

Nobody is able to give a complete definition of 'Wiener schnitzel' by specifying all of its features. Here, Wikipedia (as is so often the case) doesn't help us either, defining 'Wiener schnitzel' as 'a type of schnitzel made of a thin, breaded, pan-fried veal cutlet'.[7] For these criteria are also met by a frozen, burnt or nano-exemplar, as well as by infinitely many further variations that we just wouldn't recognize as a examples of Wiener schnitzel.

This is the precise point at which the two most important critics of so-called strong AI join the argument: the philosophers John Searle and Hubert Dreyfus, both of whom worked at the University of California, Berkeley, near Silicon Valley. They are the pioneers of the philosophy of AI. By **strong AI**, people understand the idea that we could develop an AI that is indistinguishable from human intelligence (a human level of Artificial General Intelligence). There are of course as yet no such AIs. No chatbot or other program even approximately resembles human intelligence as we know it. At the linguistic level alone, there is not yet a translation program that we can trust to produce an adequate translation of every text that's randomly fed into it.

Every AI delivers results on the basis of a restricted data pool (even if they create their own data, as in the famous game simulations of chess and Go created by AlphaZero, which run multiple bouts of those games against itself in order to create data for pattern recognition). To be sure, in the digital information age, the data pool on which AIs can draw has grown rapidly, allowing, for example, search machines to get ever better at 'anticipating' what we're searching for. Yet we should never entertain the idea that our search machines are intelligent in the same way as we are. Even if we have long since outsourced certain modules of human intelligence, such as basic mental arithmetic, to AIs like traditional pocket calculators, no pocket calculator or price-comparison algorithm has the ability to develop all the other modules. This is why a distinction is often made between the currently available forms of AI and a **universal AI**, which can, at the right moment, switch from one intelligent activity to any other. Such a universal AI has yet to be realized and, if Searle and Dreyfus are right, never will be.

Searle and Dreyfus argue against the very possibility of strong AI on the basis of the vagueness of human language. In doing so, they in fact exploit a wonderful insight, which can already be found in a small essay by the great philosopher and mathematician Georg Wilhelm Leibniz (1646–1716), one of the early pioneers in developing calculating machines (computers).[8]

We have just seen how 'Wiener schnitzel' is not fully defined and, ultimately, not fully definable. Leibniz pushes this point to its furthest consequence with an argument which, in my view, is much stronger than the formal proofs of Gödel or Turing. The argument is that we can never fully analyse a single concept. Even if we had made great strides in the definition of 'Wiener schnitzel' and attained a significantly improved understanding of the concept, we would still have to analyse all the concepts by means of which we had analysed the concept of a Wiener schnitzel. How does one now define 'schnitzel' or 'breaded'? And what about 'Wiener' (surely not by listing everything you can find in Vienna)? One could ask the Austrian Freedom Party, but they're probably not terribly advanced when it comes to foundational conceptual questions concerning the definition of 'Vienna' or 'Wiener'. And what about 'and', a little word you need to use in order to tie the elements of the definition together?

Even if you could work miracles and set out a complete definition of 'Wiener schnitzel' together with all definitions of the words needed for the definition (good luck!), you still end up with the following problem: there would be simple-meaning components that couldn't be broken down into still smaller components, so-called **semantic atoms**. If these didn't exist, we couldn't bring our definition to a clearly demarcated end and would be caught in an infinite definitional loop. But, if there are semantic atoms, we cannot grasp them by defining words that correspond to decomposable concepts.

This is the reason why Plato and Aristotle, who were the first to address this problem, both assumed that we can grasp simple concepts, semantic atoms, by means of a sense of thought. They conceived this sense as mind/intelligence (in ancient Greek: *nous*). There is an echo of this in the German word for reason: *Vernunft*. The word *Vernunft* derives from the verb *vernehmen*, which means both to interrogate or question and to perceive, specifically aurally. *Vernehmen* has an interesting history in old and Middle High German, which encompasses the idea of removal or withdrawal (abstraction) and of receiving and accepting. Reason is a thought-sense which we need in order to get into contact with semantic atoms.

Dreyfus and Searle do not go as far as our philosophical forebears Plato, Aristotle and Leibniz. Yet they are quite correct in pointing out that we can understand linguistic meaning only because we possess a background that comprises both our biological nature and socio-historically acquired capacities. Thanks to this background, we don't have to analyse expressions into their individual components in order to understand them.

Human intelligence is not digital and it works under time pressures. We don't break down our lifeworld into digital signals in order to form a picture of what we want and ought to do. Instead, we grasp it without exploiting any digital processing techniques. The resolution of our lifeworld into digital signals and its subsequent composition into a stable picture of the environment is just not an option for creatures like us: at some point or other this process has to stop, so that we can get into direct, analogue contact with the reality of the lifeworld. This does not change simply because our lifeworld is evidently populated by digital devices. I could not so much as see the screen on which I am writing this, and so articulate my thoughts in the digital code that underlies the program I am currently using, without relying on the same modes of adaption to my perceptual environment as in any other case of seeing. Screens cannot replace my field of vision; they are just more things to be seen.

Humans always understand linguistic meaning in particular contexts. And they can intelligently grasp and find their way about in these contexts without having, or even being able, to subject them to linguistic analysis. An AI cannot do this. It has to extrapolate from data that have typically already been pre-processed by humans on its behalf. How could a data-processing machine, which has no kind of interest whatsoever either in survival or in our human life form, possibly perceive its environment as we do?

We cannot solve this problem by modelling the parameters of our biological evolution, packing them into algorithms, and then installing these as a program on non-biological hardware. For, even if we thought this was somehow possible in principle, it remains factually impossible. At any given time, that is, a single human organism is far too complex to be simulated digitally. Indeed, we cannot even simulate an entire brain, as brains too develop temporally. Even if we could somehow simulate all neurons in a given brain, we would not thereby have simulated their integration into a much more complicated causal environment (which includes a human organism and much more besides). The neural processes within our skull are embedded in much larger systems, and it is a terrible mistake on the part of much contemporary neuro- and cognitive science simply to forget the fact that neural tissue is part of a highly complex ecological niche. This is just to indulge a misguided abstraction. Like it or not: we are animals and not abstract patterns of neural firing!

One of the reasons why we cannot simulate whole human brains is that our nervous system is astronomically intricate – so much so that many say the human brain is the most complex known object in the universe. Then there's the fact that signal transmission in the brain occurs biochemically and involves intensive magnitudes (such as pressure relations). Synapses are not on/off switches and our brain does not function like a Turing machine; there are no read/write heads or clearly demarcated fields offering alternatives such as on or off. The brain is in no relevant sense like a digital computer.

Even the most complete decoding of the human brain would not grasp the biological foundations of human cognition, as the nervous system is yet more ramified still, reaching through the entire organism. It is even extremely highly differentiated in the intestinal area; so the idea that gut feeling plays a role in decision making in fact has something to it. It is biologically proved that, as animals, we don't just think with our heads (and we don't think with our whole heads anyhow).

Heidegger's murmurings

Both Dreyfus and Searle build on the philosophy of Husserl and, more specifically, on that of his famous and controversial student Martin Heidegger. In his aforementioned *Crisis of the European Sciences*, Husserl had argued, with good reason, against a scientistic conception of the human being and introduced the concept of the lifeworld. He argued that we cannot fully understand the human life form through the lenses of modern natural science because of how the latter leaves out the lifeworld. Heidegger could go one step further because, in his later life, he was able to take note of the beginnings of AI research, and he reacted to this in a series of writings that centrally address the question of what 'thinking' actually means.

The origins of the sweeping claims to explanatory power that we hear so often in the information age lie in so-called cybernetics (from the Greek *kybernêtês* = steersman). Cybernetics was established as an interdisciplinary field of research at a series of conferences that took place between 1946 and 1953 in the USA and which were funded by the Macy Foundation. The leading figure was Warren McCulloch (1898–1969), and several well-known scholars were involved, such as the mathematician Norbert Wiener (1894–1964), who helped coin the term 'cybernetics', and the mathematician and logician John von Neumann (1903–1957), who counts as the most important founder of computer science besides Turing.

Cybernetics has diverse and multifaceted ramifications. It also underlies constructivism, which was developed to a great extent by the aforementioned Chilean biologist Humberto Maturana and the psychologist Paul Watzlawick (1921–2007), who was also active in Palo Alto. The basic idea of **cybernetics** is that we can describe processes as control processes, for which we can design control circuits. This is also meant to extend to the domain of human thought.

I've just been re-reading certain passages in Heidegger's lectures and essays in order to double-check that he does indeed trace out the line of thought I thought he does. In order to do so, I first had to make a plan and then walk down a flight of stairs so that I could fetch the right book from my library. My reason for doing this was that I'm currently working on Heidegger, in part to write this section. And, in order to carry out the plan, certain intermediary steps had to be taken, steps which are pretty familiar, as I know the way to the library. I thus control the entire process with reference to an overall plan, which in turn contains several component plans. As the steersman of this process, I am myself a part of a control circuit of control mechanisms that reach far beyond me and which include the book trade, Heidegger's plans to undermine cybernetics, the manufacture of bookcases, the functioning of control circuits within my organism, and countless other systems, all of which in turn produce their own control processes.

Cybernetics suggests that we should also conceive of thinking as a control process. We could, so goes the idea, then study it by means of formal methods and techniques and transfer it on to other control circuits. We thus get to the starting point of AI research, which, thanks to technological breakthroughs stemming from the military's development of increasingly sophisticated communications engineering, is able to simulate ever more domains of human thought in the form of control circuits.

Heidegger does not share this optimism regarding the explanatory reach of cybernetics. In a highly characteristic gesture, he asks us to take a step back and reflect or contemplate, using the German locution *sich besinnen*. Indeed, he does so as a friend of the festive season: in Germany, it is not unusual to wish people a 'besinnliche' Christmas. And in a letter to his brother dated 18 December 1931, with which he enclosed a copy of *Mein Kampf* as a gift, we read:

> I hope that you will read Hitler's book; its first few autobiographical chapters are weak. This man has a remarkable and sure political instinct, and he had it even while all of us were still in a haze, there is no way of denying that. The National Socialist movement will soon gain a wholly different force. It is not about mere party politics – it's about the redemption or fall of Europe and western civilization [this might sound familiar in 2020 . . .]. Anyone who does not get it deserves to be crushed by the chaos. Thinking [*Besinnung*] about these things is no hindrance to the spirit of Christmas, but marks our return to the character and task of the Germans, which is to say to the place where this beautiful celebration originates. [Was Jesus, whose birth – so far as I'm aware – is celebrated at Christmas, in fact a German?][9]

Just a few years later, Heidegger writes that he 'has joined the party', and indeed, as he adds, 'out of inner conviction'.[10] Philosophy, for him, is a form of *Besinnung* and *Gelassenheit*, often translated as 'detachment' or 'letting be'. Supposedly, one can understand this only if one puts oneself in the right mood, which Heidegger – without a trace of irony, I fear – calls 'the chiming of silence'.[11] We should always read Heidegger with the utmost caution, as his thought is permeated with National Socialism, and, without the benefit of thorough philological and historical scholarship, it is hard to determine how much we might want to take on board and how much might lead us to unacceptable consequences. Yet although he opted for a terrible, anti-modern political path, several elements of his description of modernity are still right on the mark.

Heidegger invites us to pause and pay attention to the subtle distinction between thinking on the one hand and our activities of model construction on the other. If we describe thinking as a control circuit or as a subsystem of other systems, does this then mean that thinking *is* a control circuit or a subsystem of other systems?

Heidegger cites a series of reasons that speak against identifying human thought with a control circuit. Some of these have been taken up by Dreyfus, though he misconstrues a number of Heidegger's interesting arguments which, for all their questionable political intent, are well worth considering and have lost none of their relevance. In order to understand Dreyfus's overall approach to the philosophy of AI, we thus need to take a short Heideggerian detour.

We find a good overview of Heidegger's take on AI in his lecture *What is Called Thinking?*,[12] which he delivered on Bavarian radio in May 1952. His fundamental idea can be summarized as follows: when I think through a series of thoughts and recognize a connection between them, this only works provided I can rely on something – such as the rules of logic, recognized procedures of examining and corroborating opinions, my perceptions and memories, the things taught me by my parents and teachers, and so on. Not everything I rely on will be clearly known to me in the very process of relying on it. For example, we human beings rely on the rules of grammar and the history of our natural languages, without all of us being born students of linguistics. The organization of the traffic and transport systems in my home state in Germany (North Rhine Westphalia, the most populous German state) is an unspeakably complicated occult science of which I understand only very little. Yet I have to trust that someone or other has thought intelligently about how to organize the road system. But how do I know whether the system comprising all of these presuppositions I make day in and day out is truly comprehensible, let alone explainable as a whole?

To answer this question, it won't do to try to count through all my presuppositions and then verify them one by one or in neat little packets of presuppositions. In order to do so, I would once again have to rely on a series of methods, which I cannot in turn attempt to verify by means of yet further methods. Every attempt to attain

an overall picture of our picture of the world and its human inhabitants must sooner or later come up against a boundary.

It is important to focus on our continual habit of forming pictures
of our position within an encompassing non-human environment.
In forming these pictures, we suppose that our environment is
accessible to us – that is, that it is knowable and describable, at
least to some degree or other. I assume that the Earth was not created five minutes ago by an almighty being who merely fools me
into believing that I have a set of memories and that the planet I
inhabit has a genuine prehistory. Moreover, I believe that there
is a sofa behind me at the back of the room even though I'm not
looking at it right now, and that I would see the very same sofa I
always do were I suddenly to turn around. And, more generally,
I assume that reality comprises a vast inventory in the generation
and formation of which I personally have played at most a vanish-
ingly small role.

Heidegger calls this entire system of assumptions, without
which none of us could ever think a single rational thought, our
'understanding of being'. This understanding involves generating a
picture of our surroundings and of the situations in which we find
ourselves and using this picture as a guide to action.

At the airport, for example, we follow a multiplicity of rules.
From past experience, we are familiar with situations such as going
to the check-in desk. In other words, we know our way around the
check-in process. According to Heidegger, humans from different
epochs understand themselves, and thus know their way around
reality, in ways that are often radically divergent. It is only with
considerable effort that we can even begin to understand much of
what struck people in the fourteenth century as more or less self-
evident. This is a synchronic as well as a diachronic phenomenon:
think of how people from diverse cultural spheres or people who
inhabit distant forms of life can often attain at best an inadequate
understanding of one another. Of course, we don't have to travel
all that far in space or time in order to note that humans can possess highly various standards of evaluation and utterly different
conceptions of what ultimately matters in life. It often suffices
simply to call on your next-door neighbours. Cultural otherness
has almost nothing to do with borders or spatial isolation – cultural
otherness begins at home.

Heidegger's theorization of this issue bears a famous name: 'the
turn' (*die Kehre*).[13] What he meant by this was that we moderns
are exposed to a profound transition in our self-understanding.
Today, we call this globalization. Modernity is in fact a process of

revolution, of 'turns', behind which Heidegger recognizes a unified pattern. This pattern follows the idea that everything there is (all beings) is ultimately an object. Heidegger thinks that modernity has an inherent tendency to submit everything – including synchronically and diachronically distant lifeworlds – to its conceptual rules. On his view, this is because modernity adheres to the following principle: everything there is is something about which we can essentially make true statements.

Heidegger labels this understanding of being 're-presentation' (*Vor-Stellung*). Notice that the German word he uses also has a theatrical meaning: a staging of a play is called a 'Vorstellung' in German. According to the picture of being as re-presentation, reality is conceived as a grand stage upon which everything real takes place. Reality is 'out there', as the saying goes, and it is somehow represented 'in here' (in our minds, or brains for that matter). Whatever appears on the stage hangs together according to universal (logical, mathematical and natural) laws. This overall nexus obtains independently of us human beings. It is, as Heidegger says, a *Bestand*, a term that's somewhat awkwardly rendered by his translators as a 'standing-reserve', with the aim of conveying both its relation to the verb *bestehen*, which means to exist, persist or be available, and its standard meaning of stock or inventory.[14] The suggestion is that the worldview Heidegger is criticizing understands our standing with respect to reality in terms of stocktaking or of taking an inventory. We approach the world as though we find ourselves in the midst of the so-called furniture of reality, a largely pre-arranged and pre-organized collection of entities subject to inviolable laws of nature. According to this variant of a modern scientistic account of reality (the scientific worldview), humans are just objects among objects, with the surprising additional feature of consciousness.

Heidegger encapsulates this entire world picture in the word 'technology'. He doesn't see technology as, for example, an industrial complex or as a series of instruments that we deploy in order to achieve our aims. An aeroplane is not only a mode of transport that speeds up our journey to New York; it is also a response to a felt need, to a desire to do certain things (such as flying to New York in order to do something or other). Why should we use such a means of transport in the first place? You don't *have* to fly to New York. The question, then, is why we conceive of technology as we do in the first place; why do we think of it as a set of means to achieve our goals, when this presupposes that we have a grip on what our goals are to begin with? According to Heidegger, technology is not just a bunch of cleverly designed instruments but an existentially loaded, essentially deluded relationship to human and non-human reality. Technology is not there to satisfy our needs: rather, it produces those needs so that we continue to maintain it. Here, Heidegger's description uncannily anticipates the feedback loop between digital technology and our use of it: we produce data, which are used in turn by the digital corporate world in order to nudge us into producing yet more data, and so on and so on . . .

More precisely, Heidegger is right to point out the naïvety of believing that technology is just the means in a means–end relation of our own choosing. In an age in which almost all of us have our smartphones within reach at all times, it is by now surely clear that a telephone is not merely a means for giving somebody a call or sending them a message. Rather, smartphones fundamentally transform our attitude towards conversation itself, as well as towards other processes of relating to reality. It profoundly shapes our attitudes, a fact that is seized upon by those interested in developing new methods of exploitation and manipulation. In short, technology is essentially involved in determining *which* goals we set ourselves rather than being subordinate to goals that are somehow already predetermined.

What you *can* do with a tool partly determines what it is that you *actually* do. We don't contrive to develop a new technology in order to realize determinate goals. Usually things happen the other way around: we suddenly take certain goals to be sensible and worth pursuing because a new technology has become available. The internet, for example, doesn't only lead to TV programs being downloadable at any time, in the form of Netflix or on-demand websites; it also changes the format itself. Cinematic movies are threatening to become relics of the past because the standard 90-minute film format no longer tempts enough viewers to leave their own living rooms, where it's much cosier, where the ice cream is cheaper, and where you can spend hours watching the same series.

In their heyday, cinemas too seemed to be revolutionary and were perceived as posing a threat to opera and theatre. The culture of a movie night, including the popcorn, queueing at the box office, film durations economically tailored to the format, etc., is not only a means to the end of – depending on the film – enjoyment or education. Rather, we spend time at the cinema because the enabling technology (the cinematic medium) is bound up with a conception of a certain lifestyle. We make use of technology in the light of an image of what a successful life looks like.

Yet we don't concoct this image of a successful life independently of available technology, which is why that technology is not simply subordinate to our plans, a harmless, neutral means to predetermined ends that we have selected. Instead, we find ourselves confronted with a global culture that presents us with various possible actions to choose between, options we have not usually determined for ourselves and which we would almost certainly *not* choose if we actually surveyed the overall conditions of their cultural and technological production.

Heidegger points out that we cannot think at all without there being something already given to us. He calls this '*das Bedenkliche*', the thought-provoking, that which is worth thinking about. The *Bedenkliche* gives us pause for thought. Ultimately, we are always passive in a certain respect; we depend on finding ourselves in a situation that merits reflection, thought, consideration (remember: think first, digitalize second). We don't simply reflect on anything whatsoever but receive, as Heidegger puts it, a gift in the form of a thought. As is typical of Heidegger's writing, he makes use of wordplay here. The German phrase for 'there is' is 'es gibt' which literally translates into English as 'it gives'. What there is is food for thought. It is given to us thinkers, not produced by us from off the top of our heads, as the scientific worldview wrongly has us believe.

Heideger's murmurings ultimately correspond to one of our guiding ideas: that thinking is in fact something sensory, something which we can never bring under our complete control, something which happens and by which something (namely the real) is given to us. Something always has to be given to us in the contexts of our lifeworld, something that acts as the trigger to thought.

One miracle too many

It is in this context that Heidegger develops his famous thesis of *Ge-Stell* (usually translated as 'enframing'). While we should be wary of the consequences he derives from it, his thesis is nonetheless onto a core truth. **Ge-Stell** is the idea that reality as a whole is calculable, that it stands at our disposal as a set of means for us to pursue our ends, and that we can (and, in the name of progress, should) make everything that exists readily accessible for human use. To us creatures of modernity, this at first seems reasonable enough. Reality appears to be a gigantic universe, spreading out into (possibly infinite) expanses.

Thanks to modern physics, it is well known that we are in no sense at the centre of the universe. Far from playing the lead roles in a grand cosmological drama, we are in fact cosmically insignificant. Even a layperson can be made vividly aware of how we are pretty much invisible on an astronomical scale just by contemplating the size of the Milky Way, our home galaxy.

However, the physical knowledge underlying such judgements of relative significance presupposes that enough of the universe is sufficiently knowable for us to be able, for example, to determine its approximate age or calculate enormous distances with the help of physical structures that can be used as information sources for science (such as natural laws or so-called standard candles – that is, objects with knowable absolute luminosity, which provide information about distances). One of the ways in which astrology differs from astronomy is that only the latter makes use of demonstrably precise criteria, which provide a solid framework for fallibly extrapolating truths about the universe.

That modern physics actually discovers truths about the universe can be demonstrated through experiment and technological implementation. Hilary Putnam, whose thought experiment occupied us in chapter 2 (see p. 65), talked about a 'no-miracle' argument for scientific realism – i.e. for the view that natural science actually figures out how the universe works: our ability to translate our physics into technology, which then in turn opens up further possibilities for physical science, cannot just be a miracle.[15] Even if we are far from having physically decoded every last detail of the universe, we only know that *this* is the case because we have already found out as much as we have. Thanks to modern physics, that is, we know that there are things we cannot yet know with the methods currently available to modern physics.

At the same time, we keep extending the horizon of our knowledge as far as we possibly can, and this supposes that the universe will continue to reveal itself as more or less knowable. We don't expect the universe to come with built-in traps, which catch us unawares whenever we try to find out more about it. And even if there were such traps, that wouldn't be something physics could discover.

Let us pin these insights down in the form of a **principle of intelligibility**.[16] According to this principle, the universe is knowable at least to the extent that the natural sciences have correctly grasped how it is, and this entails that there is in principle no obstacle to attaining accurate knowledge about it. The principle also entails that our perceptual systems do not just produce useful illusions or figments of the imagination, as this would undermine the knowability of the kinds of experimental conditions presupposed by any alleged empirical discovery. To be sure, the boundaries separating secure scientific knowledge from ignorance are blurry; much (but by no means everything) of what today appears unrevisable could one day be subject to revision. Besides, there are certainly further surprises lurking in dark matter or in the cosmic background radiation of the universe, perhaps even scales that are too small for our current experimental methods to access.[17]

Heidegger has his own name for the principle of intelligibility. He speaks of 'unconcealment' (*Unverborgenheit*), wanting to convey the way in which the real discloses itself to us. At the same time, we know that the real reveals itself only against the background of the as yet unknown and the in principle unknowable. Some of what we don't know we will never know, because we don't even know that we don't know it. This structure is similar to that of forgetting: when we've completely forgotten something – whether or not, for example, one afternoon 749 days ago I put milk in my coffee – we don't recall having forgotten it. Something's being truly forgotten means we don't know that or when we forgot it.

Our knowledge therefore exhibits a dynamic structure, its boundaries continually shifting into the unknown. Yet each step taken in modernity presupposes that reality consists of objects that we can discover and investigate. But how do we know that's right? What we're dealing with is a metaphysical presupposition, but a presupposition to which any alternative is currently incomprehensible to us.

And this is exactly what Heidegger sees as the source of our anxiety. We know that the boundaries of knowledge are dynamic, ever shifting. Yet our image, both of what knowledge is and of how we understand its dynamic development, can *itself* shift without our currently having the slightest inkling of what this might look like. We are confronted with a void we cannot fill. According to Heidegger, our hectic, technologically driven modern lifeworld, with all its excitements and distractions, essentially fulfils the function of diverting us from the void of our ignorance. Technology, then, is a regime of avoidance and displacement, not one of encounter with what there really is.

Rather like other thinkers critical of modernity (such as Sigmund Freud), Heidegger thinks that we developed our modern civilization in order to spare us from having to stare into this void directly. Modernity is built on the idea of banishing every secret, every mystery, from public space. Modern technology creates only the illusion of maximal transparency, most notably in the current delusion that the totality of human knowledge lies waiting at the click of a mouse and is publicly available to everyone who has access to the internet. But why would college tuition in the USA be so exorbitantly expensive if you could obtain all knowledge basically for free online? The point is: you can't. The internet is merely the illusion of omniscience.

Heidegger sees modern data infrastructure in the form of telecommunications as an attempt to escape, to flee reality. In place of an encounter with the void steps the hasty attempt to give a face to the deeply alien core of human existence and knowledge acquisition; we try to master the void by lending it the form either of an enemy or of a calculable risk.

Heidegger himself fell into the very trap he'd laid for others. He laid the blame for modernity's flight from the void at the door of 'the Jews', whom he thought were behind the modern worldview.[18] He thus committed a morally abject fallacy, which was all the more grave as it motivated membership of the Nazi Party and becoming one of their elected officials (as the first Nazi rector of the University of Freiburg). This is not to deny his many insights into the nature of technology; yet we need to separate these from the Jewish world conspiracy theory he ended up indulging, in which the figure of the Jew somehow lurks behind the emergence of modernity and the scientific worldview, an anti-Semitic story that is too absurd to require any detailed refutation here.

In the age of 'complete orderability'

In an almost clairvoyant passage, Heidegger pointed out how radio and television work to eradicate our impression of distance. Today, this process is in full flow: we are continually exposed to images from faraway crisis regions, for example, and we can form a fairly accurate picture of the location of our next holiday long before we travel to our destination. Overcoming spatial and temporal distances in this way confirms our capacity to know reality. Each successful flight is a small no-miracle argument in its own right (see p. 119); the plane flies, the image loads and the GPS functions, none of which would be thinkable without modern physics.

The digital revolution has brought about a further intensification of the way in which media structures shape modernity. These days, in order to devote more time to the acquisition of economic resources, we spare ourselves the analogue journey into the town centre and order our goods online. In general, I have nothing against this. But it is important to understand the effects of this revolution on the overall situation in which we find ourselves as human beings.

In 1949, Heidegger predicted that the global post-war order would be based on the principle of 'total availability' or 'complete orderability' (*vollständige Bestellbarkeit*).[19] The world powers (at that time the USA and Soviet Union), he thought, found themselves in an arms race of distance reduction: ever faster rockets, ever quicker deliveries of goods and information. The Cold War in its pre-1989 incarnation was in part decided by the superior speed of the then West as against the Eastern bloc.

Since then, this arms race has been displaced into cyberspace, which owes its name to cybernetics. Of course, this does not exclude a military arms race from developing at the same time, which consists in circumventing the surveillance regime of the internet via other communication channels or linguistic barriers. Because of its linguistic complexity and the vast number of communicative acts it comprises, accessing the Chinese domain of the World Wide Web from the outside is no straightforward matter. There just isn't enough manpower to keep track of developments in the online language of Chinese forums for the West to be able fully to monitor the Chinese internet. Just think of the army of skilled translators you'd need.

We are practically surrounded by data-processing apparatus. From dawn to dusk, we interact with systems that put various possibilities for action at our disposal. This was the case, of course, long before digital transformation came along: the architecture and structure of cities, for example, allows us to make certain moves and not others. Parks, bridges, forks in the road and traffic regulations steer our behaviour by presenting us with options.

The manipulation exercised by control systems is not coercive and they do not completely restrict our freedom. Without control systems, we'd lack any choices between recognizable options for action and, far from being free, we'd instead be overwhelmed. Imagine what would happen if you were to flee from the apparatus of modernity and withdraw, say, to the far reaches of the Amazon. You'd soon realize why humanity has spent millennia developing a coordination system that allows us to escape the fight for survival and to master an unpredictable environment.

Thanks to digital transformation, our lifeworld appears to be structured like a ready-made coordinate system in which we can orient ourselves. In his magnum opus of 1927,

Being and Time, Heidegger speaks of a 'context of references' (*Verweisungszusammenhang*).[20] To see what he means, think of swinging by the supermarket after work. On the way home, you want to pick up a few essentials quickly. You arrive at the supermarket, the automatic doors open, and you already find yourself in a forest of signs. Everything is ordered according to various principles, with which you are probably already familiar if you are a regular at that particular supermarket or chain. Our gaze is directed by the specific layout of the supermarket. We're incorporated into its data-processing circuitry. And because of our individual patterns of needs and interests, we leave behind a signature of our choices in that circuitry, as we ultimately have our reasons for purchasing what we do and have developed habits that are reflected in our choice of products. We thereby produce a data trace that the supermarket will use to attract more customers, who will then in turn leave their own data traces. These data traces are translated into the code of charts, so that the supermarket can adapt to consumer behaviour in order subsequently to shape it according to its fundamental need: producing ever greater quantities of surplus value. The most efficient way of producing surplus value based on data traces is the internet, as it is nothing but data traces articulating the behavioural patterns of its customers. The huge quantity of data resulting from our online activities is then easily translated back into economic value, as nothing can be more valuable than a mechanism for predicting human behaviour. This is why companies are willing to spend so much money on second-order technological devices – i.e. devices which monitor devices which monitor human behaviour.

In a number of respects, our daily lives consist in interactions with a digital environment. This does not mean, however, that our lifeworld is being digitalized. Rather, various apparatuses intrude into our lifeworld and delude us into *thinking* that it is disappearing, that it is being gradually replaced with automated processes.

At this point, Heidegger points out how the entire constellation of Ge-Stell is built on an idea that, quite incorrectly, appears to us moderns as without alternative. The error lies in our representing reality as a whole, and thus nature too, as a piece of technical apparatus or equipment. The universe – i.e. the object domain of the natural sciences – is even widely thought of on the model of a computer, as a gigantic computation connecting up basic units of information with one another. We no longer see the universe as a sort of container in which material things are pushed around according to natural laws. Physics no longer supports such a crude materialistic conception of nature. Instead, many physicists have replaced crude materialism by a less obviously false metaphysics according to which the universe is a huge information-processing machine (which is just as false).

The natural sciences deliver knowledge about reality only insofar as it supplies us with information with which we can enter into material-energetic interactions – i.e. via our measuring instruments. It is part and parcel of the nature of physics that it itself exchanges information with the universe, namely, in the form of the experiments that allow us to make discoveries about it.

In this respect, natural science functions rather like sonar. We approach the universe with questions and compel it to answer them by means of skilfully designed experiments. We thereby lay out a kind of dragnet (a particle accelerator, say) with a certain structure. Whatever gets caught up in the net has to have properties that we can theoretically derive from the properties of our apparatus together with the signature that physical reality traces within it. In his *Critique of Pure Reason*, Immanuel Kant described this as follows:

When Galileo rolled balls of a weight chosen by himself down an inclined plane, or when Torricelli made the air bear a weight that he had previously thought to be equal to that of a known column of water, or when in a later time Stahl changed metals into calx and then changed the latter back into metal by first removing something and then putting it back again, a light dawned on all those who study nature. They comprehended that reason has insight only into what it itself produces according to its own design; that it must take the lead with principles for its judgments according to constant laws and compel nature to answer its questions, rather than letting nature guide its movements by keeping reason, as it were, in leading-strings; for otherwise accidental observations, made according to no previously designed plan, can never connect up into a necessary law, which is yet what reason seeks and requires. Reason, in order to be taught by nature, must approach nature with its principles in one hand, according to which alone the agreement among appearances can count as laws, and, in the other hand, the experiments thought out in accordance with these principles – yet in order to be instructed by nature not like a pupil, who has recited to him whatever the teacher wants to say, but like an appointed judge who compels witnesses to answer the questions he puts to them. Thus even physics owes the advantageous revolution in its way of thinking to the inspiration that what reason would not be able to know of itself and has to learn from nature, it has to seek in the latter (though not merely ascribe to it) in accordance with what reason itself puts into nature.

This is how natural science was first brought to the secure course of a science after groping about for so many centuries.[21]

Nature answers scientific questions that we pose only in a methodologically controlled manner. It doesn't try to catch our attention so that it can tell us all about how it's constituted, in case we just happen to be interested. Natural science is an activity which attempts to elicit nature's secrets. And this activity always has a certain form, such that some things can be registered while others are automatically edited out of the picture through the selection mechanisms (the model) implemented in the experimental set-up.

We are indefinitely far away from having registered everything about the universe. It is in principle impossible to know whether our current methods for ascertaining its fact structure are adequate for grasping the entire universe on all of its many scales. Even though, to some extent at least, we always do know what we do not yet know, we cannot begin to know about all those different facts that slip through the cracks of our experimental apparatus.

Heidegger calls the dragnet of modern natural science the 'mathematical project of nature'[22] and also refers to the passage by Kant cited above, since it gives a significant formulation of this projection. The internet is a reality that fully corresponds to the principles of this mathematical projection: it is a technical application of the knowledge format of our advanced natural and technological sciences. This is why, for all its complexity, it is actually completely transparent. There is no real online privacy. Online, everything is public.

Digital reality is fundamentally different from nature insofar as we can know how it is constructed. This is because we constructed it: it operates entirely within the parameters of mathematical models and their logics and cannot transgress them. You can only ever protect data sets from the reach of hackers and intelligence services for a limited time. From a logical point of view, no firewall is impenetrable and no code uncrackable.

This distinguishes a firewall, for example, from the outer boundaries of the knowable universe. We cannot look further into spacetime than the Big Bang allows. At the edge of the universe that surrounds us in all directions there lies an impenetrable information barrier. Thanks to modern cosmology, we also know that nature is not exhaustively knowable at the level of the observable universe. When we reach the smallest and largest entities we can conceive of (so far, at least), we hit against boundaries that are currently unbreachable. Whether there are ultimate boundaries, behind which there is simply nothing more to discover, is not something that natural science can ever tell us. Whatever physics might discover about the universe, it can never rule out that there is more to know about physical reality. Physics cannot both achieve final closure and know that it has reached its ideal limit of enquiry. And that's simply because it's an empirical science.

By contrast, because it is a logical and mathematical artefact, the internet is thoroughly transparent, at least in principle. This is what Heidegger understands by complete availability. The fabric of cyberspace gradually spreads itself out over analogue reality, leaving ever fewer areas of our planet in which we can interact with an offline world. We retreat into a space populated by items of our own making, in the hope of taking a mental break from our own mortality. Sooner or later, however, our non-virtual mortality inevitably catches up with us.

Trapped in The Circle?

The fantasy of total transparency propagated through the digital revolution finds a powerful depiction in Dave Eggers's novel *The Circle*, which was recently the subject of a (disappointingly poor) film adaptation. The social reality in which we present ourselves as persons seems to be almost completely conquered by algorithms and data-processing systems. In this respect, we can think of the digital revolution as a restructuring of social reality, as the primary driving force of a social transformation.

The story of *The Circle* takes place in the near future in – where else? – California (the enviably beautiful caliphate of modern information technology and hedonic well-being). At its centre is the eponymous company, which brings together all the social networks and digital processes in which individuals participate into a single program, so that absolutely all of our digital activities are observable from a single control centre.

Yet as if that weren't enough, the company in *The Circle* develops especially sophisticated little cameras, which are installed as sensors all over the planet. These cameras become so prevalent that no state or other institution has the capacity to remove them all. Social reality becomes overrun with cameras directing their gaze at absolutely everything that takes place in the public (and ultimately the private) sphere. To justify this development, like the famous digital giants of Silicon Valley, the company in *The Circle* acts in the name of a false promise of democratically legitimated emancipation: by having cameras recording everything everywhere and so creating a total surveillance apparatus, every unjust exercise of state violence becomes immediately visible. In this way, the oppressed will (allegedly) instantly rise up to resist the injustice.

A central narrative axis of the novel is the relation between Mae and Mercer. Mae devotes herself to the company so that she can secure adequate healthcare for her parents – a typical problem for various social classes in the USA. Ultimately, the firm could emerge only by compensating for the analogue, material, medical and economic living conditions in California with a digital counter-reality.

The maximalist digital firm is rooted in a real historical inequality in American society – an inequality, moreover, that is reflected in more or less all of the most successful contemporary TV series and films (from *Game of Thrones* to *Breaking Bad* and *The Hunger Games*, but also in the brilliant Brazilian series *3%* or the British masterpiece *Black Mirror*). The rot of analogue inequality lurks in the undergrowth of the digital revolution.

Mae wants to fight this inequality by committing herself to the company, whose sales strategy consists in propagandizing about manufacturing equality. Mae discovers that this is mere appearance by experiencing the complete breakdown of her analogue social relations. Not only does her relationship with her parents, the very people she aimed to help with her job, go to pieces, but she also destroys the life of her childhood friend Mercer. He tries to evade the cameras and surveillance system of The Circle, only to be hunted even more persistently until he finally dies in a chase.

Ultimately at stake for Mae, therefore, are her genuine, analogue relationships, which are coupled to an analogue and ultimately biological structure. As internet users, we are all familiar in one form or another with the sense that online friendships are somehow not wholly real. Europeans like me who have had considerable and intensive contact with the USA will perhaps also have acquired the impression from their own experiences that the social systems and rituals of friendship and friendliness are established somewhat differently over there. Close and distant relationships are also regulated differently in the United States, because their socio-economic systems are spread over considerably larger geographical distances; American conurbations have a completely different structure and assume different functions because of the extent to which they are separated from other conurbations. This spatial structure is reflected in social space, a factor which lay behind the first wave of the spread of social media.

The comic potential of this transatlantic friendship gap is

exploited in the series *Episodes*, in which a British couple, both of whom are writers, find success in Hollywood with a TV series. But their European notions of friendship and honesty continually thwart them in California.

But what, from a philosophical point of view, is really behind this well-founded impression that something or other about social media is just not genuine? At this point, it is important to be clear that, as human beings, we are persons. By a **person**, I understand the image we form for ourselves of who we want to be for others. This image is in no sense private but arises essentially through our communications with others. In any given social situation, we always present ourselves to others in a particular manner, as a certain person.

The expression 'person' stems from the language of ancient theatre and originally designates the masks through which an actor speaks. Literally translated, *per-sona* (in ancient Greek: *pros-ôpon*) means 'to sound through'. In ancient theatre, the voice of the actor resounds through the immovable mask. In stark opposition to contemporary theatre, in which actors work at maximizing the expressive potential of facial gestures and bodily movements, what counted on the ancient Greek stage was the spoken word alone, which is expressed through a persona. A significant feature of this prehistory is the idea that social reality is a kind of stage on which we can express ourselves by wearing masks.

We are all familiar with the phenomenon of coming out with stock phrases in order to cope with complex emotional situations. Think of the daily rituals involved in something such as shopping: the polite clichés, the standardized smile with which one allows parents with small children to go ahead, and so on.

When we truly get to know people within the context of relationships such as parenthood, friendship or close teamwork, the effects of the mask sooner or later wear off. At some point, the same phrases, jokes and gestures become stupid and transparent, as they're always deployed in order to make social gains. We cannot keep using them to dupe the people with whom we have close relationships. In order to maintain genuine connections, we have to tear off one another's masks or remove them of our own accord.

A good presentation of this process can be found in Ruben Östlund's film *Force majeure* (2014). In the film, a married couple go on a skiing holiday with their two children in a luxury hotel and come to discover previously hidden sides of each other. After the husband leaves the family in the lurch when an artificial, controlled avalanche hurtles towards them, their masks begin to slip. Soon, their entire relationship is thrown into question. (The film does have a disappointingly implausible happy ending, but that's another issue.)

Close relationships are depersonalizing. Our reality as individuals takes the place of our practices of performance as persons. Of course, we compensate for this through everyday practices and rituals. The way in which alarm clocks, coffee breaks, working hours, family dinners and the rest lend rhythm to our everyday lives unburdens us from the experience of close relationships.

Social media are personalization machines. **Personalization machines** are systems by means of which self-dramatizations are manufactured and marketed. Within this process, what matters is not necessarily that we market ourselves through our Twitter and Instagram accounts but, rather, that others sell our self-images and thereby derive economic profit from them. Each photo we 'share' online says something about our personality. The more photos and other personal information we make available, the easier it becomes to interact with our persona.

This interaction doesn't leave us as we were before. Click by click, like by like, and link by link, data are peeled off from our lives and distributed as digitalized information far beyond our reach. Information about our whereabouts, income, interests and political attitudes can be immediately transformed into economic value: there is always someone who wants to know where we are and what we'll want next.

A fleeting visit to Winden – society as nuclear power plant

Against this background, we can distinguish between personality and individuality. **Personality** is a rehearsed role-play that varies from situation to situation, which allows us to obtain and maintain strategic advantages in social competition. It contains such seemingly unproblematic ingredients as our ability to make our way about the world while remaining bodily unscathed. After all, this ability isn't something to be taken for granted; our everyday reality is continually threatened by the outbreak of violence.

Individuality, by contrast, derives from the brute fact that each of us is irreplaceably him- or herself. With one of his countless German neologisms, Heidegger called this *Jemeinigkeit*, 'always being my own being'.[23] That I am always me and always around whenever something happens to me, so to speak, comprises my individuality. I am myself and you are yourself. This property is indivisible. In Latin, the individual is called *individuum* (and in modern Greek: *atomon*). The atoms of the social bond are individuals which enter into social relationships by way of producing a persona.

As individuals, we are pre-social atoms. This does not mean that society consists of asocial individuals. Rather, the social and the individual are two different fields of sense, which partially overlap. They are neither identical with nor fully translatable into each other. A tension constantly arises between the two, which in extreme cases discharges itself in systematic violence.

Everything we ever experience is experienced from our own perspective. This perspective is shaped by the way in which everything that currently affects us seems to bear a peculiar importance. The American philosopher Tyler Burge (b. 1947) talks in this connection about an egocentric index, which is formed through the perspective of living beings.[24] The **egocentric index** of an animal is the way in which its environment appears to it. Even at the purely sensory level of the informational exchange between creature and environment, a centre is already formed, which distinguishes between relevant and irrelevant objects: for instance, between food and mere stuff.

Every living being thus already has a perspective beneath the threshold of consciousness, which serves as an ordering principle for its relationship to its environment. For all beings, including humans, this perspective arises at a non-conscious level, because we don't have conscious access to all those processes that keep running in the background while we're consciously directing our attention at something or other. The biological background conditions of our conscious lives are not themselves entirely conscious. Life operates, so to speak, largely behind our backs. While you're busy intending to read this paragraph to the end, electrochemical processes have to keep taking place within the cranial vault. And, at the same time, your finger nails are growing too, your digestion continues to function, and so on and so on. All of these processes feed into the egocentric perspective of the animal that you are.

Pleasure and aversion accompany everything we do as living beings. This is because of our stimulus–response system, without which we humans would experience nothing like motivation. In every situation, we are threatened by illness, death and violence, and we compensate for these through a pleasure system. It is thanks to this that life takes on a certain meaning and appears to be more than just a vale of tears. In other words, we rely on what the

French philosopher Jean-François Lyotard (1924–1998) called a 'libidinal economy'.[25] This economy reaches far beyond consciousness: which actions and sensations we classify as pleasurable, and which count as permitted or forbidden, is always bound up with our infinitely complex situation as living beings.

The expression 'libido' comes from Freud and designates our psychical energy. For Freud, this did not have an exclusively sexual meaning in the usual sense of behaviour directed at sexual intercourse or self-gratification. Rather, working in the background is an idea of Kant, who investigated the 'feeling of pleasure and displeasure' in his *Critique of the Power of Judgment*.[26] Deploying his inimitable knack for precise formulations, Kant defines 'pleasure' as 'the representation of the agreement of an object or of an action with the subjective conditions of life'.[27] Something causes pleasure if it fits into our egocentric index. If it disturbs it, it causes feelings of aversion. One and the same object (an order of steak tartare, say) can give rise to pleasure in one person (a carnivore) and aversion in another (a committed vegetarian).

What triggers pleasure or aversion also depends on how we represent the object. A **representation** is the subjective conception of an object as something that is thus and so. Let's think of Stansted Airport. To do so, we represent the object as an airport. We can also represent the object as something else, as a shopping centre for example, should we for whatever reason want to go to Stansted Airport to do some shopping. The same object can be represented in various ways. I represent Stansted differently from you, even if we are both representing the same thing, namely Stansted.

Our individuality is constituted by our irreplaceable perspective. The perspective I currently adopt can be adopted only by me, because it supervenes on all those circumstances that lead to my currently adopting it. What and how we represent what we do varies to a high degree from individual to individual. This is in any case obvious from how each person tags along, so to speak, at every moment of their conscious lives, and thus undergoes experiences that nobody else accesses as a matter of principle. We can certainly share experiences, and thus representations, at least partially. But they will always remain subjective in the precise sense that they belong to an individual perspective.

The difference between social personality and non-social individuality cannot be completely bridged, and this fundamental gap results in a tension that plays itself out in a multitude of social subdomains. At the root of the tension is the fact that social systems are constitutionally incapable of grasping individuality. For even if, as subjects, our individual perspective is continually informed and transformed by our also being persons, individuality itself is not social. From the standpoint of the maintenance conditions of a given social system, the asocial individual is an insuperable source of disturbances which it needs to transform into manageable data. To see what I mean, just recall your last exposure to arbitrary bureaucratic processes, in which your individuality is reduced to the kind of person you represent in the eye of the social system.

A **subject** is an individual, minded living being. Subjects have corporal parts, but also parts that essentially resist any meaningful spatiotemporal or material-energetic classification.[28] Since we, as subjects, are also persons (among other things), our personality is part of our subjectivity. But, as subjects, we are also individuals.

Our socialized side battles with the components of our non-social side. In fact, the tension stems from both direction and manifests on different levels. Kant's description of this phenomenon is justly famous:

> *The means which nature employs to bring about the development of innate capacities is that of antagonism within society, in so far as this antagonism becomes in the long run the cause of a law-governed social order.* By antagonism, I mean in this context the *unsocial sociability* of men, that is, their tendency to come together in society, coupled, however, with a continual resistance which constantly threatens to break this society up. This propensity is obviously rooted in human nature. Man has an inclination to *live in society*, since he feels in this state more like a man, that is, he feels able to develop his natural capacities. But he also has a great tendency to *live as an individual*, to isolate himself, since he also encounters in himself the unsocial characteristic of wanting to direct everything in accordance with his own ideas. He therefore expects resistance all around, just as he knows of himself that he is in turn inclined to offer resistance to others.[29]

Social reality is marked by an antagonism, a tension that results from the conflict between personality and individuality. To this extent, society functions rather like a nuclear power plant, a comparison nicely exploited in the German Netflix hit *Dark*, in which a nuclear power plant forms the centre of a mysterious event. The narrative development of the figures unfolds the tension between their social roles as persons (teacher, policeman, student, power plant manager, hotel owner) and their individuality, by means of which they position their personalities (by having affairs, killing one another, giving false testimony, allowing themselves to act corruptly).

The town of Winden, whose society is structured round the power plant, is an ideal field of experimentation for the antagonistic structure of society as such. Whether we like it or not, we all live in Winden or, to take up the thought experiment of Lars von Trier's famous film, in Dogville.

One consciousness to go, please!

As the digital revolution unfolds, we are experiencing a transformation of consciousness with profound effects on the public sphere. We continually read both about the challenges of digital transformation and about the dangers and hopes bound up with technological developments such as AI. We all experience the digital sphere as the by now familiar acceleration of processes in the lifeworld. And this is certainly connected to the exponential increase in the processing power of our most advanced systems of consciousness extension – i.e. of our computers.

Against this background, the **extended mind thesis** seems particularly plausible. It says that our psychological, mental reality has for a long time now not been restricted to our bodies but instead extended into our technological devices and media. The quaint pocket calculator and its futuristic descendant, the smartphone, not only serve to issue helpful reminders but take over previously internal functions of memory storage: we remember having made a note of something on our smartphone without having explicitly to memorize the information we noted down; or we find that we have deposited an item in our online shopping basket or put it on a wish list and then forgotten all about it in the meantime.

Our recording systems play an essential role in determining who we are; after all, it's not as though everything that belongs to us as subjects is continually present to our conscious awareness. So why should we think that the mind is by its very nature tied to the body?[30] If my pocket calculator calculates for me and I use it to attain some arithmetical result, doesn't this demonstrate that thought is not in fact tied to a particular piece of biological hardware, or *wetware*?

With this assumption in place, we are not too far away from the idea that our mental prostheses could at some point assume control over mental reality. This assumption is partly connected to the hypothesis of superintelligence, which has been most prominently developed by Nick Bostrom.[31] We attain a superintelligence when an AI is so far superior to some or even all human mental activities that we can no longer understand or even monitor its internal thought mechanisms.

The arguments developed by Bostrom and others for and against the possibility of a superintelligence all revolve around probabilities formulated on the basis of projections of technological progress. This leads to mathematical considerations that need not detain us here, because they do not really touch on the interesting philosophical question: Can there be an AI that is sufficiently similar to our own intelligence for us to regard it as superior, be it dangerously or beneficially so?

That computer programs solve well-formulated problems more efficiently than we do is true enough, and not only when it comes to chess programs; it is also true of online programs that, for example, can find the next free table at our favourite restaurant far quicker than any human we might task with doing the same thing. The program I'm using to write this book solves the problem of writing far better than my hand and makes it far easier to translate my text into a book. Besides, you can write much quicker on a standard modern computer than on a typewriter. Perhaps you might occasionally write better if you wrote a little more slowly. But, be that as it may, the general idea here is that the digital revolution amounts to nothing less than an intelligence explosion. If the extended mind hypothesis is correct, we need not merge with AI in any fancy way (say, by connecting our brains to computing machinery or by implementing chips). We might actually have merged with AI and our digital infrastructure already. According to the extended mind hypothesis, publishing my thoughts online is even a form of literally uploading them.

If we define intelligence as a problem-solving capacity measurable relative to a time parameter, we could even say that we are all becoming more intelligent (more efficient) thanks to modern digital technology. In this sense, chess programs count as more intelligent than all human chess players, not least because they have other methods for solving chess problems at their disposal; for example, they have access to pretty much unlimited databanks and a computing capacity that far outstrips our own.

Who has a problem here?

At this point in our investigation, however, philosophical caution is called for. We ought to undertake an appropriate risk assessment and begin by taking a closer look at the very concept of a problem.

A **problem** is a task that an agent wants to solve in order to reach a certain aim – a solution. For example, getting from one side of the road to the other is a problem. There are various ways of solving this problem: using the crossing, crossing the road anywhere while looking left and right to check for cars, waiting at the lights, simply making a run for it and chancing one's luck, and so on. For every problem there are different strategies for solving it, and we can rank these in terms of their efficiency.

Yet, at this stage, the problem with problems begin. What counts as efficient depends on given interests. If I want to get to the other side of the road as quickly as possible, it's more efficient to cross the road even though a car is approaching, so long as you assume you won't get run over. But, if you want to keep in mind your own and others' safety, it is better to cross at the traffic lights, even if this represents a somewhat slower solution. The quickest way to reach a solution is not necessarily the most intelligent; it all depends on the problem space within which we want to determine the intelligence of an agent or procedure.

Think of a game, be it chess or squash. We usually don't look for an opponent we have no chance of beating. If we did, there would be little point in playing. For the same reason, we don't seek out hopelessly inferior opponents either. The aim of a game is not to attain an absolutely optimal solution as quickly as possible, say the objective 'checkmate' or '11:0; 11:0; 11:0'. Games like chess do indeed have a clear and obvious resolution, but the point is not to reach this as speedily as possible at any price. If it were, bribing your opponent at the start of the game to let you checkmate her within four moves would represent a good strategy.

There is no absolute criterion of efficiency. This goes not only for games governed by rules that can be specified with mathematical precision but for every situation in which problems arise. The life of a human being essentially consists in solving problems and in optimizing one's problem-solving competence. Yet this optimization is not subject to any absolute mode of efficient thinking. There just is no such mode. Our interests emerge from a dynamic lifeworld within which we articulate our individuality in the form of a social persona. If you abstract away from this feature of intelligence, you will not be able to understand real intelligence at all. Instead, you will confuse the phenomenon of intelligence with one of the shadows it casts over your mind.

We can see why this is so with the help of a classical existentialist consideration. **Existentialism** assumes that human life has no absolute, externally determined meaning and that we instead have to imbue it with meaning from within the contexts in which we happen to find ourselves. An example from Jean-Paul Sartre illustrates this particularly nicely:[32] to make the example a little more visual, imagine that Reinhold Messner (the most famous Alpinist in my neck of the woods) goes climbing in the Alps and comes up against a rock face that, for him, is easily scalable. Perhaps he's then seized by a burning ambition to climb it. Or perhaps the task is so easy that he just clambers up the rock face, effortlessly and without ambition. Now imagine that the elderly Mother Theresa stands before said rock face. The wall of rock will confront her as an obstacle and she will likely choose another path.

The rock face in itself, in its being-in-itself, as Sartre puts it, has neither the meaning of provoking ambition within us nor the meaning of directing us to another path. It is simply there, having somehow or other landed in its present location, perhaps due to seismic phenomena. Neither Messner nor Mother Theresa is efficient in themselves. Measuring their efficiency depends on how exactly they want to reach a goal and solve a problem. So, in a certain respect, it is much more intelligent to cheat at an IQ test, or to not bother with it in the first place, than to deploy one's spatial imagination in order to rotate a bunch of geometrical figures under time pressure so that you can tick the right box. It all depends on your goal.

Every AI system – regardless of how its internal processing mechanisms run – is internally much more like a rock face than like Reinhold Messner or Mother Theresa. We fix its solution space relative to criteria of efficiency, which is why it appears intelligent to us. Yet the system has no interests of its own and cannot itself weigh them up against one another unless criteria of efficiency have been clearly defined. Computer programs are quicker than we are when it comes to spitting out solutions whose efficiency criteria are fixed under precisely determined conditions. This does not mean that computer programs think. If thinking is indeed essentially bound to a living being who wonders, speculates and contemplates, and if criteria of efficiency arise only within the framework of such mental activities, then computers can still certainly play an important and even dangerous role in our lives without thereby being thinkers themselves. The power of computing machinery resides in the fact that they do *not* really think and are *not* really intelligent.

At this point, I'm sure many of you will object that we have for quite a while now had AI systems that can not only solve problems but even learn. **Learning** can be defined as the systematic introduction of new problems in order to solve old problems. When someone learns something, they always create new problems for themselves. Our contemporary computer programs – so goes the objection – are much more similar, and thus much more superior, to us than they are to the good old pocket calculator.

Technological progress is undeniable. Yet this does not change the fact that our intelligence is not simply a general problem-solving system but also consists in the formulation of problems. These problems place us not within an abstract problem-solving space but in the concrete framework of our survival. For computer programs, there is no question of survival, because they are not alive.

Thus far, all living entities have arisen through evolution. We can indeed clone living material and will perhaps one day be able to synthesize cells from non-living matter. Yet we would still be orienting ourselves according to the pre-settings of evolution. Life that has neither emerged through evolution nor developed within the terms set by biologically evolved life forms does not yet exist. And we do not know whether there are life forms that have arisen under conditions entirely different from those familiar from our own planet. But one thing is certain: no artificial system that's within our reach today, no system constructed from non-living matter, has any interest in its survival. And that's quite simply because none of these systems is alive.

4

Why Only Animals Think

The nooscope

Animals are complex living beings. At a certain level of complexity, they begin to think – i.e. to grasp thoughts. Currently, no one really knows at which precise level of evolutionarily produced complexity thought starts to kick in, but we can be certain about our own case. Our thought is a sense. It puts us in contact with an infinity of possibilities and actualities, the fields of sense. The peculiarity of our sense of thought is that it allows us to fathom not only deep and far-reaching structures of the universe with an impressively high degree of resolution but also the abyss of human mindedness, the history of art, crossword puzzles, and much more besides. We can all grasp the same kind of objectively existing thoughts because the objects of our sense of thought are logically structured. Logical structure cannot be subjective. It cannot be the form of our mental goggles, as it were. If it were, which thoughts follows from which would merely be a matter of opinion: your sense of what constitutes a logical connection would be something you just project on to sentences and so wouldn't carry any validity for anyone else.

Every sense modality has specific sense qualities, so-called qualia, which it takes up directly: we hear tones, see colours, feel warmth, think thoughts, and so on. Thoughts are the qualia of the sense of thought. Thoughts are vehicles of acquaintance with abstract objects, such as concepts, logical form, and so on. Without these vehicles, we could not grasp mathematical truths.

This makes the scope of mathematics and the mathematicized natural sciences intelligible. One of the greatest scientific breakthroughs of all time, the discovery of relativity theory by Albert Einstein (1879–1955), rests on a radical rethinking of our spatial and temporal concepts. And we are all familiar with the huge intellectual reorientation that this triggered, both from science fiction films and from our daily dealings with satellite-based technology.

Einstein's thought experiments led to a deeper knowledge of the fact that the universe appears differently from our provincial perspective as inhabitants of planet Earth than it does from a physical point of view. Motion and velocity are relative phenomena, meaning that, from the standpoint of physics, there is no simple thing such as motion and rest full stop, but only ever motion relative to a frame of reference. To me, for example, it currently appears as though I'm sitting on a motionless desk chair. Outside, all is equally peaceful. From another perspective, set by a different frame of reference, I am speeding around the sun together with planet Earth at over 100,000 kilometres per hour. Meanwhile, our solar system as a whole revolves around the centre of the Milky Way at even greater velocities. Yet I do not break the national speed limit by just sitting here. The rules of the road are valid relative to the frame of reference Earth, and the way we perceive the movement of this planet leaves us happily unaware of the extra 100,000 kilometres per hour.

The insights of contemporary physics involve scales describable only under extreme conditions and deal with temperatures, masses, distances, and so on, that are utterly unimaginable for our other senses. Although no human has ever left our solar system, we can peer deep into the cosmos and explore its laws. In doing so, we hit against boundaries, which for their part can be expressed mathematically. For example: we have discovered that the matter known to us (so-called baryonic matter) makes up no more than 4 per cent of the observable universe. In order to comprehend the universe through theoretical physics and experiments, be it on the very smallest or the very largest scale known to us, we are utterly dependent on our sense of thought.

'Our mathematical universe', as the MIT physicist Max Tegmark calls it, is to a large extent totally inaccessible to our classical sense modalities.[1] Mathematical advances have always laid the ground for or accompanied advances in modern physics. This is true not only of the infinitesimal calculus, which Isaac Newton (1643–1727) discovered simultaneously with Leibniz, but especially of the non-Euclidian geometry that was developed in the nineteenth century and which played an important role in Einstein's revolution.

In the end, it turns out that Plato was right all along. Plato spelled out a key idea of the so-called Pythagoreans (the students of the mathematician Pythagoras, 570–510 BC): we *find* mathematical structures by deploying our thinking; they are not simply useful tools that we use for investigating a universe that is not at all mathematical in itself. His star pupil, Aristotle, countered this with the thesis that our mathematical thought is indeed merely an aid to our five senses, which we use to categorize and master the natural environment. Actually, the truth lies somewhere in between: the universe does not consist of mathematical objects. Nature transcends our models in ways we cannot even measure in principle, since the models deployed in physical discovery are always limited. No theory is able both to cover absolutely all physical phenomena and at the same time to prove its completeness. As I have repeatedly pointed out, physics is essentially an empirical science. At the same time, however, mathematical structure is not a projection of human thought onto a mind- and structureless nature. Rather, mathematical physics captures some real features of the universe and, consequently, the universe itself has some of the abstract architecture ascribed to it by our best physical theories.

As I suggested above (see p. 11), we can see the human sense of thought as a nooscope. *Nous* is the ancient Greek word for thought, and the verb *skopeô* designates observation or exploration. We can therefore put forward the **nooscope thesis**: our thought is a sense that allows us to explore the infinite and represent it mathematically. It is thus exercises of this sense, which happens to be especially highly developed in (some) humans, that provide us with our high-level scientific expertise.

On souls and index card boxes

Plato regarded the human body as a prison or tomb of the soul. We can call this the **sôma-sêma thesis** (from *sôma* = body and *sêma* = tomb).[2] Especially in his dialogue *Phaedo*, Plato argued for the immortality of the soul, and his arguments were later taken up by the Church Fathers in the process of melding Platonism and Christianity.[3] It is worth noting that, in the canonical biblical texts as we know them today, there is no unequivocal teaching that the soul is immortal. What they do mention is the resurrection of bodies. You will search the biblical texts in vain for a heaven or hell in which entirely bodiless souls are kept in store. According to the Gospel of Matthew, for example, we even have a body in hell (how else would it be tortured there?): 'Do not fear those who kill the body but cannot kill the soul; rather fear him who can destroy both soul and body in hell.'[4] The idea of an immortal, fully incorporeal soul probably comes from Egypt. From there, it found its way into Plato's reflections, before being worked into a more elaborated theory in later ancient Platonism.

I don't want to detain you any further with the history of the idea of the soul's immortality. For both the advocates and the opponents of immortality miss the real philosophical action. And this is because they fail to recognize our thinking as a sense and instead place it in opposition to our sensory life – indeed, this is the error common both to those who take our soul to be immortal and to those materialists who believe that corporeal death spells the end of all life and thought and infer from this that our thinking too must therefore be something corporeal.

So, let's raise another fundamental philosophical question: Is it possible for something lacking any biological foundation to think? Can computers, immortal souls (were these, contrary to expectations, actually to exist) or God *think* at all?

If thinking is essentially biological, this possibility is excluded. Certainly, computers, immortal souls or God neither hear nor taste anything either, as they lack the requisite equipment and anchoring in the animal kingdom. God does not have actual ears and eyes, as this would turn him into an animal in ways that are usually not intended by monotheists. This leads us to a **second key thesis** of the current book: biological externalism. **Biological externalism** is the view that the expressions we use to describe and comprehend our thought processes *essentially* refer to something that has biological parts (cf. p. 12). Let's call these expressions **thought words**. Besides 'thinking', the following also count among the thought words: intelligence, acumen, cleverness, opining, suspecting, believing, and so on. Different languages have different thought words. Moreover, different speakers have different thought words at their disposal. The thought words of a language or speaker together comprise a vocabulary, which we can call a **noetic vocabulary**.

Noetic vocabulary varies both diachronically (over time) and synchronically (at any time there will be various languages and speakers). We cannot simply step outside of our noetic vocabulary, draw up a complete catalogue of all the thought words, and then assign unequivocal meanings to them so as to produce a perfect and complete dictionary. Because thought is a sense, we are fallible when it comes to answering the question of what thought is. Hence many like to believe (falsely, if I'm right) that thought is not a sense.

Biological externalism maintains that our thought words can, in principle, refer only to something biological, i.e. to something living. Only animals think.

The main argument for this thesis is semantic. Semantics is concerned with the meaning of expressions. It is not concerned with arbitrary stipulations; semantics is not in the eye of the beholder but in the words themselves. What expressions mean is only a matter of arbitrariness in exceptional cases, as the meanings of our expressions are fixed through linguistic usage. Language use in turn results from a vast multiplicity of concrete applications of expressions, which no single speaker can possibly keep track of. Whether or not an expression is added to a language is not up to the individual speaker but arises from a number of different contexts – such a large number, in fact, that nobody could possibly survey them all.

Think of the word 'language', for example. What does 'language' actually mean? Just try stating the meaning of this word and a few possible answers will occur to you. You might quickly be led to such concepts as syntax, grammar or meaning. When we think about language, it seems to be a kind of code that's subject to particular rules for its decoding. Yet this is of course pretty general. Indeed, understood in this sense, practically everything is language; not only the dancing of bees, which is reminiscent of our language as a means of communication, but also the order of the planets. Indeed, one might regard the latter as a code governed by natural laws, which we can decipher in order to read the heavens.

But do the orbits of the planets have meaning in the same sense as the sentences of this book? And does the choreographic language of bees really have meaning in the same sense as the sentences found in the works of the zoologist Karl von Frisch (1886–1982), who devoted himself to the study of this dance? Zoologists disagree about whether bees have a language. Several experiments and quantities of data speak against the idea. And even if there is a sense in which their movements do transmit information about food sources, this in no way means that the information displays either a grammar or a logical structure in the way a human language does.

The point here is not to cast doubt on the idea that other animals have a language at their disposal, albeit one we do not understand. For the present argument, I merely need the premise that we cannot simply know what a language is without thereby making use of linguistic meaning, which none of us produces at will. What 'language' means exactly, and what happens to be the first or even second thing that occurs to us when we ponder the question, is by no means arbitrary.

Semantics is therefore no mere matter of definition – an objection frequently levelled by non-philosophical bystanders at arguments put forward by philosophers of language. Semantic argumentation is not merely a language game. When we ask ourselves whether or not computers think, we have to know to what 'thought' refers and, therefore, that the word has a more or less determinable meaning. If 'thought' in our noetic vocabulary essentially refers to an activity of animals, we can exclude the idea that computers think, even if we might well casually talk about them 'thinking' in everyday chitchat, in the sense that they do things that *resemble* thinking.

We cannot change what expressions refer to simply by deciding that from now on they refer to something else. You might alter a word-label, but certainly not the meaning of an expression. In contrast to an 'expression', I understand by a **word-label** a sound or sign sequence that we use in linguistic contexts. We can certainly do plenty of things with these besides expressing meanings: I can find the word 'word' pleasing because of how the round 'o' follows so delightfully upon the pointy 'w'. Or we might wonder how much memory space a sign sequence, say the complete works of Goethe, would take up on a hard drive. Personally, I'm rather fond of the Devanagari script, in which Hindi, for example, is written. But this has precious little to do with the meaning of words in Hindi, but merely with word-labels.

We cannot use our thought words however we wish. Whether there can actually be something like AI is therefore not only a technological issue but a controversial question in the philosophy of language. Of course, I can call my chess program 'intelligent'. It can beat me and many far superior players at chess. And in doing so, it certainly solves certain chess problems. But if part of the point of playing chess is not only to find the quickest path through some solution space but to attain a strategic advantage through conscious reflection in a competition, we can no longer really say that chess programs play chess intelligently. If playing chess involves a set of interests grounded in the human life form, then it is a triviality that no chess program even so much as plays chess.

In fact, chess programs play chess just as little as the orbits of the planets express meanings. The planetary orbits do not speak to us in the language of physics. They don't speak at all. There is something analogous in the case of chess programs: they don't play chess at all. We can play against programs, but then only one party is engaged in playing a game. (It's rather like the situation in which someone avails themselves of the services of a sex doll. It would be false to say that this constitutes an instance of sexual intercourse.)

In the philosophy of language, **externalism** is the idea that certain expressions refer without a competent speaker having to know exactly how the target system of their linguistic reference is actually constituted (see pp. 66f.). Everyone reading this paragraph presumably knows that atoms can be combined to form molecules. Yet this hardly makes us nuclear physicists or chemists. Plus, since we don't yet know what the smallest level of the universe is, or even if there is a smallest level, we don't yet know everything there is to know about atoms. They consist of smaller parts, elementary particles, which in turn consist of smaller parts . . . but we don't know if following this path will eventually lead us to a very smallest point.

The point of this example is simply that we can master the linguistic meaning of an expression well enough to apply it competently without thereby being able to make any adequate inference to the underlying essence of whichever reality it is that we pick out by using the expression in the context of a language. There would be no prospect of understanding a language if we could not presuppose an often far-reaching historical past of linguistic usage. As the great Argentinian writer Jorge Luis Borges (1899–1986) has the narrator of his masterly tale *The Aleph* say: 'All language is a set of symbols whose use among its speakers assumes a shared past.'[5]

In the shared past of all known language communities, noetic vocabulary has always referred to a reality with a biological component. Until recently, it has pretty clearly been only living beings which have carried out those performances that we designate with 'thinking', 'cognition' and similar concepts. According to externalism, it follows that these expressions refer *essentially* to the performances of a living being. We misuse language when we ascribe thought, intelligence or even consciousness to a non-biological computer. Of course, we can use the *word-label* intelligence for AI. But his hardly means that we are using it correctly.

According to this semantic argument, it is therefore meaningless to regard machines as intelligent: they have not arisen over millions of years, let alone within the framework of processes describable in terms of the theory of evolution. The good old question of whether computers can think therefore receives a negative answer. We should not forget that Turing proposed his misguided account, according to which computing machinery can actually think, long before the most recent breakthroughs in molecular biology. And he did not even consider the option that thinking and intelligence might be tied to a specific sense modality of thought.

Computers take over various functions in our lives in order to make them easier, and because of the roles they play in our lives we endow them with quasi-mental powers. But our computers have no interests. And nor are they life forms that will either subjugate or exterminate us in any kind of *Terminator* scenario. Instead, the real danger derives from the fact that our technology *does not* think but, instead, implements value parameters under inflexible framework conditions.

This genuine problem is brought out in a particularly drastic fashion in the fifth episode of the fourth series of *Black Mirror*, which has the fitting title *Metalhead*. The episode depicts a dystopian future in which we have built perfect killing machines, somewhat resembling dogs, that go about destroying all human life that gets in their way. These machines were presumably designed for purposes such as providing protection against burglars; their sensors are highly sensitive and, without thinking or possessing intelligence, they function so perfectly that any sympathy is disabled.

Our technology throws up new dangers precisely because it is not like us, and we close our eyes to them if we indulge in anthropomorphic projections. **Anthropomorphism** is the false projection of human structures onto a non-human domain. One example of this phenomenon is the division of the animal kingdom into creatures to which we feel an affinity (such as pets, zebras, dolphins) and those that appear unimportant or even repulsive (snakes, foot fungus, insects). While we damage other animals – including ourselves in the process – through our anthropomorphism, we intervene directly in the conditions of our own lives if we conceive of machines as being like humans. It is an error to believe that computers or humanoid robots might soon think and feel like we do. They are not really intelligent. The inner life of a computer program is as exciting as that of a dusty old box of index cards. That is, it does not have one – computers are not even stupid.

As I say, none of this necessarily makes digital technology any less dangerous. But an insight into the true ontological nature of our technology can help free us from superstition and see the real dangers lying in the machines we have constructed. For these reside not in their intelligence but in their utter lack of intelligence. In this respect, we can agree with the Italian philosopher Maurizio Ferraris, whose recent book about our digital age is entitled *L'imbecillità è una cosa seria* – stupidity is a serious matter.[6] However, the 'stupidity' issue here is a human-all-too-human projection of mental features onto something that lacks them entirely.

'And now come, thou well-worn broom'

Naturally, convinced functionalists aren't going to come round to the thesis of biological externalism right away. So, to add to its plausibility, I want to make as clear as possible just how non-sensical it is to believe that computers could think and that chess programs are intelligent. But what is sense and what is nonsense?

In our language we frequently talk about reality. What is **real** is something we can be mistaken about; after all, the real tends not simply to tell us how we ought to think if we're to avoid making mistakes about it. The facts don't continually stare us in the face. Usually, reality is mute.

Insofar as we can use our language to speak about reality, we have to assume that some of our expressions refer to something real. We have to be in linguistic contact with objects and facts if we want to grasp them in a linguistically codified form. In philosophy of language, linguistic contact with the real is discussed under the heading of **reference**.

Reference presupposes that someone, in appropriate contexts, employs expressions that are directly about reality. This is how linguistic sense arises. A linguistically encoded thought has a sense only when referring expressions can be employed in suitable contexts. In his seminal *Philosophical Investigations*, Ludwig Wittgenstein discussed such contexts using the term 'form of life'. Language belongs to the 'natural history of mankind'.[7] What does and does not have sense comes out in the 'stream of thought and life'.[8]

Notice that this absolutely does not mean that we can stipulate the meaning of our expressions arbitrarily. Whether there really is artificial *intelligence* is not something we can decide simply by resolving to talk from now on as though there is such a thing. By thinking in terms of analogies with living processes, we can by all means give metaphorical descriptions of certain of the mechanisms of data storage and processing that go hand in hand with digital transformation; but this doesn't amount to generating an actual Terminator. At best, the AI systems we currently possess are a kind of Golem – i.e. a dumb, lifeless piece of material that processes information without showing the slightest trace of consciousness. A species that does not have millions of years of evolution behind it is not suitably equipped to lead an inner mental life. It simply lacks the necessary biological presuppositions.

As I've stressed above, this is to downplay neither the dangers nor the prospects of digital technology but to situate them in the right place. In programming AI systems, we in fact risk nothing less than the survival of humanity. This is not because AI is an intelligent life form, which will someday decide to eradicate us cognitively inferior human beings, as in films such as *2001: A Space Odyssey*, *Terminator*, *Transcendence*, *Her* or *Ex Machina*. Such scenarios imply that AIs constitute a kind of *human* superintelligence that does not follow any moral boundaries. They thus model AI as a decidedly insane and dangerous dictator, hell-bent on the suppression and destruction of all who think differently. But all of this misses the real danger.

A clear summary of the real danger was given by the American AI researcher Eliezer Shlomo Yudkowsky (b. 1979) at a conference on the ethics of AI held at New York University.[9] His (rather American) example is the episode 'The Sorcerer's Apprentice' from the 1940 Disney classic *Fantasia*. Actually, this episode was a filmic version of Goethe's ballad *The Sorcerer's Apprentice*. In the ballad, a sorcerer's apprentice speaks as the lyrical I (embodied in the Disney version by Mickey Mouse himself). The sorcerer's apprentice brings a broom to life, which then fulfils the task of fetching water from a river in order to fill a cauldron:

> And now come thou well-worn broom,
> And thy wretched form bestir;
> Thou hast ever served as groom,
> So fulfil my pleasure, sir!
> On two legs now stand,
> With a head on top;
> Waterpail in hand,
> Haste and do not stop![10]

The problem is that the apprentice installed an inadequate program on the broom. The program is based on a misleading user function: it stipulates that the broom should keep fetching water to fill the cauldron without stipulating that it should stop doing so once the bucket is full.

Since the broom has been programmed by a sorcerer's apprentice, it follows its program down to the last detail. It carries out its magical algorithm so perfectly that it won't be deterred by anything whatsoever; it is programmed solely to fill the cauldron with water, regardless of whether it overflows. The broom does not recognize any collateral damage, as no such thing has been programmed as relevant.

In order to put an end to the mischief, the apprentice resolves to destroy the broom and splits it in two with an axe. But the broom is so perfectly programmed that now both halves of the broom continue to carry out their task independently, which only serves to aggravate the situation yet further:

Woe, oh, woe!
Both the parts,
Quick as darts,
Stand on end,
Servants of my dreaded foe!
Oh, ye gods, protection send!

And they run! and wetter still
Grow the steps and grows the hall.
Lord and master, hear me call!
Ever seems the flood to fill[.][11]

According to Yudkowsky, the relevance of this story to the ethics of AI is that we do not know how we ought to program the value system of an AI in a way that corresponds to our form of life. By **value alignment**, researchers in this area understand the system of hierarchically ordered goals followed by a program or agent. As individuals embedded in complex social systems, we would be foolish to work on the assumption that all the human beings with whom we're in social interaction happen to share the same value system. In fact, we know this not to be the case.

In human social systems, it is impossible to guarantee a common value alignment once a certain level of complexity has been reached (as it always is once groups become sufficiently large). One reason for this is simply that we cannot even articulate our own value system with any certainty. Owing to our complex, historically shifting mindedness, we can never have the totality of our wants and wishes fully in view. Nobody has perfect self-knowledge, because too many factors participate in determining which spheres of possible action are open to us in any given situation. This is why the question of the meaning of each individual's life has to be posed anew every day.

Since we even lack sufficient self-knowledge to state which values actually orient our action, we can hardly assume that we know the value parameters of complex social systems. But then how might we program the utility function of an AI so that it cannot do us any harm without our noticing immediately?

By a **computer**, I here understand a system that we have manufactured and whose observable behaviour is governed by programs. As the term *artificial intelligence* suggests, computers are artefacts. Artefacts count as 'intelligent' because *we* have thoughts about how they should sort and process data. Data processing ultimately consists in undertaking translations – i.e. in coding and decoding data.

An AI is a program. Progress in AI results from merging different programs and feeding in vast quantities of data. Because of the processing power of modern computers, the coding and decoding of this data is performed quicker than we humans could ever manage by ourselves. The obvious reason for this is that we are not computers.

Humans are not artefacts in the sense of industrial products (we are only artefacts insofar as we are the outcome of sexual reproduction). As living beings, who receive data biologically (through our sense modalities) before storing it and subjecting it to further processing within our organism, we have arisen through natural processes, which are investigated by the natural sciences. The theory of evolution grasps the structures by which new species come into being on the basis of presently available life forms. Insofar as we are living beings – i.e. animals – we are not artificially produced by other animals.

Computers are nonsense-machines because they have no biological sense modalities. They cannot make sense of anything. They do not lead a life. At best, we can metaphorically describe them as though they were alive. To believe that they are, however, is a case of superstition. Computers produce only nonsense, which we straighten out by continually feeding them with data that does stand in contact with reality – thanks to *our* linguistic reference.

Illuminated brains

The psychologist Brigitte Görnitz and the physicist Thomas Görnitz arrive at a similar conclusion in their book *From Quantum Physics to Consciousnes: Cosmos, Mind and Matter* (2016).[12] They start from an interpretation of quantum theory that was previous suggested by Carl Friedrich von Weizsäcker (1912–2007). Summarizing this all too briefly, both authors believe that consciousness is the interior reflexive view of quantum information in a living brain.[13] Consciousness is thus like the 'folding of a protein', essentially 'involved in a process of life'.[14]

> Now, as is well known, there are artefacts that similarly react to information. Self-driving cars react to different information, which they decode and then assign a meaning, e.g. braking in front of pedestrians at a red light. Yet, despite these modes of behaviour,

which are certainly analogous to reason, the motor vehicles have no consciousness. Behind them, there is always the consciousness of their constructor, who has determined which information is assigned which meaning in the artefact's processing.[15]

Even if we ought to agree with this thesis, it raises an obvious follow-up question: if the Görnitzes are so certain that intelligent, non-biological artefacts do not possess consciousness, what do they think consciousness actually is? The philosophical weakness in their reasoning is that they simply assume that consciousness is to be found only in evolved living systems and neglect to provide any more specific arguments for this assumption (such as biological externalism). Worse still, within the framework of their quantum theoretical reflections, they take it for granted that consciousness is ultimately a receiver of information – i.e. something that allows of natural scientific descriptions. But, as the authors concede, there are other receivers too: televisions, for example. This throws up the question of whether consciousness is something different from a television. If it is not, there would be no further reason to deny consciousness to intelligent, non-biological artefacts such as my smartphone.

To deal with this issue, the Görnitzes introduce their concept of **uniware**. According to this conception, living beings are a unity of software and hardware. The authors believe that nerve cells work together with electromagnetic processes in the brain, which are 'at once senders and receivers of information'.[16] In this way, an interaction emerges between the electromagnetic processes within the skull, which we can measure using an EEG (electroencephalogram), and the biochemical processes through which the nerve cells are interconnected. This interaction undermines the idea that there is a software and a hardware of the human mind; instead, the mind is a fully biophysical phenomenon, which can be adequately grasped only through a combination of neurobiology and quantum theory. As the Görnitzes summarize their position: 'consciousness is an information structure, which can take up and experience information and thereby give it a meaning.'[17]

At this stage, I don't want to get caught up in the details of scientific speculation about the place of consciousness in the universe. From a philosophical perspective, the interesting manoeuvres contained in this kind of quantum theory of consciousness turn out to be somewhat questionable.

The first problem resides in the thesis that consciousness is a self-experiencing information structure. For this thesis just presupposes what needs to be explained. The real problem now is experience. It may well be that our conscious experience always involves a uniware of nerve cells and quantum information. Strictly speaking, this is by no means empirically resolved: we do not yet know of any exact, measurable signature (or neural correlate) of consciousness that could be used to determine, say, whether or not a patient admitted to a hospital is still conscious, even if they are currently unable to express themselves. Yet, for the sake of argument, let's suppose there is such a signature.

But even if we substitute the expression 'experience' for 'consciousness' in our definition, we have still not solved the problem of consciousness. We've just raised the problem anew. Why do 'highly complex systems'[18] such as nerve cells have consciousness while other highly complex systems such as suns, galaxies or Homer's *Odyssey* do not?

Like all other attempts to upgrade consciousness research through quantum theory, the Görnitzes' position is a further variant of naturalism and fails for precisely that reason. **Naturalism**, recall, is generally the assumption that everything that exists is explicable and comprehensible by means of the natural sciences. Consciousness causes a number of headaches from this perspective. As soon as you allocate to consciousness any kind of structure attestable in the universe (such as nerve cells or protons), you face the question of whether it is restricted to these structures. Do only mammals have consciousness? Or only creatures with certain nervous systems? Or do plants have it too? And if, say, bees and elephants have consciousness, what about bacteria or the intestinal tract? Is our intestine perhaps conscious without our realizing it, while intestinal consciousness wonders whether the brain might be conscious too?

As soon as we try to thematize consciousness in this way, we open the door to the idea of a superintelligence. Perhaps even a pocket calculator is conscious. Who knows, perhaps there has long existed a conspiracy of intelligence technology against mankind. The singularity might already have taken place. Or perhaps we are already so interconnected with our smart technologies that, far from our using them, they control us. Then it wouldn't be the Russians who hacked the US election (if they really did) but autonomous AI systems, which have consciously decided to control human history so that we keep producing hardware for them.

Of course, such speculations are nonsense. Yet we can formulate and buy into randomly many philosophical conspiracy theories so long as we simply don't know how things really are.

Consciousness first – Tononi meets Husserl

This problem was recognized by the Italian neuroscientist and renowned sleep researcher Giulio Tononi, who runs the Center for Sleep and Consciousness at the University of Wisconsin, Madison. He therefore opts for an altogether different approach, which has attracted a fair amount of attention. In January 2018, on the invitation of the Chilean senate and the then president of Chile, Michelle Bachelet, I had the pleasure of spending a few days discussing consciousness and AI with Tononi at a futurological congress held annually in Chile.[19]

Tononi takes the question of the relation between consciousness and material reality and turns it on its head. He recognizes that explaining consciousness in terms of the brain or any other complex system will never work.[20] According to Tononi, unless we take consciousness itself as our starting point, it will remain in principle impossible to answer the question of which scientifically verifiable systems in the universe are conscious.

On this basis, in a paper co-authored with Christof Koch (b. 1956), Tononi shows that both computers and deep learning systems, such as AlphaGo, are non-conscious input–output machines, which simulate intelligence without being intelligent themselves.[21] If Tononi and Koch are right, this also refutes the Turing test, because something may well *behave* in such a way that we cannot distinguish it from intelligent or even conscious life from the outside, without it therefore also being *actually* intelligent or conscious.

Besides empirical considerations, Tononi also supports this thesis with a philosophical argument. Indeed, it was primarily philosophical considerations that provoked him to change the way he previously thought about the issue. The starting point of his argument is the concept of intrinsic existence. **Intrinsic existence** consists in something's being something for itself. We all have intrinsic existence, as we all know of ourselves that we exist – whereby Tononi is of course driving at the famous declaration of René Descartes (1596–1650): *I think, therefore I am*, the **Cartesian Cogito**.

But, unlike Descartes, Tononi does not infer from the Cartesian Cogito that he is a thinker of thoughts that has somehow strayed into a body. Instead, he lingers at this starting point for a while and assumes that he is a consciousness. This is a strategy he inherits from Husserl, who also argued that, before we turn to nature and ask how consciousness can possibly fit into it, we ought first of all to give an adequate description of consciousness itself. According to

Husserl and Tononi, while Descartes certainly saw *that* he existed intrinsically, he did not grasp his own intrinsic existence correctly. Now, Husserl's philosophy of consciousness is highly complex. But, for our purposes, the advantage of Tononi's approach is that it tries to make do with just five axioms, which Tononi holds to be indubitable.

Tononi's axioms are intrinsic existence, composition, information, integration and exclusion. Intrinsic existence we've already met.

Composition consists in how our conscious experience has a structure. As I wrote these lines in my hotel room in Santiago, I saw my hands and my computer screen, and I heard the noise from the street below, all while knowing that Tononi was also somewhere in the same hotel. Every conscious state has some structure or other.

Information is the fact that every conscious experience is different from every other. Every experience is utterly individual, distinct from every further experience that I or anyone else will ever have. Tononi illustrates this axiom by way of an analogy with the individual frames of a film. Each frame contains what it contains and is thereby distinguished from every other frame.

Integration means that every conscious experience has a structure that cannot simply be traced back to its parts. Your consciousness of the word STREETCAR does not consist of a consciousness of the word STREET and a consciousness of the word CAR. And, even if this were so, you wouldn't then have a consciousness that consisted of the fragments STR, E, ET, CA and R.

Finally, Tononi sees **exclusion** in how consciousness is completely and determinately definite. It is just what it is, no more and no less.

These axioms raise a few further philosophical questions. What, for example, is the difference between information and exclusion? Tononi says that information is *specific* while *exclusion* is *definite*. If consciousness is specific, then it is seemingly also definite, unless Tononi means that there can be specific but not definite information, which is something he would have to explain. But the real problem doesn't lie in the system of axioms.

The problem that this approach creates stems from a further aspect of the theory: Tononi says that the rest of reality – that is, whatever does not exist intrinsically – can be inferred only from the standpoint of consciousness. He believes that the only epistemically secure existence is that of consciousness, meaning we have to extrapolate theoretically to the rest of reality, including to the physical realization of consciousness. He therefore concedes that there might actually be no reality outside of consciousness. To be sure, he thinks this is in fact false. But its falsity is demonstrable only by means of a so-called *inference to the best explanation*.

An **inference to the best explanation** consists in deciding which cause or causal chain most probably explains a given phenomenon on the basis of the available data. A simple example of this kind of fairly mundane inference would be leaving your house, noting the wet ground and grey sky, and suspecting that it has rained. Inferences to the best explanation are defeasible. This means that you can only draw an inference to the best explanation if you are prepared, in principle, to countenance an alternative cause. What you give as an explanation for a given state of affairs, in this framework, is always a hypothesis and not an unequivocally identifiable state of affairs. And this means that inferences to the best explanation operate under conditions that fall short of full epistemic certainty.

Yet if only the existence of consciousness is secure, and the existence of non-conscious (physical) existence is something we can only infer, we have to be prepared to acknowledge the possibility that only consciousness exists. Tononi certainly takes this to be improbable, and he is therefore in no way a solipsist. **Solipsism** is the assumption that only one's own consciousness exists and that everything else can be understood as its contents. This, to repeat, is not Tononi's view. But he does not think solipsism is incoherent; he just thinks that, as a matter of fact, it happens to be false.

The remarkable – and downright revolutionary – trick of his approach is that it allows him to formulate an empirical research program that can help find signatures of consciousness in the human brain with the help of an empirical procedure. For, within the framework of this research program, something can be a signature of consciousness only if it doesn't contravene the five axioms. Tononi has specified postulates in addition to the axioms – that is, 'properties that physical systems (elements in a state) must have to account for experience.'[22]

In conducting his research, Tononi has cooperated with a series of prominent neuroscientists, including Christof Koch, who runs the Allen Institute for Brain Science in Seattle.[23] To the extent that his mathematical model, known as **integrated information theory** (**IIT**), is empirically confirmed, Tononi can infer that no computer that has existed thus far – however much we improve on currently available hardware and software – will ever achieve consciousness.

The reason for this, according to his model (which has in fact been empirically tested to some extent), is that the information processing in our artefacts lacks the appropriate form of integration. Applying the model to artificial networks shows that these (can) have precisely zero consciousness. Yet much depends here, of course, on the details of Tononi's arguments, and these ultimately fail to prove that computers are not conscious. On the contrary, they show only that so-called feedforward networks, which process inputs to outputs, do not fulfil his postulates. But this opens up the possibility that so-called feedback recurrent networks, which are used for speech recognition, for example, could still be conscious.

None of Tononi's publications so far give any compelling arguments against substrate-dependence, something in which he does not unequivocally believe. He is currently working on a paper in which he generalizes his results to all computers. But discussion of this will have to wait for another day.

Nevertheless, it's worth underlining how, from a philosophical point of view, Tononi's approach is radically new in a number of respects. Crucially, he starts off from a basic principle of New Realism, which he deploys in his own way. This basic principle says that our thought or consciousness is in no sense less real than, say, a mountain ridge. Strictly speaking, if we want to focus on this particular case, Tononi even thinks that consciousness is *more* real than mountain ridges, because these do not fulfil his criteria for physical, independent and non-conscious existence. The information realized in mountain ridges is not sufficiently integrated to be conscious, which does in fact follow mathematically from IIT. Yet that too is a topic for another occasion. What matters here is the recognition of the irreducible reality of subjectivity – that is, of our standpoint as thinking, experiencing subjects. And on this topic too, it makes sense to follow Tononi a little further.

Inside, outside or nowhere

Leaning on his neuroscientific research, Tononi introduces a philosophical concept of consciousness that can help us on our way in the search for the meaning of thought. He directs our attention to the structure and reality of our individual subjective experience, which tends to be neglected within the contemporary scientific worldview.[24] More specifically, Tononi makes a novel contribution to our understanding of what philosophers usually refer to as *phenomenal consciousness*.[25] In order to understand his innovation, let's return to the general concept of intentionality (see p. 65). Intentionality arises in living beings. It is an actually existing structure, which connects a living, conscious system (a self) with an object (or several objects) by means of a content. Intentionality thus consists of a *self*, a *content* and an *object*.

Imagine you're in Paris, standing in front of the Eiffel Tower. The Eiffel Tower is now the object of your intentionality. You are the self that is directed towards this object. While you paint the Eiffel Tower in your imagination, it appears to you in a certain way: it has a form, a colour, relations of size, and is imagined from an optical perspective. All this belongs to the content. **Content** is the way you represent your object, in this case the Eiffel Tower. Your content and my content differ from each other. Two people (or the same person at different times) never have the same content, but they can target the same intentional object without great difficulty.

While you target the Eiffel Tower and represent it, you are conscious. Right now, you are currently experiencing all manner of things: you sense, for example, your contact with the floor, how it feels to sit with a book in your hands, and you notice certain rumblings in your stomach if you pay attention to such inner goings-on.

Now try to remember your last vivid nightmare, or one of your anxieties. During a vivid nightmare, you experience extreme emotions. Some emotions or other accompany every exercise of your intentionality (see p. 74). Not, of course, that the same feelings are always bound up with the same content and the same object: you can come to hate the very person you love, and vice versa. Moreover, our feelings are not steered exclusively by the presence of objects in our field of attention. The point of neuroscientific consciousness research is that we have subjective experience independently of the question of which objects we are thinking about. Subjective experience of intense anxiety in a dream can be just as oppressive as subjective experience undergone in the light of an actual dangerous situation.

Now, we know today that the contents we experience (such as forms, colours, smells, perspectives) can also be present when we are enjoying not waking but, rather, dream consciousness. We can elicit dream contents in a subject (at the moment we can do this only partially, but in the future perhaps fully) by placing the person's brain in certain conditions.

From this empirically confirmed fact, Tononi does not infer an identity between thinking and the brain, or that the brain causes thinking, or indeed anything similar. He merely points out that there is subjective experience that can be phenomenally – i.e. for the experiencing subject – fully identical in both dream states and waking states. This idea, a theme that today finds endless variations in film and TV, is not new. It was famously invoked by Descartes and has quite ancient origins.[26] You may have heard of the famous question by the Chinese philosopher Zhuang Zi (370–287 BC) – whether he is actually a man who dreams he's a butterfly or a butterfly who dreams it's a man.[27]

Tononi is certainly correct that subjective experience in waking and dream states can be phenomenally identical, or, rather, that this is a question to be investigated empirically. Indeed, this is precisely what he and many of his scientific colleagues in neuroscience do with some success. Nobody ought to cavil at this.

Now, Tononi does not (thankfully) infer from this that we cannot know reality as it is independently of consciousness. He is ultimately a realist who wants to introduce consciousness into reality. Consciousness is not some interior space that stands opposed to an exterior realm. It is not something that can be *located* in any meaningful way. There is, to be sure, a neural support of consciousness for Tononi, which we can find only by setting out from consciousness. But this does not mean that consciousness is to be found in the same place as its neural support. Consciousness is a reality of its own which, on the basis of its structural properties, cannot be borne by just any old material or complex system.

If we're taking consciousness in the sense of subjective experience, we have no credible reasons to ascribe any kind of consciousness to computers or manufacturable robots. This has been pointed out, incidentally, by the robotics expert Nadia Magnenat Thalmann (b. 1946), whose social autonomous robot Nadine was one of the models for the robots in the HBO series *Westworld*.[28] The belief that we will soon face a gigantic intelligence explosion and the takeover of the planet by digitally networked machines turns out to be mere science fiction.

A slimy and intricate piece of reality

After this short detour through the latest empirical research into the question of whether computers can think and feel (they can't!), let's return to the philosophical investigation of our sense of thought, of the nooscope. The philosophy of New Realism provides the model for understanding the nooscope. In general, **New Realism** asserts 1) that we can grasp objects and facts as they really are, and 2) that there are infinitely many fields of sense in which objects and facts exist. There is no single, all-encompassing reality: *The* world does not exist. I have argued extensively for this thesis elsewhere.[29] To illustrate the implications of New Realism for grasping the sense of thought, we can rehearse the following example.

Imagine you are in Naples, looking at Vesuvius. You are doing so from your vantage point, from your perspective. At the same time, your best friend is in Sorrento, also looking at Vesuvius. **Old realism** assumed that, in this case, reality contains Vesuvius, but not the two perspectives on Vesuvius. In *Why the World Does Not Exist*, I called this a 'world without spectators'.[30] For its critics, old realism raises precisely the question of the role of spectators; for it now looks as though we have the world without spectators and then, set besides it somehow, the world of 'spectators'.[31] The classical term for this situation is the subject–object divide. The **subject–object divide** is the view that there is, on the one hand, a subject-independent reality (the object or the objective) and, on the other, a subject who contemplates this reality.

The modern scientific worldview has in no way overcome the subject–object divide. Most of its propagators continue to work on the assumption that there is a fundamental difference between the external reality outside of our skulls and the internal processes taking place in the brain. In this way, the subject–object divide is replaced by the brain–universe divide, which does not make it any better.

To be sure, the brain is supposed to belong to the universe. But it is just this idea that throws up the very puzzle of consciousness that so many see as a mystery: how can it be that the brain produces subjectivity when it itself belongs to reality? How can a (slimy and intricate) piece *of* reality produce perspectives *on* reality? The British biologist Thomas Henry Huxley (1825–1895) put it this way:

> How it is that anything so remarkable as a state of consciousness comes about as a result of irritating nervous tissue, is just as unaccountable as the appearance of the Djin, when Aladdin rubbed his lamp.[32]

The subject–object divide is deeply rooted in our ways of thinking about human knowledge – but therein lies the rub. Among the uncritically absorbed hangovers of early modern philosophy, in which the subject–object divide (supposedly inherited from Descartes) played a considerable role, is a distorted picture of scientific knowledge. I'd like to set this picture straight with the help of an elementary thought experiment.

Scientific knowledge acquisition begins when we question something that previously seemed self-evident. In questioning the obvious, our aim is not to instil any sort of radical doubt about absolutely everything we believe but to gain a better understanding or theoretical explanation of how the phenomena hang together. A **phenomenon** is something that seems to appear to us utterly unmediated and unfiltered, but is in fact a sensibly mediated perception.

In the eighteenth and nineteenth centuries, the expression 'phenomenology' originally referred to a theory of illusions. The philosophical motivation for such a theory is that we cannot simply read off what is the case from our spontaneous impressions. Ultimately, we are liable to error, on account of how we all too readily lend credence to phenomena. For surely we don't get reality completely and utterly wrong, and therefore we can be certain that some phenomena place us in contact with the facts. Unfortunately, though, it doesn't follow immediately *which* phenomena these are, which is why we need a phenomenology.

Phenomenology is thus originally concerned with seeming and not being. If we treat something in a scientific manner, we have to assume that it might be a mere phenomenon, an appearance. This is how we uncover new connections in reality, which we represent in models. These models have to do away with mere seeming, so that we can secure our access to being, to the facts.

A **model** is a simplified representation of a real situation (a target system). It emphasizes essential connections which are not directly self-evident. So, the standard model of particle physics, for example, tells us which particles there are and how they generally interact with one another. However, particle physics by no means describes everything that goes on with particles in concrete situations. Because it is interested only in the essential aspects of its objects, it simplifies the reality of particles, with far-reaching consequences.

By proceeding in this way, we can better explain some actual given situation in which the properties of elementary particles play a decisive role. We can apply the model because elementary particles really have the properties which the model grasps. To be sure, the natural sciences allow a certain room for manoeuvre, because models are not simply direct copies of the properties of their objects: in order to translate properties of elementary particles into the language of mathematics, certain idealizations are necessary. From our school physics we are all familiar with the problem that cannonballs and feathers do not actually fall at the same speed; they will do so only in a vacuum, and thus under very specific conditions. A model such as Newtonian mechanics does not simply describe and explain what happens but is exactly that, a model, which allows us to make certain predictions and explanations.

For a model to be informative and deliver predictions, it cannot in fact be a straightforward copy of reality. Models are not 'mirrors of nature'.[33] If a model were a copy, it would be of no use – we could then just as well go and observe reality directly.

Think of a plastic model of the Dutch coast in a geology museum. Let's say it is used to investigate the effects of climate change. Water is slowly introduced into the model in order to determine which areas would be flooded if it came to it, and so how many Dutch refugees, say, would come over to Germany. Such a plastic model is just as little a 100 per cent accurate miniature copy of the coast as the miniature Holland in the Madurodam in The Hague is a second Holland. To a certain degree, models are permitted to distort the reality whose basic features they represent – by simplifying it, for example.

So far, so good. Yet now the epistemological fun begins. For, while you were reading the previous paragraphs, you yourself have been piecing together a model under my guidance. This model grasps essential features of models. Let's call it the simple model-model.

The **simple model-model** has two parts: models and the reality that they simplify. Now comes the decisive question: Can we also grasp the reality that a model is meant to grasp independently of any model? If it were not possible to grasp the reality that a model is meant to grasp, we would obviously face the question: How exactly can we know that there are essential features of reality at all and how can we know that we can know them? It could be, that is, that we are just hopelessly wide of the mark with our models. There would simply be no independent check on our investigations, as every check could at best consist in assembling another model, which raises the question anew, albeit in a different light. We would thus manoeuvre ourselves into a situation that Wittgenstein aptly describes in his *Philosophical Investigations*:

> Let us imagine a table (something like a dictionary) that exists only in our imagination. A dictionary can be used to justify the translation of a word X by a word Y. But are we also to call it a justification if such a table is to be looked up only in the imagination? 'Well, yes; then it is a subjective justification.' – But justification consists in appealing to something independent. – 'But surely I can appeal from one memory to another. For example, I don't know if I have remem-

bered the time of departure of a train right and to check it I call to mind how a page of the timetable looked. Isn't this the same here?' No; for this process has got to produce a memory which is actually *correct*. If the mental image of the timetable could not itself be *tested* for correctness, how could it confirm the correctness of the first memory? (As if someone were to buy several copies of the morning paper to assure himself that what it said was true.)

Looking up a table in the imagination is no more looking up a table than the image of the result of an imagined experiment is the result of an experiment.[34]

If we could know about the existence and constitution of the reality we model only within the framework of the models themselves, we could ensure neither that there is any such reality nor that we can know how it is constituted. At the end of the day, we would only ever be able (at best!) to make blind guesses about the facts. And it is just this that is the guiding wish behind today's populist defamation of facts. If we can only ever guess what the facts are, then we might as well also place bets against climate change or social progress and put our money on superstition instead.

Of course, the situation is worse still. If our experience of reality were totally restricted to the model-model, the same would also go for the model-model: we would then have a model-model-model, and then a model-model-model-model, and so on and so on. If we want to stave off the infinite regress and yet stick to the rules of the model game, the only remaining option is at some point or other to take a stab in the dark; but this really amounts to undermining all scientific objectivity. Let's call this the **sinister model regress**.

Of course, not every regress is vicious. But the sinister model regress certainly is – it deserves its name! In epistemology, a regress is vicious when we introduce a rule in order to know how knowledge is possible but have to repeat it infinitely many times before we can actually know how knowledge is possible.

The sinister model regress is one of the baleful consequences of the modern subject–object divide underlying the profoundly misguided scientific worldview. This worldview does not set out with the intention of subjecting everything to radical questioning – else there would hardly be room for scientific model-building. But, because of its experimental set-up, it produces the very result it wants to avoid: radical doubt. At first sight, this might look less radical than it really is: it seems that we can pause briefly at each individual model, take a moment for reflection, and survey the landscape of reality from the adopted perspective. But this is a mere phenomenon. The moment is fleeting, and we never arrive at a position from which we can actually observe something real.

For this reason, in the name of scientific progress we have to overcome the simple model-model together with the subject–object divide that underlies it.

5

Reality and Simulation

In the previous chapter, I tried to convince you that our thought is a real, objectively existing interface between subject and object. We humans possess a distinctly developed sense of thought, a nooscope, which allows us to browse through the reality of thoughts. Thinking and its thoughts are something real.

The task of this chapter is to paint a realistic picture of our position in reality. In this connection, we of course have to answer the question of what we mean by 'reality' or 'the real' and to what extent we are inescapably hooked up with it. We therefore need to get down to the nitty-gritty and answer the tough question: What is reality and how is our thinking in contact with it?

Neither the wings of imagination nor the modern simulations that let us experience virtual realities (such as video games) let us truly flee from reality. Imagination, simulations, video games, VR goggles and our experience are as much part of reality as bosons, fermions, mountains or what have you. The fields of sense opened up by our imagination, which we objectify as artworks, video games, novels, daydreams and ideologies, are themselves something real. Such is the contention of New Realism.

New Realism takes aim against our current alienation from reality. Iris Radisch's contribution to a series on New Realism, which appeared in a seven-part series on that topic in the German newspaper *Die Zeit*, nicely captures this alienation.[1] Radisch explains how reality has become science fiction and surprisingly accuses Maurizio Ferraris and myself of indulging a kind of postmodern nostalgia:

> Philosophers such as Markus Gabriel and Maurizio Ferraris seek a 'New Realism' that could break though the screensaver beneath which true life hibernates, as though beneath an ice sheet of a thousand constructions and postmodern rewritings.

Radisch's postmodern notion that reality has become science fiction leaves much to be desired. In reality, reality has never become science fiction and is still far from having disappeared. There is indeed science fiction, and there are technological developments that make yesterday's science fiction scenarios today's reality. But this doesn't mean that reality becomes science fiction. Looked at a little more closely, this notion is revealed as a false assumption at best.

To vary (somewhat contrary to its intentions) the title of a book by the postmodern sociologist Bruno Latour (b. 1947), New Realism says that we have never been postmodern.[2] Postmodernity never took place; we remain knee-deep in modernity, with all its pitfalls.

What is real is something we cannot delete or erase simply by piling fiction upon fiction. Spending one's life on social networks or playing video games means acting in the midst of reality, not in any way escaping from it. Technology and fictional fields of sense are not in the slightest bit less real than metabolism, stomach pains or the houses of parliament. The contrast between science fiction and reality that Radisch at once exploits and unsuccessfully denies rests on the untenable conception of reality I call 'old realism' and now want to expose as false.

Old, or metaphysical, realism conceives reality as that which is essentially independent of human beings – of our senses, for example, or of our thought and speech – without ever stating exactly what this 'independence' is supposed to consist in. Both old realism and the (supposedly) postmodern overreaction to it are a fiction, failed intellectual enterprises which operate wholly within the framework of the ultimately incoherent subject–object dichotomy. The subject–object dichotomy assumes that there are objects out there, in reality, which we grasp 'in here', in our minds or brains, by getting in touch with them (be it through our nerve endings or some metaphysically fancier activity of sending out mental rays to the universe). The obvious mistake in this dichotomy transpires once we realize that the subject (thinkers like you and me) are as much part of reality as whatever it is they perceive as being 'out there'. In other words, in here is already out there. The mind and the world are not two separate realms that need to be connected so that we might establish a fragile and fallible contact with reality.

The alienation from reality opposed by New Realism is manifest in the increasingly widespread impression that we are all trapped in media bubbles, in echo chambers of thought. At bottom, this is likely just a lazy excuse for choosing not to confront the fact that in the wake of digital revolution we have witnessed a highly complex and rapid shift to a renewed transformation of the public sphere.[3]

The transformation I have in mind finds expression in a crisis of representation (as I call it). There is at least a twofold sense in which we are witnessing such a crisis.

Firstly, a disturbing epistemological confusion concerning the relationship between thought and reality is increasingly gaining ground. Can we represent reality even approximately as it really is? Isn't everything just far too complex to be graspable, calculable and predictable, even if only approximately, in models and simulations?

Secondly, while operating within this very framework, people have the impression that our democratically chosen and legitimated representatives either stand for nothing at all or have to make compulsive attempts to address a fictional 'people', which they construct through the propagation of tasteless populist myths and propaganda.

The crisis of the *representation of reality* and the crisis of *representative democracy* hang together: by putting into question our access to objectively existing facts, it becomes much harder for democracy to survive in our alleged 'post-truth' age.

The way we experience democracy today is deeply influenced by the digital revolution. But it is an error to believe that this undoubted transformation automatically leads to the undermining of democracy. *Nothing leads automatically to the self-abolition of democracy.* It is dangerously misguided to believe that, thanks to digital transformation, or the automation of operations in the service sector, or thanks to how the internet of things is optimizing our factories, we are standing on the threshold of a beautiful new world of perfect algorithms. We cannot, and ought not, delegate our most important decisions to computer programs – whose codes, moreover, are always written by a human being, who thereby implements his or her own value system, whether explicitly or implicitly.

As is well known, democracies presuppose mature citizens and correspondingly mature representatives. Because of the recent digital transformation of the public sphere, we are continually bombarded by a whirl of newsfeeds and endlessly proliferating scandals. A case study of this problem is provided by the crazed experimental laboratory of the scandal industry that is the current US government, which unfortunately resembles a reality TV show with all too real consequences.

All of these processes that I am subsuming under the label of the digital revolution are fully real. No science fiction is involved here, just advanced communication technology and a rapidly spreading confusion among citizens when it comes to the question of what politics means today and how it can face the complex challenges of a global digital economy, as well as the more traditional but utterly serious problems arising in more classical modern industries – not to mention climate change.

In order truly to face up to the challenges of our time, we need a clear picture of how we might overcome our alienation from reality. From a philosophical point of view, what is needed is an explicit articulation of the implicit and explicit patterns of argument that lie behind that sense of alienation. It is only by pointing out the mistakes that unavoidably sneak in once we separate off our sense of thought from the facts that new paths for thinking can open up.

One of philosophy's jobs is to diagnose various ailments afflicting our sense of thought – or, as Wittgenstein put it in one of his *bon mots*: 'the philosopher's treatment of a question is like the treatment of an illness.'[4] This is ambiguous, as it could mean that the philosophical treatment of a question is itself an illness. Certainly, the self-investigation of reason, of our sense of thought, is not automatically immune from the errors we need to discover and overcome. But this is no cause for unnecessary self-doubt.

Mental cinema meets smartphone

The currently rampant alienation from reality is based on a distorted conception of what actually occurs when we perceive something. This conception takes our perceptions to be simulations visible on a mental cinema screen, which is at best more or less contingently connected with reality. According to this conception, perception is not, say, a process of grasping reality that itself belongs to the real as much as anything else does; rather, it is an illusion.

In order to dispel the illusion that our mental conscious life is by its very nature an illusion, we need to clarify quite a few concepts. Our sense modalities are media. A **medium** is an interface that transfers information from one code into another. You're currently reading a sentence. But now simply observe the following signs without asking what they could mean: σκιᾶς ὄναρ ἄνθρωπος or 道可道非常道，名可名，非常名.

If you can read these Greek or simplified Chinese characters, you can read the sentences out loud and pay attention to what they mean or to how they sound when spoken. Otherwise, look at the sentences as a graphic pattern. What you thereby see, hear or understand is on each occasion composed in a different code. The sense modalities of sight, hearing and understanding (understanding is a mode of thought) can be translated into one another. You can see, hear and understand one and the same sentence – this one, for example. Different codes present the same information in a different medium. This does not mean that we cannot directly grasp what the codes present. On the contrary, it means that in a given medium we can grasp precisely what the medium presents to us, nothing more and nothing less.

No medium can grasp everything at once. Every medium selects from everything that could be processed by some medium or other. In this sense, media are one-sided; they have a form. Yet their codes are not thereby distortions or falsifications. We can certainly distort information through translating it from one medium into another. Moreover, we can lie in any medium that is apt for expressing thoughts. However, it is not part of the very essence of a medium that it erects 'a limit which completely separates'[5] us from reality. For everything real always appears already in some medium or other. Baryonic matter is just as much a medium as the paper that's based on it – say, the paper on which this sentence is printed. Adorno captured this insight with the following formula (**Adorno's mediation principle**):

> But mediation can no more be hypostatized than can the poles of subject and object; it is valid only in their constellation. Mediation is mediated by what it mediates.[6]

Media are not filters positioned between us and reality but interfaces that ensure that something real appears to us in some specific manner (see the concept of direct realism, above, p. 41). The signs printed in different editions of this book are something real. They affect various sense modalities. How the signs are processed depends on the medium. Our sense modalities are bound up with media that we can to some extent describe in the natural sciences: you cannot hear anything in airless space (on the moon, for example) or see or read anything in the dark. Therefore, light is also a medium, as it can code information – otherwise we couldn't suddenly see things when someone turns on the light.

The way in which objects appear in a medium is their sense (cf. pp. 18f.). Our sense modalities are forms of sense which put us into contact with fields of sense – that is, with configurations of objects that can only be grasped from specific perspectives. There are no senseless objects, no objects that *just exist* without appearing in a medium.

Even those domains of the universe that are independent of human beings have a media structure, because the objects that appear in them are interconnected in a determinate manner. But this means that our senses too are a component of reality. They are themselves something real standing in contact with other components of reality. And, because of our sense of thought, this fact is in turn something accessible. We can grasp the basic structure of reality in thought, but only because thought is already in touch with it.

Both fields (think of physical fields, for instance) and sense also exist completely independently of human beings. The real is not somehow spiritually illuminated by humans, as though it were utterly devoid of sense before we evolved on planet Earth. If this were so, we couldn't know anything at all about reality as it was before there were humans. It would have been totally senseless, forever resistant to conceptual mediation.

Senseless objects would be objects that do not appear in any medium whatsoever, objects that were in no sense bearers of information. There are no senseless objects. Of course, many objects appear in media that are in principle beyond our comprehension – for example, all objects in black holes, as no information can force its way out of a black hole. And even if we could (somehow) solve this particular problem, there would still be further objects that are just too far away from us (further than, say, circa 14 billion light years away according to our present estimates) for us to possibly have any grasp of them. Yet this does not mean that these objects exist outside of any medium.

We can think of our thought as a *field-sense*: we find ourselves in the midst of fields of sense and are able to recognize them. The philosophical theory that deals with the existence of fields of sense is called the ontology of fields of sense. According to this theory, there are no raw, absolute objects existing in splendid isolation, only ever objects featuring in determinate media, which can thus be encoded and decoded. These processes of coding and decoding are real and largely independent of us human beings, as they occur everywhere in the universe as far as we can know it. They take place without our assistance. Indeed, they took place before we existed; they take place beyond our causal and cognitive reach; and they will still take place when there are no human beings left at all.

Media are not ways of standing back from reality, but real interventions into it. This holds for our media landscape too, the infosphere. Every click is an intervention in the energy balance of our planet. Think how much energy is required to power the servers needed for the World Wide Web and how frequently you charge up your phone so you can stay online. Every update of a newsfeed on an online portal costs money, time and energy. Every message that you read, however briefly it occupies you, alters the factual material-energetic situation in which you find yourself. You never look into the universe from outside, as though through some virtual peephole; instead, you already find yourself right in the midst of things. There is no escape.

A foundational error of our time is a misguided conception of our media landscape, a conception deprived of reality. It overlooks how messages are not just mental processes but intrusions into reality. Media shape what humans do by influencing how and what they think. This is to a large extent independent of whether it is real information or so-called fake news that is being propagated. What escapes our notice in particular is that our media landscape has extreme effects on our planet: maintaining the more or less global network costs time and money. This is why a select few can become incredibly rich off the back of our taking an interest in certain kinds of information. The formatting and provision of this information has a material-energetic foundation.

Today, too many humans flee to a false world of ideas. They indulge the fantasy that when we sit in front of our screens, in fear of even a single moment of boredom, we are freed from our animality and, as inforgs – i.e. information-cyborgs – placed at a distance from reality. Yet the very opposite is the case. By digitizing the real, we alter it; we create new media that are in no sense unreal.

There is hope for a better future for humanity only if we finally understand that our life, far from being a dream, is a very real biological process. To put it especially pointedly: postmodern media theory, which in recent decades has moved from literary criticism to neuroscience, behaves like a small child who believes that it can no longer see when it simply closes its eyes. It makes reality depend on our perception of it and thinks of our perception as a kind of hallucination or illusion produced by the brain (or some subsystem of it). But a crucial feature of reality is that it changes only very minimally when we look away. The sole change that we effect when we close our eyes, ears and minds (thought) is that we stultify our own faculties.

The unavoidable Matrix

The first part of the Wachowskis' famous *Matrix* trilogy was released in cinemas in 1999. It quickly established a place for itself in our cultural memory, for it managed to encapsulate the basic suspicion of postmodernity: that reality might not be all it's cracked up to be. At the centre of the film is the following construction, which I'd like briefly to recapitulate:

We are first introduced to the protagonists of the film in a merely apparent world (a simulation), which resembles a realistic video game. This seeming reality is called the 'Matrix'.

A **simulation** is generally a merely apparent reality that resembles another reality (from the Latin *simulatio*, derived from *simulare* = to make similar). Simulations are real but are generated as imitations of certain aspects of something else that, while also real, is usually not itself a simulation. Let's call anything that is itself neither a simulation nor something that came into being via a human intention to produce an artefact part of **basic reality**. Basic reality is not a 'deceased dream of elementary reality'[7] but a category that is very easy to form. There is rather a lot that is neither a simulation nor any other kind of intentionally produced artefact: the moon, Mars, the solar system, human brain tumours, leptons, prime numbers and much more besides. You can argue over particular candidates for membership in basic reality, and both the natural sciences and philosophy certainly spend much of their time doing so. But to assert that the category of basic reality is empty is a postmodern deception.[8]

The Matrix's thought experiment doesn't even come close to questioning the existence of basic reality. On the contrary. Within the film, the Matrix as a simulation is distinguished from a depressing basic reality. The film's basic reality contains machines which exploit human beings as an energy source. To keep the human organisms alive, the machines stimulate their brains in order to generate a dream-like hyper-realistic reality. To the deluded humans, this world appears fully real – in other words, it is a perfect simulation. This idea of generating a perfect simulation through brain stimulation has long been a staple of the science fiction genre. We need think only of David Cronenberg's masterpiece *eXistenZ*, which also came out in 1999. The current spearheads of this filmic genre are the British series *Black Mirror* and its sequel *Electric Dreams*.

The protagonist of *The Matrix* is a certain Neo (played by Keanu Reeves). Within the Matrix, Neo plays the role of a hacker. For various unexplained reasons, some humans have managed to defend themselves against the machines. Led by Morpheus (played by Laurence Fishburne), they enter into Neo's consciousness and free him from the simulation in order to instigate a war against the machines.

The Matrix trilogy further develops a mythology which came to epitomize the postmodern mood that was especially widespread in the 1990s. Unfortunately, this mythology has not really been overcome: what was unwillingly started by French sociology and philosophy between the 1960s and 1990s has, in our own still young century, been transferred to neuroscience and computer science, namely the illusion that reality is an illusion or a simulation indistinguishable from the genuine article of reality. A **mythology** is a narrative structure by means of which we humans construct a picture of our overall historical and socio-economic situation. Mythologies are essentially false but hide this fact by establishing certain plausible points of contact with reality.

To lay my cards on the table right away: the transhumanist image of our species that is emerging today is a dangerous illusion. This image builds on the idea that our entire life and society is potentially a kind of simulation, which we can overcome only through a thorough orientation of our humanity around the model of technological progress. It is imperative that we see through this illusion if we are not to accelerate further the destruction of the very conditions of our survival as humans, a process most alarmingly manifest in the ecological crisis we have been witnessing now for some time.

Yet the ecological crisis is by no means the only problem of our time to be exacerbated through an uncritically disseminated mythology. For this particular crisis is tightly interwoven with global systems of the exploitation and distribution of material resources which, upon closer inspection, are morally unacceptable. It is not just that exploitation leads to extreme forms of poverty and economic injustice – as is clearly visible to anyone who has travelled to Brazil, for example, or visited any of the slums spread throughout the world, the horrors of which we privileged inhabitants of Europe can hardly imagine; they also lead to crimes against humanity and to the undermining of our value systems, evils that we would find unacceptable if we were to face them in all their stark, unvarnished reality.

The popular idea that AI systems and associated technological breakthroughs, such as forms of superhuman intelligence, will sooner rather than later provide the solutions to humanity's problems is even more fatally naïve than the utopian notion that social networks would automatically lead to political liberation in the Arab world. That notion was put paid to by the aftermath of the Arab Spring and international terrorism; the other deception is still with us.

An important task of philosophical thought consists in confronting us with reality and laying bare the structures of illusion that we assemble to appease our consciences in the face of injustices that we couldn't bear to see with our eyes wide open. This is part of the philosophical mission of enlightenment, what Jürgen Habermas (b. 1929) has called the 'unfinished project of modernity'.

In our still young twenty-first century, we can trace at least three remnants of so-called post-modernity:

1   the idea that we could be living in a computer simulation programmed by an advanced future civilization (the **simulation hypothesis**);
2   the idea that our mental life is a simulation generated by our bodies in order to gain an advantage in our species' fight for survival (so-called **illusionism**);
3   the idea that society is a social construct in the sense that it is not truly real but only a kind of charade resulting from our belief-systems and manners of symbolizing and speaking. In principle, we could change the rules of this masquerade whenever we liked by changing our belief-systems and manners of symbolizing and speaking (**social constructivism**).

In memoriam: Jean Baudrillard

It is somewhat ironic that the philosopher and sociologist commonly invoked as the chief exponent of postmodernism should have explicitly attacked the mythology of social constructivism. This was the French thinker Jean Baudrillard (1929–2007), who plays a central role in *The Matrix*, even making an indirect appearance in one of the film's earlier scenes. In the film, Neo needs to hide a USB stick that he uses for his hacking activities from the powerful 'agents' who are pursuing him, and he conceals it inside a hollowed-out copy of Baudrillard's book *Simulacra and Simulation*, which first appeared in 1981.[9]

Yet the book doesn't just function as an empty case, however appropriate that might be to its content. Baudrillard claims that three major social upheavals have culminated in our present situation.

1   In *premodernity*, human societies were steered via symbols. These were fairly unequivocally differentiated from reality: a statue of a god made of clay is a symbol for a god but is not

itself a god, a point reinforced by the Old Testament's ban on divine images. The monotheistic revolution thus boils pre-modernity down to its essence.

2   *Modernity*, for Baudrillard, is connected primarily with the industrial revolution. In this period, items are manufactured in serial production. These mass-produced products, all copies of an original idea that could be patented by its inventor, are indistinguishable from their originals. Within this framework, a model, say the Mercedes S-Class or the latest iPhone, is serially manufactured in enormous quantities. According to Baudrillard, modern society is built on copying processes geared to the manufacture of mass-produced goods. IKEA is thus a paradigmatic modern invention – the idea of pieces of furniture that exist only as a series and never in original form. A textbook case in modern art would be Andy Warhol, who documented this characteristic of modern goods with his famous Brillo Boxes.

3   In comparison with premodernity and modernity, *postmodernity* is totally hollowed out, because it produces goods that are no longer characterizable as copies of reality at all. The digital commodity market supports such a diagnosis: cryptocurrencies, social networks (in which socio-economic transactions are produced in the form of likes and retweets), video games and virtual realities such as *Second Life* are contemporary examples for this stage of simulation. Postmodern symbolic systems, says Baudrillard, no longer refer to any external reality. Their ontological self-sufficiency enables them to produce new social orders.

Let's boil this down to **Baudrillard's simulation hypothesis**, according to which postmodern globalization is a process driven forward by empty sign systems that produce themselves. Platforms such as Facebook or Instagram illustrate this idea. They merely offer a means for you to share content, and this allows them to create surplus value without offering any content themselves. The images and messages you post have repercussions in reality external to the medium, simply because they arise in the context of the symbol systems of social networks. Digital commodity production, however, seems no longer to reach directly into medium-external reality, but only via the mediation of customers who, without even noticing, become employees of the social network. Heidegger coined the appropriate term for this symbolic life form: we become 'an employee of requisitioning [*Angestellten des Bestellens*]'.[10]

Baudrillard could have seen Donald Trump as virtually the

perfect confirmation of his theory – a theory, incidentally, which he developed in large part through reflecting on his experiences travelling through the USA, which are depicted in his 1986 book *America*.[11] And, indeed, Trump is a result of the US media system, which he seems to drive to a kind of frenzied extreme with his Twitter politics and incessant scandal-mongering. As a result, politics seems to transform into a postmodern 'show about nothing', to borrow one of my favourite expressions from the series *Seinfeld*. Baudrillard himself cites Richard Nixon as president of the postmodern simulation. Alongside Ronald Reagan, he provided a perfect exemplification of the US regime of postmodern simulation. Baudrillard's vivid diagnosis of the contemporary simulation process comes to a head in the following famous passage:

> Today abstraction is no longer that of the map, the double, the mirror, or the concept. Simulation is no longer that of a territory, a referential being, or a substance. It is the generation by models of a real without origin or reality: a hyperreal. The territory no longer precedes the map, nor does it survive it. It is nevertheless the map that precedes the territory – precession of simulacra – that engenders the territory.[12]

But, before we abandon ourselves to postmodern flights of the imagination, we should once again pause and take stock. Descriptions of our global order that start out from the standard ways in which it tends to be marketed in modern media overlook the simple fact that the processes that play out in reality beyond those media have hardly come to a halt. One of the election promises that brought Trump to office was to rescue the American steel industry, not to boost digital markets furthering simulated environments.

American reality bears little resemblance to the sanitized Barbie world depicted in American films, and people know it. Baudrillard's diagnosis is itself a victim of American mythology, in which the dirty reality of coal, steel plants, the car industry, fracking, oil rigs and 'Dieselgate' is about to be dissolved by a gleaming new digital world. Baudrillard partly fell for the glossy façade; he was taken in by the veneer many Americans have applied to their front teeth so that they can display a permanently gleaming smile. The veneer principle (as we might call this element of the American imaginary) should not mislead us into thinking that we are fast approaching a completely digitalized world with no external reality. This is just a silly version of the American Dream according to which everything is already a dream anyhow.

Horror and hunger (games)

There is a gaping chasm between social reality and the illusion that we stand before the complete digitalization of life and society as a whole. This gulf is made particularly visible in a new genre of horror film that shows the American symbolic order reacting to the trauma of the post-Obama era. I'm thinking in particular of films such as Darren Aaronofsky's *Mother!* (2017), George Clooney's *Suburbicon* (2017, script by the Coen brothers), Jordan Peele's *Get Out* (2017), Guillermo del Toro's *The Shape of Water* (2017), Martin McDonagh's *Three Billboards Outside Ebbing, Missouri* (2017) or Alex Garland's *Annihilation* (2018).

Get Out depicts an exaggeratedly gruesome form of racism. The black artist Chris Washington falls in love with the white Rose Armitage, who takes him to meet her parents at their remote property. Chris is concerned from the start that he might encounter racism when leaving the big city. Yet Rose convinces him that there's no chance of any racism at her parents' house: had it been possible to do so, they would have voted for Obama for a third time. Once at the property, the plot develops into a horror story, and the possibility of a wholly new form of enslavement of America's black population comes into view. For it turns out that Rose's family have for years been hypnotizing her black partners in order to transplant the brains of rich old whites into their bodies. A particularly horrifying aspect of this business is that, because certain parts of the host's nervous system are retained, some part of their consciousness remains intact. The victim therefore remains alive in the background, as it were, forced to experience how another consciousness chooses to steer around their own body. The film softens the unbearable quality of this nightmarish scenario by introducing elements of comedy and a revenge narrative: the protagonist ends up fleeing just in time and killing the sadistic family in self-defence.

A similar fantasy structure plays out in the blockbuster films based on Suzanne Collins's trilogy *The Hunger Games* (based on a Japanese original by Kōshun Takami, *Battle Royale*, which was turned into a film in 2000).[13] In the dystopia of *The Hunger Games*, the country of Panum is a dictatorship. It consists of Capitol city and twelve districts, all subject to the will of the capital. The Capitol organizes a series of games in which the youth of the districts are forced to battle for survival and slaughter one another in an arena, all in front of running cameras. Hence the name of the country, with its allusion to the Roman motto 'bread and circuses' (*panem et circenses*).

Yet, to imagine the scenario depicted in *The Hunger Games*, it is sadly unnecessary to concoct a dystopian future. A drastic real-life example of the structure of which *Battle Royale* and *The Hunger Games* provide literary and cinematic exaggerations was given by the closing ceremony of Euro 2016. The aesthetic of David Guetta's performance, with its martial rhythms and invocation of unity among the assembled spectators (*'we are in this together. . . . Our hearts beat together'*) had a cumulative effect that could have been (and maybe even was) copied right from *The Hunger Games*. The French capital in which the ceremony took place is a centre that dominates its surrounding regions economically, politically and culturally, and the belt of poverty around its periphery provides a perfect stage for such a final, in which a battle between nations (an enclosed and largely bloodless war of soccer) can take place.

Within this framework, we can borrow a concept from psychoanalysis and sociology: the symbolic order. This term was coined by Jacques Lacan (1901–1981), who used it with only slight differences. The **symbolic order** is the public exhibition of the representations we form of how society functions as a whole. The symbolic order is the medium of a social system's self-presentation. This self-presentation does not necessarily speak the truth; rather, it is symptomatic of a society's antagonisms – that is, of the tensions between personality and individuality (see above, p. 129).

Ceremonial acts such as the queen's speech, sporting spectacles, carnival, televised election debates, the inauguration of American presidents, the Olympic Games, Christmas markets and much more besides all belong to the symbolic order. The slogan of the symbolic order is: 'We're all in it together.'

The symbolic order is interwoven with socio-economic reality. After all, someone has to pay for bread and circuses. Events which act as stagings of national unity cost the taxpayer and bleed resources produced by the real economy. The symbolic order does not fall from the heavens; it is manufactured.

One of the best diagnoses of how the symbolic order of our own time functions was given by the French philosopher Guy Debord (1931–1994) in his epochal book *The Society of the Spectacle* (1967).[14] According to Debord, the symbolic order assumes the form of a spectacle, whose task is to convince those who participate in it that everything is really in order; meanwhile, the operating conditions of the social order, though reproduced by the participants on a daily basis, work against their own interests. Just think of how the interventions of the Trump administration in the tax system, infrastructure or healthcare not only do not benefit much of his electoral base but even actively harm them. Yet this segment of the population is continually bombarded with nonsense manufactured to prevent them from realizing how they vote against their own interests.

It's even more useful to Trump that worldwide news coverage chooses to report on his nonsense, thereby helping to spread it. The continual outrage at his latest comments and tweets aids his particular mode of governing. When it is reported that there are such and such quantities of ice cream for visitors to the White House, that Trump likes to eat burgers, or other such trivialities, he is symbolically re-elected, as it were, because he seeks just this kind of attention. Nothing serves Trump's purposes more than the bestseller *Fire and Fury*, a supposed exposé of his government by the journalist Michael Wolff. In contemporary digital transformation, Debord and Baudrillard would see the accelerated culmination of humanity's ultimate submission under the mandate of the simulacrum – that is, of a pure delusion that is such a successful distraction from reality that it realizes a perfect manipulation of producers and consumers.

Yet Debord's and Baudrillard's diagnoses are somewhat exaggerated. Specifically, they overlook how the structure of the spectacle is no machination of modern capitalism alone but has been around for as long as there have been advanced civilizations. The example of ancient Rome makes so much sufficiently clear. The origin of the spectacle is the division of labour, which becomes unavoidable once social groups attain certain dimensions and the exchange of goods a certain complexity.

As soon as we can no longer maintain an overview of every wheel in the mechanism of production, we humans begin to tell ourselves stories. In our consciousness, these come to take the place of actual processes. To this extent (and to this extent only), the Israeli historian Yuval Noah Harari (b. 1976) is utterly correct when, in his book *Sapiens*, he advances the thesis that humans have to depict their lives in the form of stories in order to facilitate the cohesion of groups that have exceeded a certain critical mass.[15]

The fabric of every social system that can no longer keep track of its own conditions of production has always been that of myth. Nothing can change this. And there has never been as much storytelling as there is today, because we are living through the virtually infinite replication and reproduction of the symbolic order. In fact, a historically unprecedented wave of fictionalizations of the symbolic order began to form in the nineteenth century. The literature and opera of the 1800s prepared the way for the new media of photography and film, which in turn set the stage for the digital symbolic order that is today dominated by hit TV series and social media.

Beautiful new world – welcome to The Sims

The Sims, which first appeared in 2000, is one of the most commercially successful computer games of all time. The eponymous Sims are simulated characters whose lives can be directed by the player. You can build cities and entire social structures for them. The series of games of which The Sims is a part belongs to the genre of economic simulations, as you can determine the parameters of economic developments in their world by acting as a city or even state planner.

But how do you know you're not a character in a perfect version of The Sims that has been developed by an advanced civilization? A **perfect simulation** is defined as one that you as a Sim could no longer distinguish from reality. If we could equip the Sims in our video games with consciousness, it would perhaps occur to them that the objects they perceive are somewhat pixelated. It might also be possible for them to discover the algorithms that structure their reality, so that they could then infer that they're programmed. The simulation of the Sims is thus not yet a perfect one. This wouldn't necessarily be noticeable to the Sims, because they couldn't ever tell the difference. And yet, unless we program the relevant ability out of them, they could in principle get wise to their simulated existence.

The idea that our life and the entire universe was created, and thus programmed, by God or the gods is a religious – and later philosophical – idea stretching back millennia. Monotheistic creation narratives add to this that we humans are a kind of artificial intelligence, whose software has been uploaded (breathed) into our bodies by God after he formed those bodies from clay.

Moreover, such historically significant figures as Newton and Leibniz conceived reality in something like these terms. They thought that God is active in his creation through natural laws and forces. Physics thus discovers the program that God uses to write natural history.

On the basis of such speculations, the Swedish philosopher Nick Bostrom (b. 1973) has developed his much discussed simulation argument, which he first put forward in 2003 in an article entitled 'Are You Living in a Computer Simulation?'.[16] Bostrom also achieved global fame with his book *Superintelligence*, in which he discusses the risks of an AI that is more intelligent than human beings in (almost) every respect.[17]

The conceptual heart of Bostrom's essay is an attempt to develop a probabilistic argument with the help of a few simple assumptions. His original argument contains a few errors, which he has since tried to rectify.[18] Be that as it may, we can see that Bostrom's case is untenable without expending too much intellectual effort or making too many mathematical detours. Yet, because it has attracted so much attention, and because even a Nobel Prize-winning physicist such as George Smoot (b. 1945) believes it to be quite possible that we are living in a computer simulation, we should take this opportunity to expose some of the greatest weaknesses in Bostrom's ideas.[19]

First of all, we ought to distinguish between the simulation argument and the simulation hypothesis. In his **simulation argument**, Bostrom wants to demonstrate that it's probable that we live in a simulation, and thus that it's rational to believe that we find ourselves in one. He thus poses the question:

> If there were a substantial chance that our civilization will ever get to the posthuman stage and run many ancestor-simulations, then how come you are not living in such a simulation?[20]

Then there's the **simulation hypothesis**: this consists merely in imagining that the reality we inhabit is a simulation. If one can show that the simulation hypothesis is false, the simulation argument is refuted. If we do not inhabit a simulation, the probability that we do is zero and we ought not to believe that we live in a simulation.

Several mistakes snuck their way into Bostrom's formulation of the hypothesis. On the first page of his essay, he introduces so many confused philosophical presuppositions without any clear argumentative (let alone empirical) support that it is not really worth listing them in full. If Bostrom were to have succeeded in mounting a scientifically and philosophically transparent defence of any of these presuppositions, he would already have proved a considerable amount. Instead, though, he just uncritically assumes a certain picture of humanity and a certain worldview from which he proceeds to draw quasi-religious conclusions. He states expressly that his argument 'is a stimulus for formulating some methodological and metaphysical questions, and it suggests naturalistic analogies to certain traditional religious conceptions, which some may find amusing or thought-provoking.'[21]

The real argument is ultimately meant to show that only one of the three following assumptions can be true (though he doesn't give the reader any indication of why they should comprise a complete list of options):

(1) The human species is very likely to become extinct before reaching a 'posthuman' stage.

(2) Any posthuman civilization is extremely unlikely to run a significant number of simulations of its evolutionary history (or variations thereof).

(3) We are almost certainly living in a computer simulation.[22]

The main concepts deployed in Bostrom's arguments are far too vague to be used with much logical precision. What exactly is a 'posthuman' stage? With the help of pure science fiction, he depicts this as a scenario in which silicon-based computers have attained consciousness and all humans have died out. He thus implies without any argument that consciousness is 'substrate-independent', as he calls it – i.e. that anything at all could be conscious, not just nervous systems belonging to living beings.[23] Given that no one right now has any real scientific clue as to whether consciousness is really substrate-independent, this assumption is based neither in actual scientific knowledge nor on the definition of 'consciousness'.

Bostrom's crucial assumption of substrate-independence is at best pure speculation; strictly speaking, though, it is just false (see pp. 79f.). Even if *per impossibile* it was in some sense possible for consciousness to be substrate-independent, it does not follow at all that a future computer that has achieved consciousness would have to possess anything like our mentality or attitudes and have an interest in either its ancestors or simulations. In order to undertake any kind of rationally transparent probability distribution and use it to measure Bostrom's assumptions, we would first have to deal with all these problems. Otherwise Bostrom's argument is just rationally uncontrolled speculation.

By reformulating the premises, we could of course attempt to be a little more accommodating to Bostrom. We might then try out the following assumptions:

1   Either there will or there won't someday be conscious computers which program very realistic simulations.

Let's assume this comes to pass. In that case:

2   Either they run very many perfect simulations or they do not.

Say they do run very many such simulations. In that case:

3 Either we know that we don't live in such a simulation, or we
   don't.

All along, though, we are presupposing that there can be perfect
simulations that we, as the affected party, cannot distinguish from
non-simulated reality. At this point, Bostrom would have to argue
that we cannot know that we are not in any simulation. But he
doesn't leave so much as a trace of any such argument.

At best, he might proceed as follows: let's call the way the reality we inhabit strikes us 'the appearances' = A. In addition, let us
call a non-simulated external world 'reality' = R and the illusion of
an external world a simulation a mere 'seeming' = S. Let's further
suppose that those inhabiting either a simulation or reality can
distinguish between R and S only by building assumptions about
A that could also be false. Now, there are virtually infinitely many
cases of S, virtually infinitely many simulations. The probability
that A = R therefore sinks. In that sense, one might come to the
conclusion that it would be more rational to believe that we're in
a computer simulation than to believe that reality itself appears to
us via our sense organs.

Are you awake or trapped in your dreams?

The train of thought I sketched at the end of the last section is
known in epistemology as a sceptical argument. A good **sceptical
argument** aims to show, for some putative item of knowledge, that
we cannot know that thing *in principle*. The most famous sceptical
argument is the **dream argument**, which can be found in a variety
of cultures, from east to west, north to south. In Europe, it was
made famous by René Descartes, who convincingly rebuts it in
his *Meditations on First Philosophy* (1641).[24] Descartes showed
that, even if we were dreaming, we could still know a considerable
amount about reality, as logical and mathematical truths remain
valid even in dreams. So, the hypothesis that we are dreaming does
not show that we cannot know anything about the external world
in principle. At best, it shows that we cannot know whether we are
dreaming right now.

Moreover, while we are dreaming there is in any case a reality
that is not dreamt. Descartes therefore formulated a method of
radical doubt about absolutely everything, which then proves to

be inconsistent because one cannot doubt that one doubts while one doubts. We cannot doubt everything, and we therefore have no reason to let ourselves be led by the dream problem towards universal doubt.

The dream hypothesis says that we cannot, at any point in time, say with certainty whether we are dreaming or awake. How do you know whether what you take to be the dream you had last night is not in fact reality? Perhaps you're currently dreaming that you had a dream last night, while in reality you're really recalling last night while dreaming . . .

On the basis of such puzzles, people have developed a range of **dreaming arguments**, which are supposed to show that we cannot tell whether we are dreaming or awake. These arguments always presuppose that waking appearances are indistinguishable from dream appearances. If correct, this assumption means that we cannot determine whether we are awake or asleep just by inspecting the appearances more closely. If I now pinch myself, for example, that could all just be dreamt as well.

You might object at this point that dreams are never so realistic. But we can just refine the dream argument by invoking the simulation hypothesis or hypothesizing a perfect drug that puts you in a hyper-realistic dream state. In any case, it is logically possible that all conscious life is a kind of simulation, which has altogether different origins than our being wide awake and finding our way about in reality.

Technically speaking, we do find ourselves in something like this situation. For we clearly don't know everything there is to know about the origins of appearances. In order to know everything about appearances, we would have to comprehend completely not only the physical universe, including our brain, but also its embedding in our organism and the role of the environment in determining that organism's biological processes – all of which we are miles away from achieving. How exactly appearances arise in our waking conscious state, let alone in our dream state, is something nobody yet knows.

Nevertheless, we do know the most important thing: that in our waking life we stand in connection with something real that is not entirely simulated. If something is simulated, it is an artefact – that is, something that has been created intentionally by a living being. Simulations do not simply arise but are produced. It is not possible that the entire universe is a computer game that just spontaneously emerges from nothingness or that a computer game suddenly pops up in the corner of my office where I could previously see my coat and scarf.

Likewise, it is not sensible to believe that our life could be a long dream from which we never wake up. If someone dreams, they must in principle be able to be awake. If our life as a whole were a dream and nothing but a dream, there would not be any possible waking states at all. But that would just eradicate the difference between being awake and being asleep. If everything is dreamt, nothing is dreamt – an argument that I think we already find in Descartes.

There is a yet simpler argument to block the inference from the fact that we sometimes dream to the idea that is in principle impossible for us to distinguish between wakefulness and sleep. Wittgenstein gives a condensed form of this argument in his reflections from 1950 and 1951, which were collected in the volume *On Certainty*. Indeed, he gives it in a single sentence:

> The argument 'I may be dreaming' is senseless for this reason: if I am dreaming, this remark is being dreamed as well – and indeed it is also being dreamed that these words have any meaning.[25]

If you now ask whether your whole life could be a dream, then not only would your question be dreamt, but its meaning would be too. And that would mean that you couldn't oppose dream and reality. If dreamt words have a meaning that is no different from that of non-dreamt words, then there is a reality in dreams – at least a linguistic reality.

Wittgenstein tries to take this line of thought even further. He believes that words can have meaning only when someone (a real human being) has taught them to us. This is a lesson of his famous private language argument. Philosophers disagree about how exactly this argument should be reconstructed, so I'd like here to give my own version, which is adapted to our current purposes and avoids getting us tangled up in the thickets of Wittgenstein scholarship.

According to this rendering, then, the **private language argument** says that we cannot use any single word correctly if we could not also use it incorrectly: if, that is, we weren't in contact with other speakers who correct our language use, we couldn't use any word whatsoever incorrectly. In order to be able to apply a word incorrectly, we have to be able to notice that we've slipped up. That means that there has to be a difference between our belief that we've used a word correctly and the fact as to whether we have used a word correctly. And where should this difference come from if we've spent our whole lives dreaming or have grown up in the Matrix? We would, Wittgenstein says, have no 'criterion of correctness'[26] of our linguistic usage.

One would like to say: whatever is going to seem right to me is right. And that only means that here we can't talk about 'right'.[27]

Now, quite obviously, this does not amount to showing that there is correct language use only if there are a) also other people who have b) already corrected me on an occasion. Philosophical reflection can prove no such thing. Rather, the question is why someone would ever believe that there are no other people and that they could thus correct themselves in the process of carrying out an internal conversation with their dreaming soul. For this would be a somewhat extravagant position to be in, to put it mildly. It can be refuted not by conceptual analysis but simply by pointing to the fact that other people do exist. And whoever really questions this has problems entirely different from those that an epistemologist can deal with. In any event, I have never met a real solipsist, at least none who was not profoundly mistaken . . .

The very first formulation of a dream argument goes back to Plato and is found in his dialogue *Theaetetus*. In this dialogue, Plato considers the definition of thinking as an internal dialogue of the soul with itself.[28] This idea has had far-reaching consequences. Wittgenstein knows this only too well, which is why he directly attacks the Church Father Augustine (354–430), who built Plato's understanding of the soul into the theological foundation of the Catholic Church. Plato argues that we human beings are equipped with innate ideas. Thinking, on this conception, comes ready structured from birth, so that we only have to learn our mother tongue from adults so that we can designate our thoughts and the objects of the external world. In the visual arts, this led to medieval depictions of small children as little adults.

Against this, Wittgenstein thought that we first learn how we ought to think when we learn a language. If thinking were merely a conversation that the soul carries out with itself, it would be difficult to explain how we can possibly make mistakes in our thinking. Not everything I think is true simply in virtue of my thinking it. There has to be some authority that can correct me. Wittgenstein assumes that the relevant authority is originally other members of the social group in which I grew up – members of my family, for example. The way we think is thus dependent on which social group we belong to, because our social group delivers judgements as to which words we use correctly and which we use incorrectly.

This does not mean that our upbringing imposes chains of thought on us or that social belonging deprives us of our freedom, only that we have at some point learnt a cluster of presuppositions about correct linguistic usage. During our upbringing we accept authorities and internalize them in the form of grammatical (and other social) rules. We have to believe someone or other if we're to speak any language at all and organize our thoughts.

By means of this simple reflection, Wittgenstein turns a traditional and thoroughly false picture of human thought on its head: we don't have to work our way out of the hidden inner spaces of our soul and into reality; we already find ourselves, as real beings, in the midst of reality.

Reality cannot be simulated as a whole. If it were, it would be an artefact that someone produced. There would then be a reality within which our world of appearances would have been produced, and that reality would not be simulated. For similar reasons, life cannot be a long dream. It is no accident that *The Matrix* requires a reality in which machines electrically stimulate the real bodies of the protagonists. A pure illusion machine that produces itself out of nothing is utterly unthinkable.

Do you know Holland?

The simulation argument is a postmodern version of the dream argument. Like the early modern dream argument, it uncritically presupposes the subject–object division in order to exploit its sceptical consequences. In the previous chapters, however, I've already shown that we can find reality if we locate it on one side of this split.

Let's rub the sleep from our eyes with a further philosophical exercise. We can once again take up our miniature model of Holland. In order to see that the model is a simplified version of Holland, we need to have an experience that is independent of the model. We have to *know* Holland before we can *recognize* that a Holland-model is different from Holland. Likewise, a physicist researching a refinement or extension of the standard model has to know his instruments and colleagues before she can recognize something within the framework of the model. Every model therefore presupposes that we have some familiarity with something different from the model.

Nothing can change this, regardless of how many models we assemble. It is therefore incorrect to say that we can never grasp reality independently of models. On the contrary, the way in which we can use models to grasp fundamental features of the reality they model confirms that in each case we have an experience independent of whichever model we're dealing with. Every model presupposes that there is something that is not merely a property of the model. The same goes for every model-model. We simply cannot shield ourselves from reality by piling up model upon model in front of our eyes.

Plato and Aristotle already had this insight (see p. 97). They both developed versions of the following line of thought: if we picture a particular situation, we arrange elements in thought. The state of affairs in my hotel room in Santiago in Chile is currently rather untidy. Nevertheless, I recognize my wrist watch over there, a water bottle to the right of it beside my open suitcase on the floor, and so on. In describing the scene, I distinguish different items and designate them. I express how they're ordered using words, such as 'to the right', which articulate a relation between elements.

Aristotle calls this process *synthesis*, a term still in use today. If we think about reality in this way, he says, we undertake 'some sort of synthesis of thoughts as into one'.[29] He also calls this *dia-noia*, literally: 'thinking through'. When we think through a situation, we combine elements. If this combination is successful, we've recognized the situation for what it is; if not, we've failed.

Yet, for Plato and Aristotle, this thinking through cannot be the only form of thinking. For, if – as in this book, with the exception of the odd light-hearted interlude (such as this little interpolation, for example, on which I'm currently giving a parenthetical comment) – we think about thinking, we discover something extraordinary. We discover that it is impossible to know everything only within the framework of models. Otherwise, we couldn't produce any models to begin with. If we didn't have any *knowledge by acquaintance*, as Bertrand Russell called it, we couldn't know anything at all.[30]

As conscious animals of a certain kind (the knowing ones) we can get to know reality as it really is. And we can do so only because we are conscious in two different respects. Firstly, we enjoy subjective experience; reality appears to us in a determinate fashion. Our subjective experience therefore has content. Secondly, at least when we are awake, subjective experience aims directly at (distal) objects in the form of perception, which is not automatically a distortion of those objects.

To be sure, because of our specific biological endowment, reality always appears to animals in a particular manner, which can vary from species to species, individual to individual, and even moment to moment. But this does not mean that we produce the objects of perception through neuronal activity. It is nonsense to believe that the brain is continually concocting mere models of reality on the basis of electrical signals without ever grasping reality itself. Were this the case, we would never be able to explain our acquaintance with reality or our still more intimate acquaintance with the fact of our own consciousness. The best explanation of how we develop models of reality, in a way that allows us to pierce through the phenomena and exchange them for knowledge, presupposes that we have immediate contact with the real. This immediate contact is our sense of thought.

Tononi is therefore most certainly on the right track when he makes the self-acquaintance of consciousness the starting point of neuroscientific research. If we ask ourselves how reality is constituted, we already find ourselves, just by asking, within a reality in which we pose the question. This is one of the key points of Descartes' 'I think, therefore I am.' Incidentally, Descartes also understands thinking (Latin *cogitare*) as including sensory processes; for Descartes, sensation (*sentire*) and representation or imagination (*imaginare*), as well as volition (*velle*), are all processes subsumed under thinking.[31] He absolutely does not reduce thought to *intelligere*, to the exercise of purely rational computational processes.

As my Bonn colleague Jens Rometsch (b. 1973) has shown in great detail, Descartes is therefore one of the most incisive critics of rationalism, as well as of the AI research that was already under way in the seventeenth century. Descartes himself could have taught us how to overcome the subject–object split. Yet, instead, poor Descartes was fated to become a byword for everything he argued against: rationalism, dualism, the repression of feelings, the degradation of animals, and the miserable list goes on.[32]

Matter and ignorance

Models are part of reality. You and I have together been constructing models of models for over more than a hundred pages now and testing them out with the aid of philosophical thought experiments. These models are located in the object domain of our investigation. The object domain is real. As I'll presently explain in more detail, whenever we're dealing with objects and facts about which we can be mistaken we're dealing with *reality*, because these objects and facts aren't exhausted by our having particular beliefs about them. But to see this important point more clearly, we need to make a short detour.

There are many theories of reality. The origins of theoretically sophisticated thinking about reality can once again be found in Plato and Aristotle. What will later be called 'reality' corresponds to what Plato calls *dynamis*, the word from which our expression 'dynamic' originates.[33] Plato's conception of reality is in fact dynamic. His pupil Aristotle, especially in his books *Physics* and *Metaphysics*, added an additional distinction between *dynamis* and *energeia*, the root of our expression 'energy'. This is no mere historical footnote but the starting shot of science.

Both Plato and Aristotle argue in their writings against naturalism. Specifically, they argue against the reduction of everything real to whatever we can come to know about within the framework of physics. That is why they made the first attempts at setting out not only an ambitious physics but also a metaphysics. 'Metaphysics', in this context, amounts to an investigation of those objects that essentially resist investigation by physics. In this sense, every good philosophical theory is metaphysical, because there would be no philosophy at all (and no science either) if absolutely everything we could know were physical.

The reason why Plato and Aristotle introduced the concept of reality has by no means been rendered irrelevant by the intervening centuries. By reality, Plato understood the fact that something possesses the capacity to be the ground of something else. Today, this is frequently misunderstood. He didn't see reality as a causal nexus of material objects. On the contrary! He thought that the idea of the good was the supreme ground of absolutely everything. Remarkably, Plato already argued that human decision making cannot be reduced to neuronal processes, as he rightly insisted that human decision making is oriented by considerations of value which transcend bodily and organic processes altogether. But thereby hangs a tale, and we need not get into those details here.

The word 'matter' also goes back to Plato. Matter is a Latin coinage (*mater-ia*). The expression contains the Latin word for 'mother' (*mater*) as one of its components because, in his work on natural philosophy *Timaeus*, Plato talks about how genuine reality rests upon an unreality, which he conceives as a feminine principle (the ancient Greeks were rather misogynist as well as xenophobic).[34] Aristotle too saw matter (which he calls *hyle*, meaning coppice) as something that merely underlay reality without itself being entirely real (by his standards of reality). For the ancient Greek forefathers of philosophy, the feminine principle is subordinated to true reality. Historically speaking, therefore, reflection on matter is shot through with gendered notions – but that too is a topic for another time.

In any case, neither Plato nor Aristotle saw reality as something material. Rather, they thought that something is real, or actual, if it acts as the structural condition of something else. Reality is a form of power: it decides what something really or essentially is. The ancient Greeks thought quite generally in terms of models of domination. One of the main concepts of their philosophy is empire: *archê*, which also means beginning or origin. They thought that the beginning of a thing, its origin, is that which determines what it is. This conception is echoed in the German word for cause, *Ursache*: *Ur* means original, primal or ancient, while *Sache* means thing or matter.

Returning to the present day, we still haven't shaken off this ancient Greek heritage. Think about the idea of the Big Bang. We like to think of this as the origin of everything there is, as the origin of the universe as a whole. This immediately raises the question of what came before the Big Bang and what triggered it. We thus think about the cause of all causes. Let's call the cause of all causes simply THE CAUSE.

It's clear that we have not yet discovered THE CAUSE. Indeed, current physical cosmology teaches that we cannot discover THE CAUSE of the universe, because any traces of information it might have left behind cannot reach us. This is due to the very structure of the universe brought into existence through the Big Bang. But we ought to go much further: even if the Big Bang theory in its current form were correct (which I do not want to deny), it would not follow that THE CAUSE exists or could exist. On the contrary, on the basis of the data that speak in favour of the theory, we can no longer assume that THE CAUSE exists. Given everything we know about the universe, the Big Bang could be the consequence or effect of something that is itself an effect of something else. The Big Bang theory is not a theory of THE CAUSE.

Besides, we're in any case not entitled to assume a single CAUSE. There could be many factors that together condition the Big Bang and which presuppose in turn a range of causes.

Similar considerations already led the ancients to seek THE CAUSE beyond the material universe. This is why the entire philosophies of both Plato and Aristotle were aimed in part at combating the materialism of Democritus. Democritus is commonly seen as the founder of **atomism**, the doctrine that everything that exists is composed out of the very smallest particles, between which there is nothing but pure void. Postulating the void allowed him to explain why there's not just a great, single lump of matter.

The standard model of particle physics today follows Democritus only to the extent that we now know that there are in fact elementary particles, even if we don't know whether there are smallest elementary particles. Our current ignorance about the largest physical whole, the universe, thus mirrors our ignorance about its smallest parts. There is a cognitive boundary to contemporary physics, the Planck length (circa 10^{-35} m). If you wanted to investigate objects below this scale by using measurements and experiment, you would need a particle accelerator that, given our current technological capacities, would have to be much larger than the entire planet.

Physics conducts research into elementary particles by expending energy. An experiment consists in making a physical intervention into the universe. Given the current state of our knowledge and technology, experimental research into the smallest constituents of the universe (if such there be) requires expending an untenable quantity of energy. This is why physicists keep examining cosmological models; for, shortly after the Big Bang, energies were released with effects on the Planck scale. What is biggest by our lights can therefore help us find out about what is smallest by our lights.

In short: today we know neither whether there is a physically absolutely largest nor whether there is a physically absolutely smallest. In both directions we remain in ignorance.

But even if physics gave us an answer, that answer would be restricted to the physically observable universe. Within the framework of physics, we cannot know whether what we can physically observe will ever exhaust what is real. And I haven't even mentioned the problems of so-called dark matter and dark energy, which are intrinsic to our universe.

Physics is an empirical science. It belongs to the essence of an empirical science that it can never be concluded. There will be no end to physics that gives us the final, decisive answer to the metaphysical question of THE CAUSE.

We just have to keep on enquiring. But whatever we find out within the framework of our impressively advanced empirical sciences, we will never find out what reality is *as such*. The natural sciences certainly investigate realities, real things and processes. But they don't investigate what reality *as such* is – they don't even look for this. The empirical sciences only ever answer specific, well-defined questions with empirically testable answers. They carve out individual puzzle pieces on the basis of which they can determine, with a greater or lesser degree of certainty, what can be seen on a particular region of a puzzle.

It was on this basis that the American philosopher David Lewis (1941–2001) formulated the doctrine of **Humean supervenience**, named after David Hume (1711–1776). This states that 'all there is to the world is a vast mosaic of local matters of particular fact, just one little thing and then another.'[35] Many philosophers (in particular, Hume himself) take something like this picture as grounds for the suspicion that there are, in reality, no laws of nature but merely individual events that we then put together in scientific models. These allow us to make better or worse grounded predictions. Lewis himself took a different path, providing his own theory of natural laws, which needn't occupy us here, as it presupposed complicated methods for investigating so-called counterfactual conditionals and a theory of possible worlds – ideas which are far less likely to be true than any empirical scientific theory. If we needed Lewis's metaphysics to avoid commitment to the reality and power of laws of nature, then the idea of Humean supervenience should be rejected as metaphysical poppycock.

Whether Lewis is right or not is a matter of dispute in philosophy and clearly denied by most scientists who understand his (purely speculative) ideas. All we need here is to keep hold of the valuable insight that physics has made its impressive advances precisely because it does *not* attempt to explain reality. Instead, it is content to be an empirical science, devoted to developing theoretical tools that allow it to grasp the structures of the universe with ever more precision. It is concerned not with grasping reality as a whole, or the world, but with answering well-defined questions that can be answered through experiments.

This is just what poor Faust couldn't understand. He became exasperated with how empirical research could never come up with conclusive answers to our fundamental metaphysical questions:

Well, that's Philosophy I've read,
And Law and Medicine, and I fear
Theology, too, from A to Z;
Hard studies all, that have cost me dear.
And so I sit, poor silly man
No wiser now than when I began.

They call me Professor and Doctor, forsooth
For misleading many an innocent youth
These last ten years now, I suppose,
Pulling them to and fro by the nose;
And I see all our search for knowledge is vain,
And this burns my heart with bitter pain.

I've more sense, to be sure, than the learned fools,
The masters and pastors, the scribes from the schools;
No scruples to plague me, no irksome doubt,
No hell-fire or devil to worry about –
Yet I take no pleasure in anything now;
For I know I know *nothing*, I wonder how
I can still keep up the pretence of teaching
Or bettering mankind with my empty preaching.

Can I even boast any worldly success?
What fame or riches do I possess?
No dog would put up with such an existence!
And so I am seeking magic's assistance,
Calling on spirits and their might
To show me many a secret sight,
To relieve me of the wretched task
Of telling things I ought rather to ask,
To grant me a vision of Nature's forces
That bind the world, all its seeds and sources
And innermost life – all this I shall see,
And stop peddling in words that mean nothing to me.[36]

What is reality?

Reality is the fact that there are objects and facts that we can be wrong about because their existence isn't exhausted by our having beliefs about them. What is real corrects our beliefs. Because our thoughts too are real, we can get them wrong – but also get them right. It's important to bear in mind here that reality isn't a thing or a container for things. Reality should instead be thought of as a modal category. Other examples of modal categories are necessity, possibility, impossibility and contingency (on contingency, see p. 197).

As we mentioned above, Plato and Aristotle were the first to begin making lists of modal categories and distinguishing them from one another. A **category** is generally understood as a concept without which we wouldn't be able to form other concepts. In contemporary philosophy, though, it is a matter of some debate whether or not there are categories at all, and, if so, how many.[37]

The idea operating in the background here is easy enough to understand: a **concept** is something by means of which we can distinguish something or some things from other things (see p. 19). The concept of a dog distinguishes dogs from cats, but also from lions and earlobes. Whoever has some mastery of the concept of a dog knows this much. It is not difficult to count concepts such as fish, fish fingers, fossils, financial crises, and so on. Nor is it very hard to come up with a random list of objects that aren't concepts: fish, fish fingers, fossils, financial crises . . . The concept of a fish is one thing, a fish quite another.

We can transform concepts into thoughts, fish into fish fingers. Unfortunately, you can't make any fish fingers from the concept of fish (otherwise it would be rather simple to solve world hunger or to replicate Jesus' miracles). Nor can you link fish fingers together to make a thought. This alone proves that concepts differ from non-concepts (sometimes theoretical philosophy is child's play).

Moreover, these simple considerations also prove that we do not construct reality by means of our concepts. Otherwise, it would be much more difficult to see that fish are not identical with the concept of fish. But if concepts differ from non-concepts, then – and now things get a little more dialectical – there is a concept of being a concept. Were there no concept of being a concept, we couldn't distinguish concepts from non-concepts.

In his dialogue *The Sophist* (which, incidentally, begins with a consideration of the concept of being a fisherman), Plato, who was the first to recognize all this, calls the concept of being a concept *logos*, from which logic would later be derived. There is thus a concept of being a concept. Thankfully, we do not need to answer the question of what exactly this concept consists in here. For we first of all want to know what reality is, which is already ambitious enough.

And this is precisely where Plato comes in. He notices that the concept of being a concept must be different from other concepts. There is therefore a distinguishing feature marking it off from other concepts. More precisely, he thinks there has to be a series of such features, which he designates as those 'forms . . . reckoned to be the greatest'.[38]

These distinguishing features are what his pupil Aristotle calls *categories*. The expression 'category' comes from the ancient Greek word *katēgoría*, which means accusation or bill of indictment. A category is what ensures that a concept differs from the concept of being a concept. All concepts, on this view, are determined through categories – that is, through being distinguished from the concept of being a concept.

The category of reality consists in something's participating in an idea, as Plato puts it. I, for example, participate in the idea of a living being, just as you do too. But it is rather difficult to say what the concept of a living being is. We have no universally valid real definition that tells us precisely when something is a living being. Current life science doesn't give us clear and definitive answers to such questions. They certainly give us a list of characteristic features of living beings, such as metabolism, growth, reproduction, and the like. But they do not deliver a definition of 'life' that would allow us to make a univocal division between living and non-living matter in the universe.

My reality is no more and no less than the fact that I am a minded living being – that is, a human being. There may well be other similarly minded creatures, in which case we'd have to add further concepts to characterize my being human. But, insofar as I am at least a minded living being, I am real. The reality of BMW consists in its being a company that manufactures certain products and meets a series of regulations that determine BMW's legal status. The reality of the book you're currently reading consists in its being written by me, that it expresses philosophical thoughts, which Polity Press has copy-edited and set to print.

Whatever is real is integrated in a network of concepts. Every concept refers to another. If you know a concept, you thereby know a bunch of others too. This thesis is known as **semantic holism** and says that you're able to deploy a concept only if you're able to deploy a whole battery of further concepts that stand in various logical relations to it.

In contemporary philosophy, a particularly sophisticated version of this position has been defended by the American philosopher Robert Boyce Brandom (b. 1950). He has given an accessible, introductory sketch of his position in *Articulating Reasons*.[39] Whoever knows that our pet dog Havannah is a lapdog also knows that she was bred by humans. Being a lapdog and originating via selective breeding logically hang together: you can infer the one thing from the other. Concepts thus build a network.

We might, then, attribute the unwitting discovery of the idea of the internet to Plato. He characterized the interconnectedness of our concepts as the 'connection of ideas',[40] thereby laying – far in advance to be sure – the first foundations of the information age. What we today call 'information' corresponds fairly exactly to Plato's theory of ideas. In-formation, after all, means having a certain logical form, by means of which one can describe the relation between the sender and receiver of a message as a code.

The internet is a logical space. We can travel from one position on the net to another because it contains logical addresses that can be coded and decoded through logical principles. This is also the reason, as you perhaps remember, why every code can in principle be hacked and why there can be no eternal firewall behind which to hide information once and for all. Whatever can be coded can also be decoded.

Regardless of how much information lies at our disposal, reality keeps delivering more and more. If information is to be interpretable by a receiver to begin with, something has to be left out. Interpretable information has a conceptual form. Conceptual forms are abstract; that is, they take something away from the non-conceptual (Latin *abstrahere* = to pull/draw away/off). Conceptual thought can therefore place objects into relations with one another and thereby equate what is in reality unequal. My left hand is different in several respects from my right hand, not to mention my left hand and the left hand of Heidi Klum. Yet my hands and those of Heidi Klum are all hands. To think of hands as hands is to abstract from reality. Information arises when real relations are thus simplified.

A hybrid reality

Reality has two facets. On the one hand, nothing belongs to reality that doesn't participate in some concept or other. On the other hand, nothing we can't be wrong about is real. Put in terms of a sharp contrast: on the one side we have the position of absolute idealism, represented by Georg Wilhelm Friedrich Hegel. In a famous passage, he encapsulated this conception as follows (let's call it **Hegel's principle**):

> what is rational is actual;
> and what is rational is actual.[41]

The **core idea of idealism** is that something is real only if it presents information, if it is capable of being interpreted by some system or other. Our information age builds heavily on this idea. The digital revolution and its prospect of a totally networked world uncannily resemble a technological implementation of idealism.

Yet this grasps only one side of reality. It is no accident that idealists restrict themselves to describing our capacity to grasp reality and reshape it in accordance with our representations. In the most radical variant of so-called transhumanism, idealism even strives to overcome our corporeal nature. In contemporary philosophy, this is counteracted by the Leipzig school of idealism (whose main representatives are James Conant, Andrea Kern, Sebastian Rödl and Pirmin Stekeler-Weithofer), which combines idealism with a humanism that sees our self-conscious human life as the source of the concept of being a concept.[42]

Transhumanism is the attempt to take Friedrich Nietzsche's fantasy of the superman (*Übermensch*) and make it a reality through technological progress. It aims at a higher form of human existence, an existence as pure information living in a non-biological infosphere. Think of the perfect AI named Samantha in Spike Jonze's film *Her* or any other futuristic representation from *Black Mirror* or *Electric Dreams*. Idealism gives indirect support to a transhumanist worldview, even though both Hegel and contemporary German idealists (paradigmatically represented at the universities of Leipzig and Heidelberg) try to anchor reality fundamentally in the human being as a kind of unsurpassable apex of the universe.[43]

The other side of reality, namely the side we can be wrong about, is not adequately accounted for by absolute idealism – indeed, by its very nature. Hence, from time immemorial, idealism has stood opposed to realism.

Realism sees the decisive feature of reality in how we have to adapt our beliefs to real circumstances. Reality as a whole, therefore, is not tailored to our cognitive equipment. It could even be quite different from how it appears to us (though not radically different). Realism orients its understanding of reality around the fact that it can always surprise us. According to realism, it does in fact turn out that the real is knowable and that we are not always in error; but this does not mean that reality is tailored to our epistemic purposes; it merely means that we can know some things without having to know everything.

New Realism, my own approach, gets us beyond the old question of whether reality is in principle knowable or not, because it departs decisively from the idea that reality is an all-encompassing domain of objects. Insofar as reality is a modal category, however, it is in principle knowable. The concept of reality is knowable and is thus itself something real, which does not mean that everything that is real is knowable (it isn't).

In this context, contemporary French philosophy often talks about the 'event', thereby borrowing from Heidegger, who himself borrowed freely from Henri Bergson (1859–1941), albeit while at the same time distancing himself from him. Bergson remains underappreciated in Germany, precisely because Heidegger talked him down. In his own day, Bergson debated on equal terms with Albert Einstein and others, and on account of the quality of his writings he was awarded the Nobel Prize for literature in 1927. Einstein and Bergson were not on the best terms either, which also (quite unjustly, in fact) contributed to the decline of the latter's reputation.

According to realism, reality has the character of an event. This means that quite how reality will unfold can never be entirely predictable. However precisely our models are adapted to those segments of reality the structures of which they are supposed to grasp, they will never allow us to render reality fully transparent. Reality might well be structured through and through – but it will never be possible for us to determine its exact constitution. This is why Heidegger had no faith in the ability of traditional philosophy to grasp reality as such; in his view at least, it had no room for the event. He therefore hoped to overcome traditional philosophy and replace it with an altogether different form of thinking, which he referred to as the 'other beginning'. But this is yet another path down which we ought not to follow him.

In recent years, reflections on the event and the scope of realism have led first to speculative and then to New Realism. In his epochal book *After Finitude*, the French philosopher Quentin Meillassoux (b. 1967) has pushed the theme of the event to its logical endpoint.[44] **Meillassoux's speculative realism** assumes that at each and every moment reality could become radically different from how it has seemed until now. Without any reason, Aladdin could suddenly appear beside my sofa and contravene all the natural laws whose validity we currently take for granted. The universe could suddenly come to a standstill, a new god emerge out of nothing, and so on and so on. The only thing we can know for sure, he thinks, is the radical contingency of reality.

Contingency is being able to be otherwise. Whatever is contingent can be this way or that way. This means that it is in any case not necessary that it be as it currently is. The sole necessity, for Meillassoux, is the necessity of contingency.

Yet absolute idealists and speculative realists each overextend one side of reality. One group (the absolute idealists) overestimates the knowability of reality, while the other (the speculative realists) underestimates it. This is why New Realism seeks a middle position that acknowledges the hybrid nature of reality. Reality need not be one thing or the other, which is why I call my own contribution to epistemology **neutral realism**, the thesis that reality is neither knowable in its entirety to us humans nor by its very nature something that eludes human cognition.[45] Reality is what it is, and 'that is its definition' as the French philosopher Jocelyn Benoist (b. 1968) ironically remarked.[46] It is for this very reason that we can be mistaken about reality; for we can't get rid of it just by changing our beliefs about it.

Fish, fish, fish

The expression 'fish' can be used in at least three different ways:

1 'Fish' can designate a *word* which has four letters. In this sense, 'fish' can be spelled.
2 The word 'fish' can express the *concept* of being a fish, as in the sentence 'dolphins are not fish.'
3 In thoughts about fish, the concept of being a fish refers to certain living creatures, namely fish. Let's call this the *matter* delineated by the concept of being a fish.

A **word** is something that one can spell and translate into other languages. 'Fish' is '*Fisch*' in German and '*pescado*' in Spanish. A *concept* is an element of a thought, which allows us to establish logical relations (see pp. 58f.). The concept of a fish differs from the concept of a mammal, for example. It encompasses many species. You cannot translate a concept from one language into another because, while they are expressed in language, concepts are not themselves linguistic in nature. A **matter** (*Sache*) that we can designate by means of a word is what a concept is about, where the concept is part of a thought.

We think in concepts about a variety of matters, which we then express using words. Our thoughts are conceptual, but not linguistically formatted. Nobody thinks in Spanish or German, even if you might occasionally dream in Spanish. Thoughts are, if you like, speechless.

The natural languages that we speak as native speakers – in my case, for example, German – inform our thinking. But they don't restrict it. Hence, we can learn foreign languages and invent new sentences. Most of the sentences identifiable in the book you're currently reading have never before been printed or otherwise expressed. Every day, countless speakers of German or English use countlessly many sentences that nobody before them has ever used.

This is possible because language does not limit our thoughts. The decisive connection between natural language and thought is that the former helps us more finely to delineate, distinguish and shape our thoughts, which often come to us in a hazy or confused form. Take as an example the extraordinarily precise expression of a thought in Rainer Maria Rilke's eighth *Duinese Elegy*:

And how confused is anything that comes
From a womb and has to fly. As if afraid

Of itself, it darts through the air
Like a crack through a cup, the way a wing
Of a bat crazes the porcelain of night.

And we: spectators, always, everywhere,
Looking at everything and never from!
It floods us. We arrange it. It decays.
We arrange it again, and we decay.[47]

Here, Rilke describes what it's like to be a bat. In one of the most famous philosophical essays of the last century, the American philosopher Thomas Nagel maintains that he cannot imagine what it would be like to be a bat.[48] Yet this is because he lacks the necessary language. Of course, none of us can currently be a bat, or replicate the felt experience of a bat from within, so to speak. Something like this might be possible in the distant future if we ever manage, through surgical interventions, to manipulate the neurophysiological basis of our conscious life in a way that allows us to hallucinate or dream of really being a bat. But this is just pure science fiction and, strictly speaking, would actually let us become bats rather than merely feeling like one.

Rilke succeeds in pulling off what seems to be impossible if we restrict our linguistic expressive capacities: he captures a feeling. The flight of the bat interrupts the monotony of an evening, which Rilke describes as 'porcelain'. Several resonances are in play here: it's easy enough to imagine a summer's evening, sitting silently on a terrace and sipping tea from a porcelain cup. There's a certain way it feels to sit, relaxed, drinking one's tea. Suddenly, a bat flies into view and you're startled. Perhaps the cup smashes. But it suffices that the peaceful, smooth flow of our experience is disrupted spontaneously by the bat. Rilke makes an analogy between this break in the surface of experienced reality and the presence of the bat. The bat itself leaves behind a trace of its experience in our own, just like the fly addressed at the beginning of the stanza I cited above:

Oh, blessed are the *tiny* creatures
Who *stay* in the womb that bore them forever;
Oh the joy of the gnat that can still leap *within*,
Even on its wedding day; for the womb is all![49]

The poetic expression facilitates the clearer articulation of a series of thoughts. Poetry is not an exercise in imprecision but, on the contrary, frequently an attempt to exhibit thoughts that have previously been left unsaid. It extends our thinking, because our minds contain a tumult of countless thoughts that we never consciously grasp; they literally leave us speechless.

The concept of being a concept, which has now been our central focus for several pages, can be grasped too. We need only to find a suitable language. 'Concept' in German is *Begriff*, which is originally a metaphor, having something to do with *greifen*, grasping, reaching for. In English too, we *grasp* thoughts, and can have a grip on and access to reality. 'Metaphor' is itself a metaphor.

We have already seen how many expressions of philosophy and science are metaphorical. Throughout the history of thought, articulating a new thought has invariably required the coinage of new expressions that originally function as metaphors, as bridges between thoughts and sentences. Literally translated, a **metaphor** (from the ancient Greek *meta-pherein*) is a transferral. A metaphor transfers something from one shore to the other (to use a metaphor for the concept of a metaphor). The one shore is the reality of thought, the other the reality of language. Without metaphors, we couldn't express any new thoughts.

As soon as metaphors have been expressed, we can translate them. We can therefore develop formal systems that count as translations of natural language sentences. I can translate the sentence 'two plus two is four' into the sentence '2 + 2 = 4'. The thought that 2 + 2 = 4, however, can also be expressed completely differently, by counting on one's fingers, for example, or by setting a pair of apples and a pair of pears together.

Our capacity for expression belongs together with our capacity for language. But this does not mean that language determines what we think. Ludwig Wittgenstein was wrong when he wrote his famous sentence '*The limits of my language* mean the limits of my world.'[50] He himself later came to see the problems with this view, which is why he then developed a philosophy of language that is truer to our actual language use. However, this landed him in the opposite extreme of (almost) denying that we express thoughts in language without thereby turning thoughts into linguistic items (such as mental utterances).

Concepts such as the concept of a concept itself are concepts we can express only in metaphor. This explains why the first philosophical utterances both in ancient Greece and in ancient China or India are all poetic by contemporary standards. The earliest philosophical theories of the West, of which only fragments have survived, speak in verse or riddles. The pre-Socratics first had to invent a fitting language – that of philosophy – before Plato and Aristotle could describe and systematize this activity as 'philosophy'. To this end, they applied new metaphors in order to bring new thoughts to expression, a process that the Platonic dialogues time and again bring out using the metaphor of birth. The Romantic philosopher Friedrich Wilhelm Joseph Schelling (1775–1854) went so far as to describe thinking itself as a perpetual delivery room:

> All birth is birth from darkness into light; the seed kernel must be sunk into the earth and die in darkness so that the more beautiful shape of light may lift and unfold itself in the radiance of the sun. Man is formed in the maternal body; and only from the obscurity of that which is without understanding (from feeling, yearning, the sovereign [*herrlich*] mother of knowledge) grow luminous thoughts.[51]

One of the greatest errors to have plagued theoretical philosophy in the twentieth century was the idea that formal mathematical logic represents the paradigm of the clear expression of thoughts. It's especially conspicuous that there is not a single theory of clarity that shows this assumption to be correct.

And what is clarity anyhow? The history of philosophy contains several significant contributions to answering this question, including from Descartes, Leibniz and Wittgenstein. In contemporary philosophy, by contrast, the expression 'clarity' unfortunately tends to be used with comparatively little clarity. The clarity of clarity is simply taken for granted, which ironically has a blinding effect. The underlying error is easy enough to identify: it stems from the fact that we today have advanced formal tools at our disposal, which allow us to clarify logical connections between thoughts at an abstract level.

Think of a simple example from back at school: at some point you learn that $2 + 3 = 3 + 2$, $7 + 4 = 4 + 7$, and $5 + 1 = 1 + 5$ have something in common. This commonality can be expressed as follows: $a + b = b + a$. The algebraic expression shows us something that was previously hidden from view, a mathematical law that determined our thoughts about numbers before we even noticed it. We arrive at clarity when we understand that $a + b = b + a$, which then spares us a great deal of intellectual effort.

We can call this process abstraction. **Abstraction** is the grasping of a general rule on the basis of a series of examples. Because we can abstract, we can express abstract thoughts. This is a matter of undertaking a process of translation: we translate thoughts that we would previously have expressed differently in a formal language.

But there is also the converse thought process, which is at least as important. Call it concretion. **Concretion** is the process of finding an appropriate example for illustrating a rule or a theoretical connection.

The task of philosophy is not restricted to abstraction. Concretion is just as important. The sense of philosophical thought consists, at least in part, in acting as a diplomatic mediator between the realm of abstract and the realm of concrete thoughts.

Kant begins his wonderful essay 'What Does it Mean to Orient Oneself in Thinking?' with his version of this distinction:

> However exalted the application of our concepts, and however far up from sensibility we may abstract them, still they will always be appended to *image* representations, whose proper function is to make these concepts, which are not otherwise derived from experience, serviceable for *experiential use*. For how would we procure sense and significance for our concepts if we did not underpin them with some intuition (which ultimately must always be an example from some possible experience)? If from this concrete act of the understanding we leave out the association of the image – in the first place an accidental perception through the senses – then what is left over is the pure concept of understanding, whose range is now enlarged and contains a rule for thinking in general. It is in just such a way that general logic comes about; and many *heuristic* methods of thinking perhaps lie hidden in the experiential use of our understanding and reason; if we carefully extract these methods from that experience, they could well enrich philosophy with many useful maxims even in abstract thinking.[52]

Philosophy is neither as abstract as mathematics nor as concrete as poetry, however much many thinkers in the twentieth century wanted to identify it with either the one or the other. Both, equally misguided, extreme positions had prominent advocates: Bertrand Russell and Rudolf Carnap (1891–1970) for the first, Ludwig Wittgenstein and Martin Heidegger for the second. Russell held philosophy to be a kind of mathematics and so coined the misleading term 'mathematical philosophy'. Heidegger, by contrast, wanted to equate poetry and thinking, and thereby follow in Nietzsche's footsteps. Nietzsche, after all, said of himself that he was 'Only a fool! Only a poet!'.[53] Russell attempted to get philosophy to be committed to abstraction, Heidegger to concretion, which Wolfram Hogrebe has analysed as 'risky proximity to life'.[54]

Both manoeuvres are impermissible, landing us in each case with a form of bad reductionism. **Bad reductionism** reduces one way of thinking to another by leaving out something essential and thus leads to a blinkered perspective. A currently rampant example of bad reductionism is what in *I am Not a Brain* I called 'neurocentrism' – that is, the identification of thought processes with neuronal processes. If you think of Germany, Germany features in this thought. Germany belongs to the thought about

Germany. Otherwise, it would be a thought about something else. But Germany does not belong to my brain. There simply isn't any place for a territory the size of Germany within my skull. I encompass Germany in thought without having literally to embrace it.

If we reduce thinking to our capacity to grasp mathematical thoughts through abstraction or, conversely, to our capacity to understand abstract thoughts through concretion (by means of examples), we commit the error of bad reductionism. Philosophy remains philosophy, even if some members of the academic guild of philosophers would prefer to have become mathematicians or poets.

The shimmering spectrum of reality

Back to reality! It should by now be clear that 'fish' is not the same as fish (not to mention *fish*). Let's now apply the distinction between word, concept and matter (see p. 198) to reality. The word 'reality' expresses the concept of reality. I will call the matter it concerns *the real*, in order to avoid an all too widespread confusion. This confusion is the product of a worldview. A **worldview** is a conception of how everything there is hangs together with everything else. Worldviews work at achieving a theory of absolutely everything. They emerge when people pick out something real (baryonic matter or genes, for example) and then use this as a basis for forming a picture of absolutely everything real. That is, they take something real and then apply it as a universally valid model. Worldviews suppose that there is one reality and identify it either with a huge container or at least with some common feature shared by everything real.

Today, two worldviews are particularly widespread: crude materialism on the one hand and religious fundamentalism on the other. **Crude materialism** thinks that reality consists solely of material-energetic structures. **Religious fundamentalism** thinks that material-energetic structures are just a world of sensory appearances that God has put in place to test us. Behind this veil of appearances is supposed to be another world, which Nietzsche already mockingly called 'a world behind' (*Hinterwelt*).[55]

Both parties to this quarrel are in the wrong and indeed commit the same error: they choose something that really is real and infer from their (pretty arbitrary) choice that they've found the paradigm of everything real. They then set about piecing together a worldview. It is within this framework that they get the idea of a gigantic object domain called *reality*, where this singular reality is the all-encompassing total mass of all things. But this just confuses concept and matter.

The concept of reality is itself not any old piece of furniture. Of course, reality as a concept belongs to the real, since we can be wrong about it. Since there are various mutually exclusive theories of reality, it might well be that one party has got it right, meaning the others have got it wrong (needless to say, it's New Realism that's got it right . . .). It follows that reality is certainly something real, but not merely that alone. For, without reality, we couldn't think at all.

Crude materialism sometimes appeals to the notion that anything that exists has to be bound up in cause–effect networks. The technical term for such networks is **causality**. Crude materialism thus reduces reality to causality. Yet this doesn't get it very far. In order to infer back to reality, you need a theory of causality. And there are many competing theories, which are discussed and developed not only in philosophy but also in the natural and social sciences.[56] It would lead us too far afield to run through all these theories here. For our present purposes, the most relevant point in such theories is that we mustn't understand causality in terms of some material thing being pushed and pulled around by another material thing (see pp. 86ff.). For not every case of causality is a process of energy transfer.

Causal relations between two systems A and B are in any case more than mere correlations. A simple example suffices to show this: for as long as I've been alive, the sun has risen every morning; for as long as I've been alive, I've eaten something almost every day. Yet the daily rising of the sun is not the cause of my daily bread (even if there would be no bread if it were not for the sun). To be sure, the sun's rising correlates with my eating habits, but it doesn't cause them. Conversely, neither do my eating habits cause the sun's rising. Not everything that occurs at the same time stands in a cause–effect relation. Hence, we distinguish between *mere correlation* (a regular co-occurring of events) and *genuine causation*.

Genuine causation exists not only in the domain of the physical. The South African cosmologist George Francis Rayner Ellis (b. 1939), who co-wrote a highly respected book together with Stephen Hawking in the 1970s, has recently been arguing that there is top-down causation.[57] The decision of a court to hand someone a prison sentence, for example, can lead to this person being in a particular location (in prison). Thus, the abstract process of passing a judgement can also cause an alteration in the spatiotemporal distribution of matter. It is therefore a mistake to think that all causation runs from the material to the mental (bottom-up). And it is even further wide of the mark to think that everything that exists is material. People arrive at this senseless idea only after already having concocted a false theory of causality, one that seduces us into recognizing only the material energetic as real.

Instead, the context determines the behaviour of elements embedded within it, and this goes for the universe too: the universe does not consist simply of elementary particles, since these originate from the initial conditions of the Big Bang, which in turn forms a context that exhibits a top-down organization (from the whole to its parts).

The genuine natural, social and human sciences just don't offer any support for a materialistic worldview. And nor, conversely, are they supported by such a view. Crude materialism certainly doesn't want for adherents, but that alone doesn't make it a scientific theory worth taking seriously. Rather, crude materialism is a form of superstition, which at best draws pseudoscientific conclusions from scientific results. It typically hides this uncomfortable truth about itself behind an uninformed and misguided attack on 'religion', but without bothering to give an account of religion and religions that meets the standards of those humanities disciplines that actually specialize in dealing with this deeply important topic (including the philosophy and sociology of religion, not to mention religious studies and systematic theology, which is still practised widely in German public universities).

No single result in either the natural and social sciences or the humanities has ever entailed a metaphysical thesis about the structure of reality as a whole. The increasingly rampant naturalism of our times, which, in the service of crude materialism, would fit all of reality to a natural scientific format, is no genuine scientific theory but, rather, pseudoscience and should be rejected by all honest scientists.[58]

But this is no reason to defect to the other side and embrace religious fundamentalism. It is just as superstitious to believe that the falsity of materialism entails that God is the quasi-material, ghostly cause of the existence of matter or the universe. The classical creation narratives of the monotheistic and polytheistic religions (such as Hinduism) do not contain any scientific theories about the origins of the universe. The concept of the universe as the object domain of scientific investigation was simply unknown at the time of their composition. The holy texts of the world's great religions do not contain scientific accounts of the nature of the universe.

This is itself an unscientific and uninformed claim that makes sense only from within the so-called scientific worldview, which is itself a crude form of religious superstition.

It's obviously no good appealing to how the authors of the various holy scriptures were directly inspired by God or the gods. Neither these authors nor God himself had (or has) a materialist worldview. So, even for a religious fundamentalist, the creation narrative cannot constitute a description of the purely material universe. A creation narrative is not physics in verse form. And, in any case, there is not simply one valid creation narrative; several narratives combine in the Bible or the Koran, not to mention the various stories that underlie Hinduism. Creationism is thus idolatry by religious lights: it thinks of God as a craftsman who intervenes causally in the universe by shaping matter. Yet, the entire tradition of religious metaphysics as developed in all the world religions that have creation narratives avoids a scientific understanding of God's role in the universe. This should be obvious, as what we're dealing with here are meta-physical topics.

It is the job of theology, philosophy of religion, literary studies, religious studies, history and a range of further disciplines to tell us about the meaning of the creation narratives and myths bequeathed to us by advanced premodern civilizations. I do not want to tie myself here to any particular philosophy of religion, let alone a given religion. Rather, I want to underscore just one point: to believe that the God of the monotheistic religions is a kind of magician who, in an utterly incomprehensible act, pulled baryonic and dark matter out of a hat is a form of superstition. That God in the beginning created heaven and Earth evidently does not mean that God created baryonic and dark matter. None of the relevant texts mention any such thing. Monotheism designates God as creator, which in no way means that God produced purely material reality. For God is also regarded as the creator of living creatures and human beings, whereby the latter, according to many among the faithful, were in receipt of an immortal soul – and this is hardly supposed to consist of baryonic or dark matter.

The conflict between a supposedly scientific and a supposedly religious worldview – a fight carried out today with considerable verve and socio-political consequences especially in the USA – is therefore a conflict between two forms of superstition. Neither genuine science nor genuine religion is committed to a materialistic (or any other) worldview.

There is much that is real, not just matter. Call this fact the

heterogeneity of the real (from the ancient Greek *heteros* = other, various, and *genos* = kind). The real is of various kinds. Yet we have a homogeneous *concept* of reality. At its core is the idea that, while we can make mistakes about the real, we can also comprehend it correctly. We moderns have indeed come to know much of the real. Much, though, remains unknown. And among that which remains unknown there is much that we will never know and, for various reasons, will remain forever unknowable.

Caesar's hairs, India's manhole covers and Germany

The class of the forever unknowable contains not just spectacular mysteries but entirely mundane matters. Think of Caesar – that is, Gaius Julius Caesar. As far as we know, he crossed the Rubicon on 10 January in the year 49 BC, an event that played a role in the history of the Roman civil wars. Let's imagine how he places his foot on the riverbank as the wind rushes through his hair. At this precise point in time, provided he wasn't bald, Caesar had a certain number of hairs on his head, and this number will forever remain unknown. And, even if he was bald, the number of hairs on his head would still have been an utterly precise one: zero. I'm supposing that nobody actually counted the number of hairs on Caesar's head at the very moment he was crossing the Rubicon. If someone did, for whatever reason, their report of the matter has in any case vanished without a trace.

Let's take another example, which doesn't take us all the way back to ancient Rome. While I write this sentence, there are manhole covers in India. But how many exactly? I am writing this sentence on 2 February 2018 at 11:39 (CET). Imagine you wanted to find out precisely how many manhole covers there were in India at the time of the composition of the sentence you've just read. It doesn't take much reflection to realize that it is quite impossible to discover the answer to your question. And, even if you somehow managed to find out the answer, there would still be the question of the number of manhole covers in China, in North Korea, in Hamburg, in Rome, and so on. We know that there is an exact number of manhole covers on planet Earth; but we also know that nobody knows what this number is.

You've perhaps already sussed what I want to get at. There are very many facts that are unknowable for us humans, even though they don't concern any transcendent states of affairs. A whole host of completely mundane processes remains beyond the scope of our knowledge on account of the sheer complexity of the factors we'd have to take into account.

We have developed methods for dealing with this uncertainty. For as long as there has been the idea of taking censuses, one function of bureaucracy has been to record as many relevant facts as possible. In the digital age, this has become somewhat easier, because it is now simpler and less costly to determine figures. The very earliest advanced civilizations already kept data on clay tablets in the form of figures about socio-economically relevant objects, even if these could hardly have been complete.

Today's globalized economic order, which piles products upon products, results in a simply unsurveyable division of labour. Global concerns take advantage of this by trying to create facts beneath the level of bureaucratic observation and regulation, facts which cannot be registered. The immensely powerful Californian quasi-monopolies of the beautiful new world of the digital age generate new products (such as social media or the products of the 'sharing' economy such as apartment rentals and car-sharing) for which we still lack any kind of halfway sufficient legal or fiscal regulatory systems. They thus benefit from a leap forward in knowledge. And, at the moment, they are the only ones who know certain facts (algorithms, for example, or legal traps laid for us customers), from which they literally derive capital.

And now imagine just how complex a situation governments find themselves in, say the German government. Obviously, no single member of the government enjoys a total overview of the social system called 'Germany'. Nobody knows even approximately everything about Germany at any given time. Every government therefore operates under circumstances of extensive ignorance. For this reason, a functioning government requires ministers, secretaries of state, governmental panels, committees, ministries – in short, a bureaucratic apparatus. This apparatus in turn filters available information according to criteria of relevance, which are determined partly by the government so that it can intervene in turn in the manufacturing of facts. In doing so, they follow certain representations of value, which are specified in part by party manifestos. This structure would collapse in on itself if it weren't for how information is transferred and communicated at every level, even though the people working at any given level know perfectly well that there is always an indefinite, but gigantic amount that nobody knows.

There's no escaping from this situation. The fascination for totalitarian models of the state, which bequeathed us the humanitarian disasters of the previous century, derives in part from totalitarianism's promise of an omniscient bureaucracy engaged in the total surveillance and control of all social transactions. This holds out the prospect of order. Yet such omniscience is in principle impossible.

The German sociologist Niklas Luhmann (1927–1998) coined the term 'demobureaucracy',[59] in order to designate a structure that we might see as characteristic of the federalist republican idea. In place of the fantasy of a single centre of power from which an entire state is to be governed (on the model of Paris or London) step a variety of largely independent centres and decision-making processes.

This structure functions only for as long as it generates knowledge that can be filtered through suitable procedures and transported across a multitude of different levels. The politics of education thus plays an important role, which is why it can generally be regarded as sensible to have a strong state school and public university system. For, especially within a globalized economy, we expect a government to possess knowledge and expertise that, in a well-functioning democracy, can be deployed to protect us citizens from damaging intrusions into the socio-economic order. In the digital age, this goes in particular for digital encroachments. Many believe, for example, that the American election of 2016 took place within a context of cyber-warfare conducted in order to influence the result. This, of course, has been the subject of extensive and still ongoing investigations in the USA itself.

Determining how exactly we should assess this specific situation is not my role as a philosopher. What matters for present purposes is the essential connection between knowledge and power. The sense of thought is tasked with generating a clear picture of the pitfalls that plague reflection on social and political reality. The decisive point is that we really live in a knowledge society, which generates surplus value through science, technology and bureaucracy. This surplus value can be put to meaningful further use provided other forms of knowledge are consulted.

If we simply let natural science and technology drive ahead without confronting questions of universal moral value, the next atom bomb or the next 'Dieselgate' is just around the corner. Harun Farocki's influential 1969 film *Inextinguishable Fire* gives us a particularly impressive illustration of the responsibility of science against the background of the Vietnam War. Questions of value cannot be answered by scientific or technological methods. Who we are as human beings and who we want to be, how we're to behave towards other animals, towards our planet, towards humans who speak a different language and come from other countries, towards the diverse forms of life that are all gathered beneath the gappy and fragile shelter of our atmosphere, can only be determined with the help of knowledge gained through philosophy and the humanities. Nobody knows, for example, what Germany or England is. Whether we like it or not, Germany and England are incalculably complex and not reducible to some simpler set of factors. In this respect, they are like Caesar's hair and the manholes in India. And that's not even to mention the complexity of the processes driving globalization, which cannot be reversed by searching for the essence of the West or the East – there is simply no such thing.

Frege's elegant theory of facts

Gottlob Frege, whom I have mentioned several times already (see pp. 51ff.), was one of the greatest logicians of all time. As a mathematician he made significant contributions to the discovery of modern symbolic logic – i.e. to the mathematical sign system that we still use today to express mathematical thoughts. Frege invented his own symbolic language in order to present logical relations between thoughts in a more lucid fashion. He called this language the 'concept script' (*Begriffsschrift*).[60]

Without Frege's concept script there would be no digital revolution today. Thanks to the formalization of logic in the nineteenth century, which he helped advance substantially, new encoding possibilities arose. And, thanks to these, we could for the first time present logical connections between thoughts in a simple and programmable fashion.

Frege also wrote one of the most important texts on thinking, his unprepossessingly short essay 'The Thought' of 1918. People like to overlook how Frege concedes in this essay that we can speak of thought only metaphorically. By 'thinking', he understands 'the grasp of a thought'.[61] Let's call this **Frege's theory of thought**. Frege distinguishes between three different attitudes to thoughts, which helps bring us a few steps further:

1 the grasp of a thought – thinking;
2 the acknowledgement of the truth of a thought – the act of judgement;
3 the manifestation of this judgement – assertion.[62]

This simple distinction underlies Frege's ingenious thought about thoughts. In his view, thoughts are truth-apt entities. Who or whatever is truth-apt has by no means to be true, but only capable of being true.

> Without offering this as a definition, I call a 'thought' something for which the question of truth can arise at all. So I count what is false among thoughts no less than what is true. So I can say: thoughts are senses of sentences without wishing to assert that the sense of every sentence is a thought. The thought, in itself imperceptible by the senses, gets clothed in the perceptible garb of a sentence, and thereby we are enabled to grasp it. We say a sentence *expresses* a thought.[63]

To cut a long story short: a **thought** is something that is either true or false (see pp. 51ff.). If we grasp a thought, we think about something. Think about the question whether Beijing or New Delhi has more inhabitants. If you've just done what I've asked you to do, you've grasped a thought. This thought is, among other things, about Beijing, New Delhi and inhabitants. If this thought made its way through your consciousness in English, so to speak, you might have had the impression that a barely audible voice (presumably sounding much like your own) popped up in your stream of consciousness and whispered: 'Does Beijing or New Delhi have more inhabitants?' The point of thoughts is that we can grasp them in a range of ways – in different sentences, languages, and sign systems of all kinds. The sentence

(S1) 'Beijing has more inhabitants than New Delhi'

and the sentence

(S2) 'More people have a fixed abode in Beijing than in New Delhi'

express a similar thought. This thought deals with a subject matter. We can grasp it both in the form of questions and in the form of assertions.

On this basis, Frege delivers one of the most elegant theories of facts. With the trademark precision and argumentative acuity that was so admired by many of his contemporaries, he refuted in less than a page the very notion that there could ever be a post-truth age. Before we go on to take Frege's idea a step further, it's best to savour the following passage:

> To the grasping of thoughts there must then correspond a special mental faculty, the power of thinking. In thinking we do not produce

thoughts, we grasp them. For what I have called thoughts stand in the closest connection with truth. What I acknowledge as true, I judge to be true quite apart from my acknowledging its truth or even thinking about it. That someone thinks it has nothing to do with the truth of a thought. 'Facts, facts, facts' cries the scientist if he wants to bring home the necessity of a firm foundation for science. What is a fact? A fact is a thought that is true. But the scientist will surely not acknowledge something to be the firm foundation of science if it depends on men's varying states of consciousness. The work of science does not consist in creation, but in the discovery of true thoughts. The astronomer can apply a mathematical truth in the investigation of long past events which took place when – on Earth at least – no one had yet recognized that truth. He can do this because the truth of a thought is timeless. Therefore that truth cannot have come to be only upon its discovery.[64]

With Frege, we can now hold on to the idea that reality consists essentially of thoughts, namely of true thoughts. In this respect, he is certainly an idealist. However, thoughts for Frege are not contents of consciousness. They do not belong to any thinking creature. Rather, thoughts are objectively existing structures through which objects stand in relation to one another. If we grasp a thought, we can thus be wrong, because the real can be other than we believe. Thoughts can be false. In this respect, Frege is certainly a realist.

The thought that 2 + 2 = 5 is false. If I take it to be true, I commit an error. The thought itself does not commit any error; it is simply false. We humans are liable to error because we make assertions. As soon as I assert that a thought is true or false, I can be making a mistake. Fallibility comes into play via our human thinking. Frege is quite right when he understands thinking as the grasping of thoughts, but he sadly misses the point that our fallibility does not consist in some of our thoughts being false. For a thought's being false is not yet an error. Error comes into play when our sense of thought can be exercised or impaired.

The Leipzig philosopher Sebastian Rödl (b. 1967) is completely right when he points out that, while there is an explanation of how and why someone is in error, a true thought has no other explanation besides its truth.[65] When I am wrong about some matter, this is because I have miscalculated, held on to a superseded view, have not looked closely enough, been blinded by my prejudices, etc. There are countless ways of getting some matter wrong, but there is only one way of getting it right. If we think a true thought, the reason the thought is true and that we do not err is nothing other than the thinking of this particular thought with this particular content. In the successful case, no further explanation is needed. If you speak the truth, you need no excuse.

On the limits of our knowledge

Because we are fallible there must be facts. It is impossible to be fallible if there are no facts for one to grasp, rightly or wrongly. If we keep this in mind, we can shoot down radical scepticism in just a few steps. **Radical scepticism** is the view that we cannot know anything at all. If it were true, then we obviously couldn't know *that* it was true. But let's set this notorious difficulty to one side and try to imagine what it would be like if radical scepticism were true. If it were, every single one of our judgements would be false. To judge means to carry out an act of thinking that regards a thought as true. Regarding a thought as true presupposes that we have an idea of what it would be to confirm its truth – otherwise, we wouldn't have understood it to begin with.

Let me explain. Take any old banal thought, say

The sky over Paris today (2.2.2018, 3.52 pm) is overcast; at the moment, it is not raining in the rue Suger where I am writing this sentence.

I can easily confirm that the thought is true by looking out of the window of the apartment where I'm currently working. There are many (unlimitedly many, even) possibilities for confirming this thought. If you understand the thought, a bunch of ways of verifying it will occur to you. To understand a thought typically means being able to conceive what it would take to find out whether or not it is true.

Incidentally, this is a key idea in the philosophy of religion. In his book *Thought and Reality*, the Oxford philosopher Sir Michael Anthony Eardley Dummett (1925–2011) even took it as the basis for arguing that we can and must be able to imagine a divine standpoint.[66] For there are unlimitedly many thoughts the truth of which no human being will ever be able to confirm or refute. But we can nevertheless formulate and understand sentences about these facts. For example, we can understand the **very general fact sentence (VGFS)**:

There are unlimitedly many thoughts, the truth of which no human being will ever be able to confirm of refute.

VGFS does not say much more than that we humans do not know everything there is to know. It confirms that we are not omniscient. In order to understand that we are not omniscient, we have to understand sentences that nobody will ever actually confirm or refute.

According to Dummett, however, this means that we can imagine that someone or other (even if it's God) could, in principle, confirm or refute these facts. Our understanding of sentences therefore extends indefinitely further than our actual cognitive achievements. This is why we can make progress in knowledge in the first place and why our thought reaches far beyond our demonstrable cognitive achievements. Without this assumption, we could not explain knowledge acquisition.

Now, using these premises, Dummett pieces together a proof of the existence of God. But we needn't go along with this. At best, he shows that we can think of a being that knows of every fact that obtains. It evidently does not follow that such a being exists. And, even if you could somehow prove that it does (which you cannot!), you would not by a long chalk have proved that this being is God.

The topic of God, though, is one for another day; for the time being, we can happily return to earthly matters. We know that we do not know everything. In knowing this, we also know that we understand a sentence only provided we can imagine what it would take to confirm or refute it.

One of Dummett's recognized contributions to philosophy was his supplementation of Frege's theory of thought with a theory of understanding. After all, how could we grasp a thought if we could not understand any sentences?

The scholarly term for the theory of understanding is **hermeneutics**. The term for the theory of linguistic meaning is **semantics**. There can be no sensible semantics without hermeneutics. It is impossible to effect any clean separation between a theory of linguistic meaning and our ability to understand words and sentences in the first place. In this regard, the late Dummett agreed with the Heidelberg philosopher Hans-Georg Gadamer, who throughout his life pointed out that there are boundaries to knowledge. These boundaries, however, do not separate reality into two permanently fixed domains: the knowable and the unknowable. What we do not yet know today, we might well know by tomorrow. There are no stable boundaries to knowledge. And it is precisely for this reason that we never know exactly what we do and do not already know.

One of the first attested uses of the ancient Greek word for linguistic meaning is found in a saying of the philosopher Heraclitus. In what is traditionally classified as fragment 93, we read:

> The lord whose oracle is in Delphi neither indicates clearly nor conceals but gives a sign (*sêmainei*).[67]

Linguistic meaning resembles the process of expressing riddles. Everything anyone says, that is, can be understood or misunderstood. There's no way of ruling out each and every possible misunderstanding of an expression in advance. Our thought and speech therefore belong to reality. We can be wrong about what we think and say and even about what we mean by our words. Nobody is ever infallible when it comes to the question of how some real thing really is – and that includes our thought.

Do thoughts lurk within the skull?

Thinking is not a process occurring within your skull, one known to you and you alone. Insofar as thinking consists in grasping thoughts, it has to have structures that are not our own private mental property. Thinking is something real. It really takes place. That's why we can sometimes better understand how and what another person thinks than they do themselves. Without this presupposition, the entire scientific discipline of empirical psychology would be ruined, and there would be no hope for psychotherapeutic interventions in the psychical lives of people who wish to change their thought processes. They would not even be able to express them meaningfully to their therapist.

The way we think about things has effects, particularly in the domain of introspection. Who we are at a particular point in our mental lives is tightly bound up with how we think about ourselves and our social and natural (non-social) environment.

This simple fact undermines a currently popular conception of thinking. Thanks to certain influential pronouncements and observations by Sigmund Freud and, more generally, to developments in empirical psychology and neuroscience in the second half of the nineteenth century, it is frequently acknowledged that our thought processes are by no means always as we believe them to be. We can't get them transparently in view just by turning our mental eye inwards, as it were.

This is easy enough to see. Every sentence I'm writing right now comes from somewhere or other. The sentences that make up this paragraph did not pop up on my screen before I typed them, else

I'd have saved myself the trouble of writing the book. So where do the sentences of this paragraph come from?

It is natural to assume that, before I wrote the sentences down (or even while I was writing them down), I formed them in my inner mental space (in the silent chamber of my soul). But then how is this meant to take place? Surely not by my somehow envisioning them or bringing them to mind *before* they arise in my inner mental space. But this means that I cannot intentionally form the sentences by summoning them before my mental eye, because I already have to know which sentence I want to summon forth. I would then have to have access to the sentences before they are even there.

Let's go through this once more: here is a sentence (the one beginning 'Let's go through . . .'). I have written it (and it was then reproduced multiple times at the printer). This sentence occurred to me at some point. Now this cannot mean that I wrote it in my soul, so to speak, or that I said it to myself before typing it out; else it would have had to occur to me prior to my mentally writing it down.

But now it suddenly seems open to doubt whether I can actually be the author of my linguistically coded thoughts. The naturalist and mathematician Georg Christoph Lichtenberg (1742–1799) had this very suspicion, from which he drew the following consequence in a famous aphorism:

> *It thinks*, we should say, just as one says, *it lightnings* [*es blitzt*]. To say *cogito* is already too much if we translate it as *I think*. To assume the *I*, to postulate it, is a practical necessity.[68]

Schelling went even further, writing in his Munich lectures *On the History of Modern Philosophy*: 'it thinks in me, thinking goes on in me, is the pure fact.'[69]

We can be just as wrong about our own thoughts as about the thoughts of others. What and how we think is not just a matter of our thinking something about it. If I think some particular thought T, I cannot ensure that I think T without thinking in addition that I am thinking T and not T*. We can therefore experience our thinking as something alien which simply befalls us. Our thinking belongs to the order of things; it is no ethereal process at one remove from reality, like a kind of mysterious mental breathing.

Lichtenberg and Schelling, however, are guilty of exaggerating a truth that has been frequently repeated from the origins of depth psychology right through to contemporary neuroscience and cognitive science: we never completely govern our own thought. We think what occurs to us. After all, we cannot step behind our own thought processes in order to monitor them. Yet none of this means that our thoughts simply pop up at random. Free will and conscious decision making are not threatened by the fact that we are not absolute masters of our own mental processes – an idea, by the way, which no one in the history of philosophy ever believed.

So long as we are conscious, thinking occurs uninterrupted. If psychoanalysis is right, there are also unconscious thought processes, which find expression in our consciousness without our so much as noticing. Because thinking is something real, the conditions of its emergence are not known to us in their entirety. How exactly a particular thought occurs to us and how we then process it, i.e. how exactly a concrete thought process unfolds, is something it takes a further thought to grasp. No thought can catch itself in the act.

The difference between cauliflower, cognac and the thought of thought

Ever since depth psychology discovered the unconscious in the nineteenth century, it has been widely acknowledged that how our thought processes actually run is one thing and how we *believe* they do when we report them quite another. This corresponds to the common conception that psychoanalysis has proved that our ego is not 'master in its own house'.[70] Of course, thanks to advances in empirical psychology (which led in part to psychoanalysis) we do in fact know that all our thought processes have presuppositions that are not fully transparent to us in the very act of thinking. It might be tempting to infer from this that our conscious thought and experience is a kind of simulation, something our body generates together with its unconscious processes in order to get a conscious grip on itself, so to speak.

Nietzsche, in calling 'The intellectual [*das Geistige*] . . . the sign-language of the body',[71] did much to contribute to this kind of conception. Might our mental processes be symbols that our body generates in order to steer itself through the world? Right now, for example, I am experiencing thirst and, sooner or later (most likely sooner), I'll go to the fridge and get something to drink. – Done. Now I'm back at my desk. While those pangs of thirst grew gradually stronger, my thoughts were distracted by them without my intending this. Thirst didn't pop up in my consciousness like any old random object but, once a certain stimulation threshold was reached, drew my attention towards it.

We cannot have full and complete control over what we think about or how we think about it. Proof: think about the fact that you are reading this sentence. As you can see, I have some (pretty minimal) control of your thoughts, even if I do not even know you personally.

In a way, we are continually distracted and keep having to pull ourselves together so that we fix our concentration on something, which we see now from this perspective, now from that. Our entire mental life is an arena of diverse tensions, which is for psychological theory and experiments to investigate.

There is a deep philosophical reason for this. It is essentially impossible to think about something that is not itself a thought (say cauliflower or cognac) and thereby, in the very same breath, think about the thought thinking about something that is not itself a thought. Let's call objects that aren't themselves thoughts **non-thoughts**. If you reflect on non-thoughts, you're obviously not reflecting on your own thoughts.

Most of the time, we think about non-thoughts. Even professional philosophers who spend their working lives thinking about thoughts have to wonder now and again about non-thoughts ('Who's calling?', 'Where's my notebook?', 'I hate it when my laptop crashes!', 'Oops, I've spilled my coffee!'). There is of course much more that goes on in our psyche. Thoughts that we can immediately transfer into simple sentences are not the standard case when it comes to mental processes. Most of these processes, in fact, run like imprecise and out of focus search processes.

Aristotle coined the definitive term for this: *orexis*, which is tantamount to desire. The corresponding verb *oregomai* means to reach out for something. In the Latin philosophy of the Middle Ages, one outgrowth of reflection on this category was what we today call intentionality (see p. 65). At every moment of our lives, we humans are seeking something out. In dreamless sleep our organism maintains itself in a state of dreamlessness; right now, I'm seeking to bring this sentence, which is part of my intention to express a thought about thoughts, to an end. Of course, in the course of this book I would only ever mention my more or less innocent intentions or come up with pretty anodyne examples of what we humans desire. According to psychoanalysis, what I'm leaving out is, in part, an effect of my unconscious on my thought-world. That which I am reporting here of my mental processes is subject to a psychical – if not, mercifully, a Prussian or North Korean – censor. This is not a flaw but a sign of the psychic normality that's required for going about one's daily tasks.

A characteristic of Freud's writings is that his case studies tend to break off just when they start to get exciting for the reader. Even text production in the field of psychological theory-building rests on psychical censorship. But as if that weren't enough, both the psychotherapeutic process and every psychological experiment presuppose that all participants submit themselves to a censor. What Freud calls the 'ego' is the arena in which the censoring process is carried out, the process by which relations of psychical force emerge. In this way, Freud's theory generates an idea of normal thought processes: 'It is impossible to define psychic health except in terms of metapsychology, i.e. of the dynamic relations between those institutions of the psychic apparatus, the existence of which psycho-analysis has discovered, or, if our critics will have it so, has inferred or conjectured.'[72]

Remember, in contemporary philosophy, *intentionality* is the term for the directedness of our thoughts towards objects, and the theory of intentionality tends to be interested primarily in thoughts about non-thoughts (see p. 65). The connection between Aristotle's theory of desire and the modern theory of thought gained prominence, moreover, through Franz Brentano (1838–1917), who was Freud's philosophy professor at the University of Vienna. All of modern psychology rests on the simple thought that our acts of thinking are directed at something and that we cannot infer why these acts are directed at precisely what they are merely from our experience of them. In thinking about non-thoughts, thinkers of thoughts are partially unknown to themselves.

Yet we can't just leave things there. It's no good just crawling away into our own unconscious. We are not passive victims of the unconscious. Conscious thought is not a simulation run (for whatever reason) by the unconscious. If all thought processes were controlled by impulses inaccessible to the thinker – if, that is, we were literally never masters in our own house – it would be fully incomprehensible how anyone could ever find this out.

In this connection, we can speak of **the alienation theory of thought**. This theory maintains that all of our chains of thought are determined by unconscious processes together with unconscious biases that have been fixed in place in early childhood, be it genetically, through our motor-sensory wiring, or whatever. According to this model, whatever occurs to us here and now has to come as something of a surprise. The impression that we lead a rationally controllable mental life would be just an illusion, an effect generated by the inability of our thoughts to reach through to their own true origin.

The problem is that this theory fails as soon as we apply it to itself: if *all* of our thought processes were really steered by unconscious impulses, the same would go for thought processes about thought processes. If anyone managed to arrive at a psychological discovery, that would always be just a lucky find to which they themselves couldn't have made any real contribution. Either you become a psychologist or you don't, and if you do thanks to your biographical circumstances, then it's a completely contingent matter what, if anything, happens to occur to you.

If this were right, you wouldn't be able to study psychology – or any other discipline for that matter. There would be no methods, no standards, no universally valid insights, but only the random whimsical notions of individual research personalities. Many of these would perhaps have sufficient charisma that they would gain followers, creatures who secretly crave their own submission, like a pack is to its leader.

I am not denying that the business of scientific knowledge acquisition can, with some plausibility, be explained as a battle between competing egos. The enterprise of academic self-assertion involves trials of strength, which cry out for at least partly psychological explanations. It fits the pattern of what the Frankfurt philosopher Axel Honneth (b. 1949) has called the 'the struggle for recognition'.[73] But no sociology of knowledge will explain how theory construction actually functions. At best, it explains which social and psychological conditions underlie the acceptance of results and systems of thought, and this has little to do with the question of whether the systems of thought under investigation from the sociological standpoint are actually true.

The entire vulgar Nietzschean constellation that traces every will to knowledge back to a will to power results from the problematic alienation theory of thought. Reducing thinking to thinking about non-thoughts ends up ensnaring itself in the logic of the unconscious. For, in thinking about non-thoughts, we do indeed draw on biophysical parameters without which we human beings could not think about or know anything at all. But it is fundamentally impossible to get a complete overview or full grip on the activation of these parameters.

Yet everything looks quite different if we think not about non-thoughts but about thoughts – i.e. when we do philosophy. In the heyday of Greek philosophy and German idealism, our intellectual forebears even allowed themselves to regard philosophers as divine; for, by reflecting on reflection, they step outside the familiar structures of our everyday cares and concerns. Philosophers thus became the model for medieval monasticism, and it is no accident that it was the medieval monastery (with some substantial help from the Muslim world) which preserved the treasures of ancient knowledge over several centuries, subjecting it to ever new interpretations, finally culminating in the advances of modern Enlightenment.

Whether we like it or not, the European Middle Ages are the intellectual and cultural foundation of modernity, and countless 'non-European' influences from the Islamic world and even from Asia cannot be left out of the picture either. Europe was never sufficiently isolated to develop a modernity entirely of its own making, which is one of the reasons why it is also nonsense to think of European civilization as automatically leading to brutal imperialism and colonialism. Brutally subjugating human groups in order to exploit them is, unfortunately, a rather universal phenomenon.

In the German-speaking world, the medieval intellectual prehistory of modernity has been skilfully reconstructed in the writings of Hans Blumenberg (1920–1996), Kurt Flasch (b. 1930) and my Bonn colleagues – especially Ludger Honnefelder (b. 1936) and Wouter Goris (b. 1968). In the posthumously published final volume of his history of sexuality, *Confessions of the Flesh*, Foucault derives our modern psychical situation entirely from medieval practices, seeing the entirety of the sociology and psychoanalysis of his own time as an echo of earlier confessional practices, however much these contemporary disciplines take themselves to be modern – that is, above all, not to be medieval.[74] If Foucault is right, this too undermines the usual boundaries drawn between modernity and the Middle Ages.

Be all of that as it may: thinking about thinking functions completely differently from thinking about non-thoughts. In the books that have been passed down bearing the titles *Metaphysics* and *De anima*, Aristotle develops a theory of thinking about thinking. Its basic ideas remain unsurpassed. The ninth chapter of the twelfth book of the *Metaphysics* contains some of the most influential sentences in all of philosophy. As I've already mentioned, these have echoed through the millennia in everything that's been said about thinking (including in this book).

Aristotle poses the question of why we actually value thinking. Ultimately, human beings to this day understand themselves in terms of their capacity for thought, their intelligence. This is why we're confused and disturbed by the advances of AI research and technology; the prerogative of the human is suddenly being transferred to the non-human. Our artefacts seemingly surpass us in domains in which humans previously enjoyed exclusive privileges.

But what is actually so special about thinking? Why is it even seen as 'the most divine of all phenomena',[75] to quote Aristotle? At this point, Aristotle distinguishes three aspects of the process of thought:

1   thinker (*nous*);
2   what is thought (*noumenon*);
3   the act of thought (*noêsis*).

That which we think about, what is thought, cannot be the reason why we value thinking. After all, we are able to think about 'the worst thing'[76] – for example: totalitarian dictators, waterboarding, brutal violence and much more besides that is better left unmentioned. In Aristotle's laconic words: 'There are in fact some things that it is better not to see than to see.'[77] Thinking wouldn't be such a wonderful thing if we always dwelt on such horrors. So it must be either because of thinkers (*nous*) or because of the act of thought (*noêsis*) that we value thought.

And here Aristotle comes to the remarkable conclusion that, in the best case, our thinking is so constituted that it thinks itself. If we think of ourselves as thinking – in distinguishing, say, between thinker, that which is thought, and the act of thought – we thereby grasp the reality of thought. 'It is itself, therefore, that it thinks, if indeed it is the most excellent thing, and active thinking is active thinking of active thinking.'[78] We can call this **pure thought**. Pure thought consists in the act of thought grasping itself as such. Thinkers of a thought encounter themselves as thinkers by way of thinking about thinking.

Philosophy is a kind of theory construction that investigates all other thoughts from the standpoint of pure thought. Philosophy is the exercise of thought thinking itself. If you've been following me this far, you'll by now be used to thinking about thinking. The meaning of the sentence from Aristotle quoted in the last paragraph might be more or less obvious to you. But then it should also have become clear that not all thinking is concerned with non-thoughts and, therefore, that not all thought can be explained in terms of unconscious processes. We have to assume that we can develop theories of thinking that are not themselves playthings of unconscious forces, else we would no longer have any standard by which to distinguish between genuine gains in knowledge and intellectually sublimated struggles for power.

This undermines the anti-philosophical projects of people such as Foucault and his master, Nietzsche, who cannot explain how they arrived at their alleged insights into the unconscious will to power or into the subterranean disciplinary practices that are supposed to structure our entire conscious thought. They exempt themselves from the scope of their own speculations, which, it's worth mentioning, Nietzsche used for his shameless justification of slavery.[79]

We thus have a choice: either we completely abandon the idea that we, as rational, minded beings, are at least sometimes able to prioritize truth and the facts over our egoistic interests, or we recognize that there is pure thought.

Pure thought is an accomplishment of living beings. Being human does not boil down to exercises of reason or pure thought, because we are animals whose mode of living occasionally has the form of reflecting on their own thought processes: 'For the reality of thinking is life.'[80]

Human AI

As animals, we are endowed with a species-relative set of sensory equipment. That is, we possess a basic set of sensory faculties without which we couldn't be in contact with reality. This basic equipment is by no means fully known to us. Nor will we ever be able to map it completely. It is inseparable from our ecological niche and ultimately interwoven with unsurveyably many conditions of survival, many of which have developed over millions of years through the evolution of countless species and through their interaction with the atmosphere on our planet (to which they in part contribute). Then there is the role played in evolution by cosmic rays, of which we as yet understand only very little (though we do now know that they influence biological processes on our planet), by the geological phenomena that codetermine our atmosphere, and by the climate change to which human beings make a decisive contribution.

All of this is reflected on the level of our conscious experience of reality without our having anything like a complete grasp of the individual factors that cooperate in determining that experience. It belongs to the essence of reality that we can never simulate it completely.

But the human being is on no account an animal stuck in its cognitive niche, frantically building models in a desperate attempt somehow to work its way out of it. Our biological component is not a restriction; it does not put blinkers on us that we cannot tear off. On the contrary, it is the presupposition of our having created a form of intelligence that has emancipated itself from its biological foundation: our very own, actually existing artificial intelligence.

It is a matter of debate whether there is a psychometrics of general intelligence which could measure the intelligence of a human or other creature.[81] It is by no means proved that what we capture when performing intelligence tests on humans is something that might be traced in other creatures too. There is obviously a difference between human intelligence and the intelligence of other animals: we move around in fields of sense from which other creatures are precluded. One aspect of this is that we carry out intelligence tests while other creatures do not. We investigate the migration patterns of whales, while whales don't bother to track ours. We are presumably the only living beings on our planet who even know that they are animals whose destiny unfolds on a planet.

This is not to denigrate other life forms. I mention these things only in order to point out the following: our human intelligence is not biological through and through, even though it would not exist if it were not grounded in a biological prehistory.

The human being is an essentially historical creature. As the animal that doesn't want to be one, the human invents stories about how the various episodes of its life hang together. Over thousands of generations of recitation, these stories have led to the blossoming civilizations that speak to us from the depths of the past from the time of the invention of writing. The Gilgamesh epic, the Old Testament, the epics of Homer and Hesiod, the Mahabharata and Ramayana in India, etc., all attest to a deep structure of human self-exploration, the sophistication of which has barely been matched since. You can spend a whole lifetime uncovering the narrative structures and highly complex languages of these epics and holy scriptures. Indeed, from its beginnings, depth psychology has scanned the archaeological and written testimony of our ancestors for clues as to the inner life of the human soul.

What the great epics document is how humans form an image of who or what they really are. In these works, the human confronts us as a being enmeshed in a dense network of narratives that serve to differentiate human from non-human reality. The human being becomes who she is through recounting stories about why she is not only an animal – and not a stone or a god either. She becomes a teller of stories.

We can never fully escape from our stories. Yet in modernity we have managed to come closer to the infinite, which cannot be grasped through stories; it can only be comprehended through scientific theory-building. This process itself begins in the age of great myths, in Greece, through the distinction between mythos and logos, between stories and pure thought.

By drawing this distinction, the human being invents a new form of intelligence, one that previously did not exist. Through education and upbringing, we program our descendants and pass on to them those algorithms that we have invented in order to optimize our pattern recognition. The mathematics taught today in schools is beyond anything our most intelligent forebears could have known, because we hand down our artificially acquired intelligence through systems of education.

The scientific progress of humanity rests upon our possession of an artificial intelligence. *Our* intelligence, that is, is to a great extent an artefact of our cultural and thus social environment. Of course, our particular modes of access to humans' artificial intelligence have biological presuppositions. But that does not mean that intelligence is innate. What is innate are the biological presuppositions that can make it easier or harder to grasp the logical structures underlying a given domain of human thought and storytelling. The sense of thought is innate, though how it comes to be trained and exercised is not.

The programs that we humans install on a non-biological foundation are models of the relation between human biological and artificial intelligence. What is today called AI is therefore really a second-order AI. We can call this the **AAI thesis**. An AAI is a *thought-model*, not a *thought-copy*. We have developed these models. They are artefacts of human beings, whose own intelligence is an artefact.

The human being has two components. Each of these, however, influences the other, and they cannot, as dualism would have it, be distributed over two separate domains of reality.

Let's call the one component the human animal. The **human animal** is a biological species, which as such emerged through evolution. We are still the very same species as our ancestors from way back. If we could take the bards who sung the earliest orally transmitted forms of our epics and transport them to present-day Tokyo in a time machine, we could pretty quickly teach them to ride the subway. They would be no different from us biologically. By contrast, we cannot ever hope to explain to elephants that Tokyo is the capital of Japan. A *Homo sapiens* from the twentieth century BC, however, could in principle understand us.

This is not mere speculation. In modern times, contact has been and continues to be established between premodern and modern humans. This has unfortunately had fatal consequences for our pre- or non-modern fellow species members, the reason being that modernity is literally the outcome of an arms race. It represents a further optimization of our artificial intelligence, which aimed at subjugating and destroying our political enemies and those who had to suffer from brutal forms of conquest, capture, enslavement and exploitation.

Modern technology emerged in the historical laboratory of modern European wars, which in the twentieth century became world wars. Yet there were already predecessors in the early modern period, in which the 'alien peoples' encountered by explorers from the Iberian peninsula were subject to imperialist subjugation. Unfortunately, our own human artificial intelligence develops not only in the realm of storytelling but simultaneously on the battle-field. And so it is no wonder that the topic of all great epics is war: wars between human beings or between non-human beings, gods, powerful mythical creatures and ourselves.

The second component of the human being is the image that each of us has of who or what she is, the image from which every human derives instructions for who or what she ought to be. Call this **the human self-portrait**. Humans are reluctant animals because it is not possible for us to identify ourselves with the human animal. As humans, we are not merely a species that has developed on some particular evolutionary branch. For we cannot avoid coming to terms with our sense of thought – a sense that, as a historical, socio-cultural artefact, cannot be fully described in evolutionary terms. Which human self-descriptions, which human self-portraits come to assert themselves are subject to a high degree of both diachronic and synchronic variation. Changes in the human self-portrait are not subject to the principles of slow biological selection; they are not subject to the principle that living beings are geared towards their self-maintenance, as is unfortunately clear from how most human self-portraits lead to human self-destruction.

The current development of AAI is no exception to this rule. Our stories about the future of intelligence are distinctly martial. We imagine that every intelligence we can construct could be deeply interested in the eradication of humanity. This speaks volumes.

This is not an exclusively European affair: it can be studied just as well by turning to the history of Asia. Zen Buddhism is closely implicated with the culture of the sword, as is Hinduism, whose holy scriptures contain a vast epic relating a brutal battle between warring families. The Asian martial arts loved around the world are also a practice in AI; they rehearse the basis of teaching and instruction at a sensomotoric level. And we ought not to forget that the Second World War was not fought in Europe alone. We need to overcome the stereotypical explanations of modernity according to which it is a kind of European attack on the rest of the world, passively suffered by otherwise morally advanced peoples. Modernity – including projects of colonialism initiated and run by kings, emperors, etc., from the European continent – is a complicated global meshwork of different events and not a single, unitary process. It is blatantly false to assume that there is such a thing as Europe and that this thing has been a unified force of colonial modernity. This does not correspond to the facts and is thus a poor basis for fighting for the rights of those who suffered from colonial projects.

Our current stories about the AAI that threatens us humans is a transferral of our own violent fantasies onto machines of our own creation. For we know that AAI has emerged and developed principally in military contexts and is now spreading itself over human society in the form of a global network of surveillance. The digital revolution is by no means a purely economic process and certainly not any kind of liberation of humankind from the yoke of its physical limitations. It is a gigantic war machine, and our best hope is that it is kept in check by the spread of horror scenarios, which thus function rather like the fear of nuclear war in the latter half of the twentieth century. Just as the nuclear deterrent, thanks to countless apocalyptic films and stories, has thus far contributed to delaying the self-eradication of humanity, we can today only hope that the regular invocation of the threats of AAI will have a comparable effect.

To a considerable extent, the human being is its own worst enemy. We have created autonomous weapons systems, which we fear precisely because they are thought models of our own strivings after power and destruction.

The end of humanity – tragedy or comedy?

The word 'machine' stems from the ancient Greek expression *mêchanê*, which means instrument (a means to an end), but also cunning and stratagem. Our machines fulfil the function of outwitting nature, other creatures and, above all, other people.[82] The training in algorithms we receive at school provides us with ways and means of gaining competitive advantage. This is why education is a good for which, in certain countries at least, one has to pay good money. In countries such as Germany and France, education is broadly seen as a right, one to which residents from other countries are also entitled, albeit with certain restrictions. This is an achievement of modernity. The idea of equality of opportunity is not simply self-evident but a realization of the insight that the greatest threat to the human being is the human being itself. This is also the reason why we have created social systems to provide for our mutual protection. Equality of opportunity means risk minimization; in the ideal scenario, no one is excluded from the possibility of developing their sense of thought for the sake of ethically guided action-coordination.

Modernity brings with it genuine progress. Genuine progress does not consist solely in combinations of science and technology with industrial applications. If we neglect to reflect on what we're really doing when we take scientific and technological steps forward, we will destroy ourselves sooner rather than later and, on our way to self-destruction, spread calamity wherever human beings lack the capacities to defend themselves against the superior technological power of advanced industrial nations. This is the state of affairs we have to confront today; we cannot choose simply to avert our gaze. But this does not mean that the modern notion of universal moral progress, which is based on rational moral insight and emotional sensitivities available to all humans, is somehow a direct or indirect justification of unjust acts. That line of thought is simply nonsense, as it confuses the fact that modernity is not driven by moral progress alone (but by capitalistic greed, racism, exploitation, and so on) with the misguided claim that there are no universally valid moral standards. If that were true, what reason would the next generation of European (more likely: North American) imperialists have not to subjugate and shamelessly exploit peoples who have already suffered from earlier waves of colonization?

Kant regularly asked himself how the human being can be 'always only a link in the chain of natural ends', on the one hand, while falling outside the natural order, on the other, by working against its own self-preservation. Self-preservation and the will to survive are not natural properties of humanity as a whole. In lugubrious tones, Kant therefore describes how, due to 'the conflict in the *natural predispositions* of the human', this creature

> reduces himself and others of his own species, by means of plagues
> that he invents for himself, such as the oppression of domination, the

barbarism of war, etc., to such need, and he works so hard for the
destruction of his own species, that even if the most beneficent nature
outside of us had made the happiness of our species its end, that end
would not be attained in a system of nature upon the earth, because
the nature inside of us is not receptive to that.[83]

Humanity's natural end is not happiness. Humanity as a whole
can never achieve a permanent state of happiness if the systems of
our need-satisfaction at the same time lead to our dehumaniza-
tion of other people. Hence social justice remains an important
shibboleth. In an unjust society, in which goods and opportuni-
ties are distributed in the way we find in contemporary Brazil, for
example, human beings' worthiness of happiness is put at risk, to
borrow another expression from Kant (somewhat contrary to his
intentions). For those who consciously profit from extreme injustice, those whose activities directly or indirectly condemn innocent
people to suffering and an undignified death, have renounced their
worthiness to be happy. And this means that the reason why equality of opportunity is a value not to be sought in any kind of
strategic calculus of suitable means towards a maximally stable
state of coexistence; rather, it is anchored in the concept of humanity itself insofar as we human beings are capable of moral insight.
And this capacity belongs together with our sense of thought.

It is therefore a central idea of the Enlightenment that we attain
genuine progress only if we bring humanity forward. This presupposes reflection on the part of philosophy, the arts and the
humanities, which in turn has to be the foundation of our thinking about genuine social justice. Only within this framework can
we begin to determine how we ought to deal with the digital
revolution.

In this book, I have attempted to construct a path through the
labyrinth of thinking – a path that anyone can follow. In doing so,
my hope has been that we might together rediscover our sense of
thought. And, if we can, we can calibrate it in a way that lets us
begin to clear away the errors generated by the industrial mechanisms of unbridled technological progress.

At this point I'd like to take stock and remind you of a well-
known thought experiment: theatre. We first need to go back to
antiquity. The first ever democracy was famously established on the
soil of Athens – though it was anything but perfect since, for one
thing, it could not function without slaves. This society engaged in
multiple forms of self-observation, including mathematics, logic,
philosophy, physics, political theory, architecture and, above all,

theatre. The result was **humanism,** the discovery that the human being itself is at stake in all its activities. What we do is a mirror of who we are – whether we notice this or not. This idea has not been superseded in the course of subsequent history but remains as valid as it did in the age of Pericles.

Plato had an ingenious interpretation of the structure of theatre which, it's worth noting, he set out in the form of plays – that is, in the form of dialogues. His dialogue *The Symposium* (in modern English: party) takes on the topics of love and friendship. In particular, it deals with philosophy, because philosophy is the love of wisdom. The dialogue culminates in Socrates' insight that a genuine tragedian must also be a comic poet.[84] I interpret this as follows: *who* the human is depends upon *how* we determine ourselves. Whether the future will be a tragedy or comedy lies in our hands.

If we decide in favour of tragedy, we will perish of our own blindness in believing that a further acceleration in technological progress will somehow rid us of today's problems. We fail to realize that this way leads precisely to those social models depicted with shocking realism in such masterpieces of self-knowledge as *Black Mirror* and *Electric Dreams*.

If, by contrast, we decide in favour of comedy, we have to create the conditions of a society in which all people are afforded the opportunity to exercise their self-determination with their human rights fully intact. But, to achieve this, we first of all have to see that there is a universal core of being human: the wish not to be an animal. This wish connects us to immaterial reality, the current object of our shameless technocratic exploitation. This functions so well because the (in fact superseded) materialist worldview of the nineteenth century has lodged itself in our modes of thought.

We have to defend ourselves against post-humanism's attempt to abolish humanity. For it is based on a delusion, which only advances the self-annihilation of the human being by means of the digital military juggernaut it has itself created. Whoever wants to overcome the human in favour of the *Übermensch* is in fact guilty of a contempt for life. Yet the only meaning of life, its very sense, lies within life itself. The conditions of a successful life are explored in part through thinking about thinking – thinking that, through our sense of thought, makes contact with the fact that we cannot escape from life. We are and remain the minded living being that does not want to be an animal and yet all too often uses its reason to 'be beastlier than a beast'.[85]

The End of the Book –
a Pathos-Laden Final Remark

This book completes a trilogy in which I've tried to argue against a powerful but mistaken conception of the world and the human being. Exposing the philosophical foundations of this image has led me from the question of the world as a whole (*Why the World Does Not Exist*) to the question of the self (*I am Not a Brain*) to the task of understanding *The Meaning of Thought*. While writing this trilogy, New Realism has, if anything, become even more relevant. Looking back, it seems as though the global crisis of representation and the mistrust of the idea of ethical universalism have only intensified since the realistic turn in contemporary philosophy.

The nonsense of alternative facts and of a post-truth age, the scorning of the media, and the abolition of a free press in several countries over the past seven years make it quite clear that New Realism has a moral mission too. Humans cannot successfully determine themselves if they flee from reality. It is then easy to sow discord by perpetuating the lie that we humans are essentially distinguished by our skin colour, gender, religious affiliation, nationality or cultural tradition. Yet humans are different simply because they distinguish themselves from one another.

Today, we find a whole catalogue of putative distinguishing characteristics of different human beings or groups, none of which stand up to any historically or culturally informed scrutiny. Whoever knows their history will know that there never was any primordial people – never. They will also know that there is no unequivocal cultural identity and never has been – never. Whoever believes, like Viktor Orbán, that Europe has a Christian foundation demonstrates a total ignorance of the history of both Europe and Christianity – a religion, moreover, founded in the Middle East by a Jew who was executed by that very European empire that was subsequently conquered for several centuries by Christianity. Christianity is a consequence of a migration flow of people and ideas that has absolutely nothing to do with the essence of Europe. Europe has no essence.

What Europe can be in the future depends upon whether we can develop successfully and in accordance with the standards of morality. The exclusion of entire population groups whose ancestors decisively shaped European civilization (among whom, as everyone should know, were a number of Islamic scholars) does not meet the standards of universal human reason and is therefore to be rejected (not only, but certainly also) philosophically. In any case, to be a human, and thus to enjoy human rights in Europe, one need not have any ancestors who achieved something or other for Europe. Being human is not measured in terms of achievements.

Europe finds itself in crisis. This crisis is part of a global process which is enmeshed, at least in part, with the digital revolution and the cyber-warfare currently being waged all around. In times of crisis, one can never know how things will develop. In every life crisis we ask ourselves who we really are and who we want to be. We think about ourselves. And when our self-reflection is defective, we do not come out of the crisis unscathed. Who are we Europeans really, and who do we want to become?

It would be somewhat presumptuous to end this book by attempting to develop a vision for Europe. But it is vital to make one thing clear: Europe is neither a technocratic construct – Brussels in the eyes of its critics – nor the Christian West. Strictly speaking, nobody knows what it really is. Hence the pressing question: What should it be?

To end on a somewhat pathos-laden note, I would like to bang the drum for an unconditional universalism. There is an essential universal core of the human being: its capacity for self-determination. The capacity for self-determination expresses itself in our pathogenic self-definition as the animal that doesn't want to be one. All humans experience reality in fundamentally the same way, on the basis of their shared senses – including thought. This is why we have the capacity to imagine what it would be like to be someone else. This capacity is the source of morality. An action is morally relevant when performed in the knowledge that I could also be another – that is, that what I do could also be done to me.

The foundation of morality, the good, is derived from the fact that everyone is an other. Everyone is a foreigner to the foreigner. How we think about foreigners reveals who we really are. Addressed to Christians: this means precisely loving one's neighbour as oneself. At this point, therefore, I can only hold up a mirror, so that we can take a look at ourselves and work out the extent to which each of us shares the (fallacious) view that we possess a fixed and valuable identity that entitles us to a derogatory view of foreigners.

The current crisis in Europe is a consequence of the pathology of xenophobia, of fear of the other. Like arachnophobia or claustrophobia, xenophobia is the expression of an impaired self-representation. It is therefore more vital than ever to reactivate the sense of thought, so that we can find possible cures for the prevailing intellectual errors of our age. It is time for a European philosophy, something that has previously existed just as little as a truly unified Europe.

Glossary

AAI thesis: our own intelligence is an AI, while what are usually called AI systems are artefacts, which merely represent models of our own intelligence. An AAI is a *thought-model*, not a *thought-copy*.

Abstraction: grasping a general rule on the basis of a series of examples.

Adorno's mediation principle: mediation can no more be hypostatized than can the poles of subject and object; it is valid only in their constellation. Mediation is mediated by what it mediates.

AI, strong: the idea that we could develop an AI that is indistinguishable from human intelligence.

AI, universal: an AI that, at the right moment, can switch from one intelligent activity to any other.

Alethic transparency (from Greek *alêtheia* = truth): to say that something is true is merely to underline an assertion but not to alter its content. The statement 'It's true that it's raining' therefore ultimately says the same as 'it's raining'.

Algorithm: a rule that prescribes how a process is to be carried out in well-defined steps in order to arrive at a certain result, a solution to some given problem.

Alienation theory of thought: the theory that all of our thought processes are determined by unconscious processes together with unconscious biases set in place in early childhood, be it genetically, through our motor-sensory wiring, etc.

234

Animism: the belief that nature as a whole is ensouled; today this belief is also called **panpsychism.**

Anthropological constructivism: the view that the human being entirely produces itself. There are no truths about us independent of our self-constitution.

Anthropological principle, first: the human being is the animal that doesn't want to be one.

Anthropological principle, second: the human is a free, specifically minded animal (*freies geistiges Lebewesen*).

Anthropology: the discipline tasked with figuring out what precisely distinguishes the human both from other animals and from the lifeless expanses of the inanimate universe.

Anthropomorphism: the false projection of human structures onto a non-human domain, for example, the division of the animal kingdom into creatures to which we feel an affinity (such as pets, zebras, dolphins) and those that appear unimportant or even repulsive (snakes, foot fungus, insects).

Aristotle's definition of truth: to say of what is that it is not, or of what is not that it is, is false, whereas to say of what is that it is, or of what is not that it is not, is true. So he who says of anything that it is, or that it is not, will say either what is true or what is false.

Atomism: the doctrine that everything that exists is composed out of the smallest particles, between which there is nothing but pure void. Postulating the void explains why there is not just a great, single lump of matter.

Basic principle concerning the relation between so-called artificial intelligence (AI) and human intelligence (HI): AI relates to HI like the map to the territory. With AI, we are dealing not really with *thought*, but with a *model of thought*.

Basic reality: the domain of that which itself is neither a simulation nor something that came into being via human intentions to produce an artefact.

Baudrillard's simulation hypothesis: globalization is a process driven forward by empty sign systems that produce themselves.

Binding problem: we do not perceive isolated qualities but enjoy experiences that form (or at least seem to form) a unity. The connection between our brain and the combination of the various sensory modules remains unexplained.

Biological externalism: the thesis that expressions we use to describe and understand our thought processes are essentially related to something biological.

Biological naturalism: identifies all the mental states of human beings with neuronal processes.

Broad concept of information: we are dealing with information wherever a question can be answered with a 'yes' or a 'no'.

Cartesian Cogito: 'I think, therefore I am'.

Category: as a concept without which we wouldn't be able to form other concepts.

Causal theory of perception: according to this theory, the external world, the world located outside of our consciousness or of the surface of our bodies, contains things that stimulate our sense organs. These sensory stimulations are processed internally within the organism and formed into impressions via information processing in the brain.

Causality: the technical term for a cause–effect connection.

CAUSE: the cause of all causes.

Chinese room argument: a thought experiment designed to show that no computer can processes information in an intelligent manner because no computer understands anything and, for that very reason, cannot possess a capacity to think.

Civilization: the organization of human coexistence via explicitly formulated rules transmitted in linguistic codes.

Cognitive penetration: the way in which our sense modalities influence one another (e.g. when a plane takes off, we have the impression of suddenly glancing upwards even though nothing has altered in one's line of sight, because our sense of balance penetrates our visual field).

Coherent: a system of thoughts (a theory) is coherent if its parts hang together in a rational manner.

Colour constructivism: a colour constructivist believes that colours do not really exist. Rather, colours are supposedly generated by animals with certain neuronal equipment in order to facilitate their conscious dealings with an in-itself colourless world.

Composition (Giulio Tononi): consists in how our conscious experience has a structure.

Computer: a system that we have manufactured and whose changes of state are governed by programs.

Concept: something that we can separate out from a thought in order to use it in further thoughts.

Concretion: the process of finding an appropriate example for illustrating a rule or a theoretical connection.

Consciousness, higher-order: consciousness of consciousness.

Consciousness, object-level: consciousness of something in our environment or in our organism that is not itself a consciousness.

Consciousness, phenomenal: what it is like to be who you are at any given moment; the background noise of our entire organism, to which countless factors contribute, including what is colloquially known as our abdominal or 'second' brain, the enteric nervous system located in our gastrointestinal tract.

Consistent: a system of thoughts (a theory) is **consistent** provided it neither contains an explicit contradiction nor allows one to be derived from it by its own lights.

Constructivism, hyper-radical: argues that reality itself is not as described by either physics or the natural sciences as an ensemble, because these disciplines too are merely a construction of the human mind or brain or – as one sometimes reads – of a certain social system (viz. science).

Constructivism, radical scientific: claims that there aren't *really* colours and geometrical forms; what physics tells us about the objects of the external world is all there really is. According to this view, there are not any different shades of red but only a spectrum of wavelengths which appear to us as red.

Contact theory: introduced by Hubert Dreyfus and Charles Taylor in their book *Retrieving Realism*. Perception is not a way of gradually grasping our way towards an alien external world; rather, thanks to perception we are already in touch with the real.

Content of a thought: the way in which a thought is about its object.

Contingency: being able to be otherwise. Whatever is contingent can be this way or that way. This means that it is in any case not necessary that it be as it currently is.

Continuous differences: intensive differences. For example, the red covers of two books can each feature a differently intensive red. Our red experience is continuous: there are various grades or intensities of being red, just as a tone can be louder or softer without there being two clear classifications (the loud and the soft).

Contradictions: thoughts that are necessarily false.

Cybernetics: the basic idea of cybernetics is that we can describe many processes as control processes, for which we can design control circuits.

Digitalization: the realization of the logical insights of the late nineteenth and early twentieth centuries on a newly developed technological basis.

Discrete differences: things sorted into clearly demarcated domains.

Disjunction: a statement of the form that something or something else is the case.

Dream argument: is supposed to show that we cannot know whether we are dreaming or awake. Such arguments presuppose that waking appearances are indistinguishable from appearances in dream states.

Dream hypothesis: we cannot, at any point in time, say with certainty whether we are dreaming or awake.

Egocentric index: the egocentric index of an animal is the way in which its environment appears to it.

Empiricism: thesis that everything we can ever know about reality boils down to an interpretation of data delivered to us by our senses.

Enlightened humanism: is based on an image of the human (such as that developed in this book) that from the very outset allows no room for doubt that everyone, whether foreigner, native, friend, neighbour, woman, child, man, coma patient or transsexual, ought to count as human in the full sense.

Epistemology: the philosophical subdiscipline concerned primarily with the question of what (human) knowledge is and how far it extends. What can we know and how can we justify knowledge claims?

Ethics: the philosophical subdiscipline that asks what a good life looks like. It distinguishes permissible from impermissible actions and establishes logical relations between actions of these types.

Exclusion (Giulio Tononi): consciousness is completely and determinately definite. It is just what it is, no more and no less.

Existential generalization: a logical law – e.g. if something (call it: a) has a property (P), then it follows that something (x) has the property P. From 'a is P', we can infer 'some x is P'.

Existentialism: assumes that human life has no absolute, externally determined meaning and that we instead have to imbue it with meaning within the contexts in which we happen to find ourselves.

Extended mind thesis: the view that our psychological, mental reality has for a long time now not been restricted to our bodies but has, instead, extended into our technological devices and media.

Externalism: the idea that certain expressions refer to something without a competent speaker having to know exactly how the target system of their linguistic reference is actually constituted.

Externalism, semantic: is based on the idea that many elements in the expressions we use in directing our thoughts at things that aren't themselves expressions are given their direction from outside, so to speak. 'Meaning ain't in the head' (Hilary Putnam).

Factivity: from the fact that someone perceives something, it follows that things are as the person perceives them to be. Objectivity and factivity belong together: wherever we're in a position to know how things really are, we can also be deceived.

Field of sense: an arrangement of objects where these objects hang together in a particular manner. I call the manner in which they hang together a **sense**.

Frege's theory of thought: thinking is the grasping of a thought.

Functionalism: the thesis that human intelligence is a rule-governed system that processes data with a view to solving certain specific problems. This system does not have to be realized on biological hardware.

Functionalism, main problem of: the theory doesn't give us any description of what human thinking really is.

Fundamentalism, religious: holds that material-energetic structures are just a world of sensory appearances that God has put in place to test us.

Geist: the capacity to lead a life in the light of a representation of who the human being is.

Ge-Stell: the idea that reality as a whole is calculable, that it stands at our disposal as a set of means for us to pursue our ends, and that we should therefore make everything that exists readily accessible for human use.

GOD: a program that, for every single program, can determine whether *it* does or doesn't terminate.

Halting problem: it is impossible to write a program that cannot possibly run in an endless loop.

Happiness: the name for a successful life, for which there are no universally valid standards – no set of principles of which we might somehow draw up a catalogue.

Hegel's principle: what is rational is actual; and what is rational is actual.

Hermeneutics: the theory of understanding.

Heterogeneity of the real (from the ancient Greek *heteros* = other, various, and *genos* = kind): The real is of various kinds.

Holism (from the Greek *to holon* = the whole): traces all of the events and structures of the universe back to its overall maximal cosmological structure. Reductionism, by contrast, tends to want to explain all complex structures in terms of the interaction of simpler ones – in the ideal reductionist theory, this will boil down to an explanation of the smallest building blocks of the universe.

Holism, semantic: states that you're able to deploy a concept only if you're able to deploy a whole battery of further concepts that stand in various logical relations to it.

Human animals: a biological species, which emerged thus through evolution. We are still the very same species as many of our paleontological ancestors.

Human self-portrait: the image that each has of who or what she is; the image from which every human derives instructions for who or what she ought to be.

Humanism: the discovery that the human being reflects itself in all its activities. What we do is a mirror of who we are – whether we notice this or not.

Humean supervenience: states that 'all there is to the world is a vast mosaic of local matters of particular fact, just one little thing and then another' (David Lewis).

Idealism, core idea of: something is real only if it presents information, if it is capable of being interpreted by some system or other. By contrast, realism assumes that there are realities that will never be graspable for any intelligent system.

Ideology: a distorted conception of the human that fulfils a socio-economic function, usually the implicit justification of an ultimately unjust distribution of resources.

Immaterialism: thinking is the grasping of immaterial thoughts. Thoughts are neither brain states nor any form of information processing that we measure physically. Yet humans cannot have any thoughts without being living creatures who find themselves in certain brain states – or, more generally, in certain physiological states.

Individuality: derives from the brute fact that each of us is irreplaceably him- or herself.

Individuation, condition of: a set of rules that determine when something is identical with something else, and therefore with itself.

Inference to the best explanation: consists in deciding which cause or causal chain most likely explains a given phenomenon on the basis of the available data.

Inforg: a cyborg, consisting purely of digital information.

Information: the fact that every conscious experience is different from every other. Every experience is utterly individual, distinct from every further experience that I or anyone else will ever have.

Infosphere (Luciano Floridi): our digital environment.

Integrated information theory (IIT): a theory of consciousness developed by Giulio Tononi. On this account, consciousness is a highly unified phenomenon which cannot be broken down into parts and which exhibits a high information density.

Integration (Giulio Tononi): every conscious experience has a structure that cannot simply be traced back to its parts.

Intelligence: the capacity to think.

Intentionality (from the Latin *intendere* = to hold out, to stretch out): philosophers understand the way in which mental states are directed at something that is not necessarily a mental state itself.

Intrinsic existence: consists in something's knowing of itself that it exists.

Key thesis of the book, first: thought is a sense, just like our sense of hearing, touch, taste, our sense of balance, and everything else that we nowadays count as belonging to the human sensory system.

Key thesis of the book, second: *see* **Biological externalism.**

Learning: the systematic introduction of new problems in order to solve old ones.

Lifeworld: our everyday understanding of the things that surround us, of the persons and cultural relations that we negotiate as soon as we have undergone even minimal education. It is what allows us to avoid running to our deaths the second we cross the road, to learn to feed ourselves, etc.

Linguistic turn: the transition from investigating the real to investigating our linguistic tools for investigating the real.

Logic: studies the laws of thought insofar as this consists in grasping thoughts. It thereby determines the ways in which thoughts are related.

Magical theory of reference: the idea that we can refer to something mentally without having any knowledge of it. So, ants could happen to draw an outline of Winston Churchill in the sand without having a clue who Churchill is (the example comes from Hilary Putnam).

Materialism: encompasses both the doctrine that everything that exists consists of matter and the ethical conception that the meaning of human life ultimately consists in the accumulation of goods (cars, houses, sexual partners, smartphones) and their pleasurable annihilation (burning fossil fuels, ostentatious luxury, gourmet restaurants).

Materialism, crude: reality consists solely of material-energetic structures.

Matter (*Sache*): that which a concept is about, where the concept is part of a thought.

Medium: an interface that transfers information from one code into another.

Meillassoux's speculative realism: assumes that at each and every moment reality could become radically different from how it has seemed until now.

Metacognition: the traditional philosophical designation for which is **self-consciousness** – i.e. consciousness of consciousness.

Metaphor (from the ancient Greek *meta-pherein*): is a transferral of a statement of one form into another.

Metaphysics: a theory of reality as a whole, which distinguishes between a real world (being) and the appearance and deception that supposedly has us humans caught in its snares.

Minimalism: the view that a few easily comprehensible principles hold good for truth and establish what propositional truth consists in.

Model: a simplified presentation of a real situation.

Model-model, simple: a model of models that divides them into two parts: models and the reality that they simplify.

Model regress, sinister: if our experience of reality were totally restricted to the model-model, the same would also go for the model-model: we would then have a model-model-model, and then a model-model-model-model, and so on and so on. If we want to stave off the infinite regress and yet stick to the rules of the model game, the only remaining option is at some point or other to take a stab in the dark; but this really amounts to undermining all scientific objectivity.

Multiple realizability: a system of rules is multiply realizable if it can be installed in different pieces of hardware.

Mythology: a narrative structure by means of which we humans construct a picture of our overall historical and socio-economic situation.

Naturalism: in its standard form, it maintains that human beings, and thus our thinking, are fully describable in the terms of natural science and therefore, at least in principle, possible to re-create.

Noetic vocabulary (from the Greek *noein* = thinking): the thought words of a language or speaker together comprise a vocabulary.

Non-intentional environment of our lives: comprises those facts that obtain without anyone having planned for them to obtain.

Non-thoughts: objects that are not themselves thoughts.

Nooscope thesis: our thought is a sense that we can use to scout out the infinite and then depict it in various ways, mathematically for example.

Object of a thought: that which a thought is about.

Objectivity: that feature of an attitude which means we can get things right or wrong, be correct or incorrect.

Objectivity, contrast of: the characteristic feature of a thought is that it is either true or false regardless of our opinion on the matter. The contrast of objectivity consistently distinguishes between truth and holding-true.

Objects, senseless: objects that do not appear in any medium whatsoever, that would in no sense be bearers of information.

Panpsychism: the view that everything that really exists exhibits a kind of consciousness.

Perceptual constructivism, modest: our concepts alter our perception.

Perceptual constructivism, radical: the concepts we have at our disposal not only alter our perceptions but affect the things themselves.

Perceptual selectionism: the view that, thanks to our acquired conceptual capacities and other modes of registration (which include our sensory and physiological endowment as higher primates), we can only ever perceive some things at the expense of others.

Perfect simulation: is defined as a simulation that you can no longer distinguish from reality.

Person: the image we form for ourselves of who we want to be for others.

Personality: a rehearsed role-play that varies from situation to situation and by means of which we obtain and maintain strategic advantages in social competition.

Personalization machine: systems by means of which self-dramatizations are manufactured and marketed.

Phenomenon: something that seems to appear to us utterly unmediated and unfiltered.

Principle of intelligibility: the universe is knowable at least to the extent that the natural sciences have correctly grasped how it is.

Private language argument: we cannot use any single word correctly if we could not also use it incorrectly: if, that is, we could not be in contact with other speakers who correct our language use, we could not use any word whatsoever incorrectly.

Problem: a task that an agent wants to solve in order to reach a certain aim – a solution.

Problem of weird realizations: imaginability is no guarantee of real possibility.

Program (from the Greek *pro* = pre-, and *graphein* = write): literally translated, a pre-scription. Every instruction that can be carried out in explicable steps is a program.

Projection thesis: We endow reality with a meaning it would not have without our own mental endowment.

Property: something in virtue of which something differs from something else.

Pure thought: consists in the act of thought grasping itself as such; this occurs only when we occupy ourselves not with non-thoughts but with the form of thinking itself.

Quale (pl. **qualia**): an individual qualitative experience.

Real: something is real if we can be mistaken about it, because the real tends not simply to tell us how we ought to think if we're to avoid making mistakes about it.

Realism: sees the decisive feature of reality in how we have to adapt our beliefs to real circumstances.

Realism, neutral: the thesis that reality is neither knowable in its entirety to us humans nor by its very nature something that eludes human cognition.

Realism, New: maintains 1) that we can grasp objects and facts as they really are and 2) that there are infinitely many fields of sense in which objects and facts exist.

Realism, old: reality consists of things and contains no perspectives on things. Reality = the world without spectators.

Reality: the fact that there are objects and facts that we can be wrong about because their existence isn't exhausted by our having beliefs about them. What is real corrects our beliefs.

Reality, object-level: that which statements are about in the case where what they are about is not itself a statement.

Reductionism, bad: reduces one way of thinking to another that leaves out something essential and thus leads to a blinkered perspective.

Reference: linguistic contact with reality.

Sceptical argument: aims to show, for some putative item of knowledge, that we cannot know that thing *in principle*.

Scepticism, radical: the view that we cannot know anything at all.

Self-consciousness: consciousness of consciousness.

Semantic atoms: simple meaning components that cannot be broken down into still smaller components.

Semantics: the theory of linguistic meaning.

Sense modality: a fallible mode of establishing contact with objects which can recognize objects across gaps in conscious awareness.

Set: any assortment of objects that we find and simply gather together.

Simulation (from the Latin *simulatio*, derived from *simulare* = to make similar): a merely apparent reality that resembles another reality.

Simulation argument (Nick Bostrom): wants to demonstrate that it's probable that we live in a situation in the sense that it is rational to believe that we find ourselves in a simulation.

Simulation hypothesis: consists in imagining that the reality we inhabit is a simulation. If one can show that the simulation hypothesis is false, the simulation argument is refuted.

Singularity: the point at which our AI systems will have become so advanced that they are able to develop themselves automatically, without any involvement on our part.

Social constructivism: the idea that society is a social construct in the sense that it is not truly real but only a kind of charade resulting from our belief-systems and manners of symbolizing and speaking, whose rules we could, in principle, change whenever we liked by changing our belief-systems and manners of symbolizing and speaking.

Social ontology: the philosophical subdiscipline that addresses the question of why many objects and facts count as 'social'.

Solipsism: the assumption that only one's own consciousness exists and that everything else can be understood as its contents.

Sôma–sêma thesis (Plato) (from the Greek *sôma* = body and *sêma* = tomb): according to Plato, the human body is a prison or tomb for the soul.

Statements: sentences with which we claim to describe what is actually the case.

Subject: an individual minded animal.

Subject–object divide: consists in the false notion that we as thinking subjects confront an alien reality, a world we don't really fit into. It arises from the assumption that there is, on the one hand, a subject-independent reality (the object or the objective) and, on the other, a subject who contemplates this reality.

Subjectivity: consists in the way in which we can be deceived and go wrong.

Substrate-independence: the assumption that a function can potentially be fulfilled by things that have completely different material foundations – that is: different substrates.

Symbolic order: the public exhibition of the representations we form of how society functions as a whole.

Tautologies: thoughts that are necessarily true.

Technological imaginary: an attitude to the manufacture of technological artefacts.

Technology: the actualization or implementation of ideas; the process by which we produce things that were not already there as parts of the natural order.

Thesis of derived intentionality (John Searle): thoughts and sentences (and thus texts and computer programs) are about something only because we lend them our human intentionality.

Thing: a meso- or macroscopic spatiotemporally extended object. Things are those objects with which we make contact through our nerve endings. These objects are the cause of our perceiving them.

Thought: something that is either true or false.

Thought, meaningful: a thought that is neither necessarily true nor necessarily false.

Thought, senseless: a thought that is either a tautology or a contradiction.

Thought words: besides 'thinking', these include intelligence, acumen, cleverness, opining, suspecting, believing, and so on. They designate processes of grasping thoughts.

Tononi's axioms: Tononi provides five axioms: intrinsic existence, composition, information, integration and exclusion.

Transhumanism: the attempt to take Friedrich Nietzsche's fantasy of the superman (*Übermensch*) and make it a reality through technological progress.

Truth argument: the starting point of the argument is the observation that we can use sentences to express what we take to be real. Let's call sentences with which we claim to establish what is actually the case **statements**. Statements are usually either true or false (setting the senseless ones aside for the moment). They are, in any case, something that fundamentally raises a question as to their truth. It cannot be that all our statements and sentences are false.

Truth-apt: A thought is **truth-apt** if it can be true or false. If a thought is truth-apt, it is about something. What a meaningful thought is about is its object; the way in which it is about what it's about is its content.

Turing machine: Originally, 'computer' simply meant 'someone who computes', primarily a human being. Since Turing, the expression has been applied to machines that share certain features with human computers. Turing described these machines, thus laying the foundations of computer science.

Universe: the object domain of physics.

Uniware (Brigitte and Thomas Görnitz): animals are unities of software and hardware – i.e. a uniware.

Vagueness: natural languages are not formal systems. The meaning of most expressions (most likely of all expressions) is not precisely defined. In the philosophy of language, this is known as **vagueness.**

Value alignment: the system of hierarchically ordered goals followed by a program or agent.

Very general fact sentence (VGFS): There are unlimitedly many thoughts, the truth of which no human being will ever be able to confirm or refute.

View from nowhere: the assumption that objectivity consists in assuming a fully neutral standpoint. The view from nowhere assumes that genuine objectivity is utterly a-subjective.

Word: something that one can spell and translate into other languages.

Word-label: a sound or sign sequence that we use in linguistic contexts; we can do many things with these besides expressing meanings (e.g. aesthetic formations).

Worldview: a conception of how everything there is hangs together with everything else.

Notes

Acknowledgements

1 Georg Wilhelm Friedrich Hegel, 'Hegel an Schelling [End of January 1795]', in Johannes Hoffmeister (ed.), *Briefe von und an Hegel* (Hamburg: Meiner, 1969), pp. 15–18, here p. 18.

Preface

1 Immanuel Kant, *Lectures on Logic*, ed. and trans. J. Michael Young (Cambridge: Cambridge University Press, 2004), p. 537 (9:23).
2 Ibid.
3 Ibid.
4 G. W. F. Hegel, *The Phenomenology of Spirit*, trans. Terry P. Pinkard (Cambridge: Cambridge University Press, 2018), p. 50 (§74); Paul Artin Boghossian, *Fear of Knowledge: Against Relativism and Constructivism* (Oxford: Clarendon Press, 2007).

Introduction

1 In the main body of the text, I define bold expressions as precisely as possible. The definitions are also collected in a glossary at the end of the book to provide a clear overview of the most important concepts I'm working with.
2 The questions of what we owe ourselves and one another, and of what in general is truly significant, are central to two of the most important positions in current philosophical ethics: that of Thomas M. Scanlon (b. 1944) and that of Derek Parfit

252

(1942–2017). See Thomas M. Scanlon, *What We Owe to Each Other* (Cambridge, MA: Harvard University Press, 2000); Derek Parfit, *On What Matters*, 3 vols (Oxford: Oxford University Press, 2011–16).

3 For a more detailed account, see Markus Gabriel, *Neo-Existentialism* (Cambridge: Polity, 2018) and *I am Not a Brain* (Cambridge: Polity, 2017).

4 Luciano Floridi, *The Philosophy of Information* (Oxford: Oxford University Press 2011).

5 Markus Gabriel and Frank Thelen, 'Schöne neue Welt?', *Philosophie Magazin* 02 (2018), pp. 58–65.

6 Jean Baudrillard, *Simulacra and Simulation*, trans. Sheila Faria Glaser (Ann Arbor: University of Michigan Press, 1994).

7 Immanuel Kant, 'On the Different Races of Human Beings', in Kant, *History, Anthropology and Education*, trans. Mary Gregor, Paul Guyer, Robert B. Louden, Holly Wilson, Allen W. Wood, Gunther Zöller and Arnulf Zweig (Cambridge: Cambridge University Press, 2007), p. 93. The 'Negro' is therefore meant to be 'strong, fleshy, supple, but who, given the abundant provision of his motherland, is lazy, soft and trifling.' Among other practices, Kant here justifies the introduction of 'Negroes' as slaves, as the 'red slaves (Americans)' 'are too weak for field labour, for which one uses Negroes.' He believes that 'all Negroes stink' on account of the putative effects of 'phosphorous acid' on their skin.

8 *Caroli Linnaei Systema naturae: A Photographic Facsimile of the First Volume of the Tenth Edition, 1758* (London: British Museum, 1939). On this, see Gabriel, *I am Not a Brain*.

9 See Plato, *The Last Days of Socrates: Euthyphro, Apology, Crito, Phaedo*, trans. Hugh Tredennick and Harold Tarrant (London: Penguin, 2003), 20e–23c.

10 Jean-Paul Sartre, *Being and Nothingness*, trans. Sarah Richmond (New York: Routledge, 2018), p. 577.

11 Durs Grünbein, *Zündkerzen* (Berlin: Suhrkamp, 2017), p. 132.

12 Saul A. Kripke, *Naming and Necessity* (Cambridge, MA: Harvard University Press, 1980), pp. 20–1.

13 Georg Ephraim Lessing, *Die Erziehung des Menschengeschlechts und andere Schriften* (Stuttgart: Reclam, 1980).

14 Peter Sloterdijk, *You Must Change Your Life*, trans. Wieland Hoban (Cambridge: Polity, 2013), p. 451.

Chapter 1 The Truth about Thought

1 See Markus Gabriel, *Why the World Does Not Exist* (Cambridge: Polity, 2015), and *Fields of Sense* (Edinburgh: Edinburgh University Press, 2015).

2 Mark Johnston, *Saving God: Religion after Idolatry* (Princeton, NJ: Princeton University Press, 2009), pp. 131f.

3 Theodor W. Adorno, *Negative Dialectics*, trans. E. B. Ashton (London: Continuum, 1973). See too his unfortunately nowadays little read *Against Epistemology: A Metacritique: Studies in Husserl and the Phenomenological Antinomies*, trans. Willis Domingo (Cambridge: Polity, 2013).

4 Willard van Orman Quine, *Ontological Relativity and Other Essays* (New York: Columbia University Press, 1969), pp. 45–6: 'On deeper reflection, radical interpretation begins at home.'

5 David Deutsch, *The Beginning of Infinity: Explanations That Transform the World* (London: Penguin, 2011).

6 Ibid., pp. 107–24.

7 Ibid., p. 114.

8 Aristotle, *De anima*, trans. C. D. C. Reeve (Indianapolis: Hackett, 2017) p. 45 (424b22 f.).

9 Immanuel Kant, *Critique of Pure Reason*, trans. Paul Guyer and Allen Wood (Cambridge: Cambridge University Press, 1998), A110–11.

10 Wolfram Hogrebe, 'Risky Proximity to Life: The Scenic Existence of Homo Sapiens', trans. Adam Knowles, *Graduate Faculty Philosophy Journal* 31/2 (2010), pp. 219–312.

11 Aristotle, *De anima*, p. 46 (425b12).

12 Gabriel, *I am Not a Brain*, ch. 3.

13 See Aristotle, *De anima*, p. 46 (425a27 and, at greater length, 450a9–15).

14 Ibid., p. 48 (426b3 and 426b8).

15 On the contact theory, see Charles Taylor and Hubert Dreyfus, *Retrieving Realism* (Cambridge, MA: Harvard University Press, 2015).

16 Thomas Nagel, *The View from Nowhere* (New York: Oxford University Press, 1986).

17 Willard van Orman Quine, *Word and Object* (Cambridge, MA: MIT Press, 2015), p. 254.

18 See Liu Cixin, *The Dark Forest*, trans. Joel Martinsen (London: Head of Zeus, 2016), and *The Three-Body Problem*, trans. Ken Liu (London: Head of Zeus, 2015).

19 For a more extensive engagement with epistemology, see Markus Gabriel, *The Limits of Epistemology* (Cambridge: Polity, 2019).

20 See Gabriel, *Why the World Does Not Exist.*

21 For a good overview of different currents of constructivism and their foundational claims, see Ian Hacking, *The Social Construction of What?* (Cambridge, MA: Harvard University Press, 1999).

22 See Donald Davidson, 'On the Very Idea of a Conceptual Scheme', in *Inquiries into Truth and Interpretation* (Oxford: Oxford University Press, 2001), pp. 183–98, here pp. 196–7.

23 Aristotle, *Metaphysics*, trans. C. D. C. Reeve (Indianapolis: Hackett, 2016), p. 65 (1011b26–28).

24 A comprehensive sketch of the terrain can be found in Wolfgang Künne, *Conceptions of Truth* (Oxford: Oxford University Press, 2005). The standard presentation of minimalism is Paul Horwich, *Truth* (Oxford: Oxford University Press, 1999).

25 Michel Foucault, *The Order of Things: An Archaeology of the Human Sciences* (London: Routledge, 2002), p. xxv.

26 Ibid.

27 See Michel Foucault, *The History of Sexuality*, trans Robert Hurley, Vol. 1: *An Introduction* (New York: Vintage, 1990); Vol. 2: *The Use of Pleasure* (Harmondsworth: Penguin, 1992); Vol. 3: *The Care of the Self* (Harmondsworth: Penguin, 1990); *Histoire de la Sexualité*, 4: *Les Aveux de la chair* (Paris: Gallimard, 2018).

28 Michel Foucault, *The Archaeology of Knowledge*, trans. A. M. Sheridan Smith (London: Routledge, 2002).

29 See Gottlob Frege, 'Thought', in *The Frege Reader*, ed. Michael Beaney (Oxford: Blackwell, 1997), pp. 325–46.

30 See Gabriel, *The Limits of Epistemology*; Anton Friedrich Koch, *Versuch über Wahrheit und Zeit* (Paderborn: Mentis, 2006), *Hermeneutischer Realismus* (Tübingen: Mohr Siebeck, 2016).

31 Ludwig Wittgenstein, *Tractatus-Logico-Philosophicus*, trans. D. F. Pears and B. F. McGuinness (London: Routledge, 2001), p. 14.

32 An initial overview of various theories of information can be found in Luciano Floridi, *Information: A Very Short Introduction* (Oxford: Oxford University Press 2010). He works out his own impressive theory in Floridi, *The Philosophy of Information*. For an exciting history of the concept, see

James Gleick, *The Information: A History, a Theory, a Flood* (London: HarperCollins, 2011).

33 Floridi's argument is rather technical but also extremely sophisticated. For those who want to make the effort, see especially Floridi, *The Philosophy of Information*, pp. 93–107.

34 Frege, 'Thought', p. 342.

35 John R. Searle, *Seeing Things as They Are: A Theory of Perception* (Oxford: Oxford University Press 2015).

36 Pedro Calderón de la Barca, *Life's a Dream*, trans. Frank Birch and J. B. Trend (Cambridge: W. Heffer & Sons, 1925).

37 If you're interested in the further details of this argument, see Markus Gabriel, *Die Erkenntnis der Welt: Eine Einführung in die Erkenntnistheorie* (Freiburg im Breisgau: Alber 2014), where I discuss the three steps of Cartesian scepticism.

Chapter 2 Thought Engineering

1 Michel Houellebecq, *The Map and the Territory*, trans. Gavin Bowd (London: Vintage, 2012), p. 19.

2 Ibid.

3 Ibid., p. 49.

4 Luciano Floridi, *The Philosophy of Information* (Oxford: Oxford University Press 2011), p. 61.

5 Gottlob Frege, 'Thought', in *The Frege Reader*, ed. Michael Beaney (Oxford: Blackwell, 1997), pp. 325–46, here p. 325.

6 Houellebecq, *The Map and the Territory*, p. 268.

7 John Searle, 'Minds, Brains, and Programs', *Behavioral and Brain Sciences* 3 (1980), pp. 417–57.

8 For a detailed deconstruction of Searle's arguments, see Martin Dresler, *Künstliche Intelligenz, Bewusstsein und Sprache: Das Gedankenexperiment des 'Chinesischen Zimmers'* (Würzburg: Königshausen & Neumann, 2009).

9 John Searle, *Intentionality: An Essay in the Philosophy of Mind* (Cambridge: Cambridge University Press, 1983).

10 Ibid., pp. 27f.

11 Hilary Putnam, *Reason, Truth and History* (Cambridge: Cambridge University Press), pp. 1–22.

12 Ibid., p. 1.

13 See Charles Travis, *The Invisible Realm: Frege on the Pure Business of Being True*, forthcoming.

14 Xenophanes of Colophon, *Fragments*, trans. with a commen-

tary by J. H. Lesher (London: University of Toronto Press, 1992).

15 For the current state of discussion, see the contributions in Friederike Schmitz (ed.), *Tierethik: Grundlagentexte* (Berlin: Suhrkamp, 2014).

16 Floridi, *The Philosophy of Information*, pp. 7–12.

17 Ibid., p. 7.

18 Martin Heidegger, *Being and Time*, trans. Joan Stambaugh (Albany: State University of New York Press, 1996), §15.

19 Lawrence M. Krauss, *A Universe from Nothing: Why There is Something Rather than Nothing* (London: Simon & Schuster, 2012).

20 Sigmund Freud, *Civilization and its Discontents* (London: W. W. Norton, 2005).

21 Ludwig Feuerbach, *Principles of the Philosophy of the Future*, trans. Manfred H. Vogel (Indianapolis: Hackett, 1986), p. 53.

22 On this, see Markus Gabriel, *I am Not a Brain* (Cambridge: Polity, 2017), ch. 2.

23 Gottlob Frege, 'On Sense and Reference', in Beaney (ed.), *The Frege Reader*, p. 155: 'To the possible differences here belong also the colouring and shading which poetic eloquence seeks to give to the sense. Such colouring and shading are not objective, and must be evoked by each hearer or reader according to the hints of the poet or the speaker. Without some affinity in human ideas art would certainly be impossible; but it can never be exactly determined how far the intentions of the poet are realized.'

24 Humberto R. Maturana and Francisco J. Varela, *The Tree of Knowledge: The Biological Roots of Human Understanding*, trans. Robert Paolucci (London: Shambhala, 1992).

25 Hans Jonas, *The Phenomenon of Life: Toward a Philosophical Biology* (Chicago: University of Chicago Press, 1982).

26 For detailed counter-arguments, see Holm Tetens, *Gott denken: Ein Versuch einer rationalen Theologie* (Stuttgart: Reclam, 2015). And, for opposition to Dennett's worldview, see Markus Gabriel, *Neo-Existentialism* (Cambridge: Polity, 2018).

27 Max Tegmark, *Life 3.0: Being Human in the Age of Artificial Intelligence* (London: Penguin, 2018), pp. 65–7.

28 See, for example, Ned Block, 'Troubles with Functionalism', *Minnesota Studies in the Philosophy of Science* 9 (1978), pp. 261–325.

29 On the beer can example, see John R. Searle, 'The Myth of the Computer', *New York Review of Books* 29/7 (1982), pp. 3–7.

30 David Chalmers, *The Conscious Mind: In Search of a Fundamental Theory* (Oxford: Oxford University Press, 1996).

31 Humberto R. Maturana, *Biologie der Realität* (Frankfurt am Main: Suhrkamp, 2000), p. 11 [trans. A. E.].

32 Aristotle, *Physics*, trans. C. D. C. Reeve (Indianapolis: Hackett, 2018), p. 24 (194b).

33 David Deutsch, *The Beginning of Infinity: Explanations That Transform the World* (London: Penguin, 2011).

34 Maurizio Ferraris, 'Total Mobilization', *The Monist* 97/2 (2014), pp. 200–21. See also Ferraris, *Mobilisation totale: l'appel du portable* (Paris: Presses Universitaires de France, 2016)

35 Ray Kurzweil, *The Singularity is Near: When Humans Transcend Biology* (London: Penguin, 2006).

36 Maurizio Ferraris, *Documentality: Why It Is Necessary to Leave Traces* (New York: Fordham University Press, 2012).

37 John R. Searle, *The Construction of Social Reality* (London: Penguin, 1995), and *Making the Social World: The Structure of Human Civilization* (Oxford: Oxford University Press, 2011).

38 Maurizio Ferraris, *Manifesto of New Realism*, trans. Sarah De Sanctis (Albany: State University of New York Press, 2014); John R. Searle, 'Aussichten für einen neuen Realismus', in Markus Gabriel (ed.), *Der Neue Realismus* (Berlin: Suhrkamp, 2014), pp. 292–307.

39 Searle argued for this claim in a series of public debates that we conducted at Berkeley in the spring semester of 2013.

40 Maurizio Ferraris, 'Was ist der Neue Realismus?', in Gabriel (ed.), *Der Neue Realismus*, p. 58.

41 An excellent overview of the current state of our historical knowledge about pre-literate societies is given in Hermann Parzinger, *Die Kinder des Prometheus: Eine Geschichte der Menschheit vor der Erfindung der Schrift* (Munich: C. H. Beck, 2015).

42 Hilary Lawson, *Closure: A Story of Everything* (London: Routledge, 2001).

43 Jean-Gabriel Ganascia, *Le mythe de la singularité: faut-il craindre l'intelligence artificielle?* (Paris: Éditions du Seuil, 2017).

44 Ibid., p. 75 [trans. M G.].

Chapter 3 The Digital Transformation of Society

1 A drastic example of everyday nonsense is the genre of political speech-making and discussion. A TV debate during an election doesn't really do anything to put the logical competence of the candidates to the test. Today, this is unfortunately a problem. What we observe instead is a series of fallacies of half-baked thoughts combined with baseless accusations against members of other parties. What is said serves the sole function of maintaining or increasing political power. Of course, genuine political issues are addressed now and again, since politics belongs to reality; it is not just mere unrelenting discourse but about the tangible distribution of resources. Such distribution is governed by value parameters, which tend not to be articulated with anything like sufficient logical clarity. Because resource distribution is an ongoing business, we *fight* elections instead of making rational decisions. Whether that is a good thing is another question, one for political philosophy.

2 *The Holy Bible containing the Old and New Testaments with the Apocryphal/Deuterocanonical Books* (Oxford: Oxford University Press, 1995), Titus 1: 10–14.

3 For more details, see Dirk W. Hoffmann, *Theoretische Informatik*, 3 (rev. edn, Munich: Hanser, 2015).

4 See, especially, Graham Priest, *Beyond the Limits of Thought* (Oxford: Oxford University Press, 2001), and Anton Friedrich Koch, *Versuch über Wahrheit und Zeit* (Paderborn: Mentis, 2006). For a development of Koch's theory in connection with New Realism, see Koch, *Hermeneutischer Realismus* (Tübingen: Mohr Siebeck, 2016).

5 Joachim Bromand and Guido Kreis (eds), *Gottesbeweise von Anselm bis Gödel* (Berlin: Suhrkamp, 2011).

6 A. W. Moore, *The Infinite* (London: Routledge, 1990).

7 https://en.wikipedia.org/wiki/Wiener_schnitzel.

8 See G. W. Leibniz, 'Meditations on Knowledge, Truth and Ideas', in *G. W. Leibniz: Philosophical Essays*, ed. Daniel Garber and Roger Ariew (Indianapolis: Hackett, 1989), pp. 23–8; and, on this, Markus Gabriel, 'Ist der Gottesbegriff des ontologischen Beweises konsistent?', in Thomas Buchheim, Friedrich Hermanni, Axel Hutter and Christoph Schwöbel (eds), *Gottesbeweise als Herausforderung für die moderne Vernunft* (Tübingen: Mohr Siebeck, 2012), pp. 99–119.

9 Luisa Zielinski, 'In His Own Words', *Paris Review*, 18

October 2016, www.theparisreview.org/blog/2016/10/18/in-his-own-words.

10 Walter Homolka and Arnulf Heidegger (eds), *Heidegger und der Antisemitismus: Positionen im Widerstreit, mit Briefen von Martin und Fritz Heidegger* (Freiburg im Breisgau: Herder, 2016), p. 36.

11 Martin Heidegger, *Unterwegs zur Sprache (Gesamtausgabe,* I. Abteilung, Band 12) (Frankfurt am Main: Vittorio Klostermann, 1985), p. 27.

12 Martin Heidegger, *What is Called Thinking?*, trans. F. D. Wieck and J. J. Gray (New York: Harper & Row, 1968).

13 Martin Heidegger, *Bremer und Freiburger Vorträge (Gesamtausgabe* III. Abteilung, Band 79) (Frankfurt am Main: Vittorio Klostermann, 2002).

14 Ibid., p. 28.

15 See Hilary Putnam, *Meaning and the Moral Sciences* (London: Routledge & Kegan Paul, 1978), pp. 18f.

16 Markus Gabriel, 'What Kind of an Idealist (if Any) is Hegel?', *Hegel Bulletin* 27/2 (2016), pp. 181–208.

17 See the wonderfully clear accounts in Lisa Randall, *Warped Passages: Unravelling the Mysteries of the Universe's Hidden Dimensions* (London: Allen Lane, 2005); and Brian Greene, *The Elegant Universe: Superstrings, Hidden Dimensions, and the Quest for the Ultimate Theory* (London: Vintage, 2000).

18 A good overview of current positions surrounding the topic of Heidegger and anti-Semitism can be found in Homolka and Heidegger, *Heidegger und der Antisemitismus.*

19 Martin Heidegger, *Bremen and Freiburg Lectures: Insight into That Which Is, and Basic Principles of Thinking*, trans. Andrew J. Mitchell (Bloomington: Indiana University Press, 2012), p. 29.

20 Martin Heidegger, *Being and Time*, trans. Joan Stambaugh (Albany: State University of New York Press, 1996), p. 70.

21 Immanuel Kant, *Critique of Pure Reason*, trans. Paul Guyer and Allen Wood (Cambridge: Cambridge University Press, 1998), BXII–BIV.

22 Heidegger, *Being and Time*, p. 331.

23 Ibid., pp. 40f.

24 See Tyler Burge, 'Self and Self-Understanding', *Journal of Philosophy* 108/6–7 (2011), pp. 287–383.

25 Jean-François Lyotard, *Libidinal Economy*, trans. Iain Hamilton Grant (London: Athlone Press, 1993).

26 Immanuel Kant, *Critique of the Power of Judgment*, trans. Paul

Guyer and Eric Matthews (Cambridge: Cambridge University Press, 2000), 20:207f.

27 Immanuel Kant, *Critique of Practical Reason*, trans. Mary Gregor (Cambridge: Cambridge University Press, 2000), 5:9fn.
28 Markus Gabriel, *I am Not a Brain* (Cambridge: Polity, 2017).
29 Immanuel Kant, *Political Writings*, ed. Hans Reiss, trans. N. B. Nisbet (Cambridge: Cambridge University Press, 1991), p. 44.
30 David Chalmers and Andy Clark, 'The Extended Mind', *Analysis* 58/1 (1998), pp. 7–19; Andy Clark, *Natural-Born Cyborgs: Minds, Technologies, and the Future of Human Intelligence* (Oxford: Oxford University Press, 2004), *Supersizing the Mind: Embodiment, Action, and Cognitive Extension* (Oxford: Oxford University Press, 2008), and *Surfing Uncertainty: Prediction, Action, and the Embodied Mind* (Oxford: Oxford University Press, 2016).
31 Nick Bostrom, *Superintelligence: Paths, Dangers, Strategies* (Oxford: Oxford University Press, 2014).
32 Jean-Paul Sartre, *Being and Nothingness*, trans. Sarah Richmond (New York: Routledge, 2018), pp. 67–70.

Chapter 4 Why Only Animals Think

1 Max Tegmark, *Our Mathematical Universe: My Quest for the Ultimate Nature of Reality* (London: Allen Lane, 2014).
2 Plato, *Gorgias*, trans. Donald J. Zeyl (Indianapolis: Hackett, 1986), 493a.
3 On this, see Werner Beierwaltes, *Platonismus im Christentum* (3rd edn, Frankfurt am Main: Klostermann, 2014).
4 Matthew 10: 28.
5 Jose Luis Borges, *The Aleph and Other Stories 1933–69*, trans. Norman Thomas Di Giovanni (London: Bantam Books, 1971), p. 13.
6 See Maurizio Ferraris, *L'imbécillité est une chose sérieuse* (Paris: Presses universitaires de France, 2017).
7 Ludwig Wittgenstein, *Philosophical Investigations*, trans. G. E. M. Anscombe (Oxford: Blackwell, 1974), §451.
8 Ludwig Wittgenstein, *Zettel*, trans. G. E. M. Anscombe (Oxford: Blackwell, 1967), §173.
9 The talk can be viewed on YouTube: www.youtube.com/watch?v=93sYbHDtv9M. See also Nick Bostrom and Eliezer Yudkowsky, 'The Ethics of Artificial Intelligence', in Keith Frankish and William M. Ramsey (eds), *Cambridge Handbook*

of Artificial Intelligence (Cambridge: Cambridge University Press, 2014), pp. 316–34.

10 Johann Wolfgang von Goethe, *The Complete Works of Johann Wolfgang von Goethe in Ten Volumes*, Vol. 5: *Poems*, trans. various authors (New York: P. F. Collier, 1900), pp. 132–4.

11 Ibid.

12 Brigitte Görnitz and Thomas Görnitz, *Von der Quantenphysik zum Bewusstsein: Kosmos, Geist und Materie* (Berlin: Springer, 2016).

13 Ibid., p. 120: 'Consciousness is a special form of protyposis, namely quantum information that can experience and know itself as part of an information-processing process carried by a living brain' (trans. A. E.).

14 Ibid., p. 161.

15 Ibid., p. 160 (trans. A. E.).

16 Ibid., p. 174.

17 Ibid.

18 Ibid., p. 175.

19 www.congresofuturo.cl/.

20 See, especially, Giulio Tononi and Christof Koch, 'Consciousness: Here, There and Everywhere?', *Philosophical Transactions of the Royal Society* B370 (2015), https://royal-societypublishing.org/doi/full/10.1098/rstb.2014.0167.

21 Ibid., pp. 13–15.

22 Ibid., p. 7.

23 For Koch's current position on consciousness, see, for example Christof Koch, 'Lasst uns aufgeschlossen bleiben und sehen, inwiefern die Wissenschaft eine fundamentale Theorie des Bewusstseins entwickeln kann', in Matthias Eckoldt (ed.), *Kann sich das Bewusstsein bewusst sein?* (Heidelberg: Carl-Auer, 2017), pp. 179–196; and, at greater length, in *Consciousness: Confessions of a Romantic Reductionist* (Cambridge, MA: MIT Press, 2012).

24 At this point I should stress that Tononi is no advocate of neurocentrism, a position which I criticized in *I Am Not a Brain*. Rather, he overcomes neurocentrism on a neuroscientific basis and thereby effects a paradigm shift – i.e. a radical change of perspective. Just as contemporary physics is ultimately no longer naturalistic, contemporary neuroscience is on its way to overcoming neurocentrism from within. This is an exciting development, which could lead to a completely new convergence between philosophy and natural science.

25 For an introduction to the topic, see Gabriel, *I Am Not a*

Brain. And for an accessible overview of current positions in the discipline, see the entry on 'Consciousness' in the online *Stanford Encyclopedia of Philosophy*.

26 Markus Gabriel, *Antike und moderne Skepsis zur Einführung* (Hamburg: Junius, 2014).

27 Zhuangzi, *Chang Tzu: Basic Writings*, trans. Burton Watson (New York: Columbia University Press, 1964).

28 Thalmann has assured me in an email exchange that social robots are not conscious and that *Westworld* is an unrealizable fiction. I mention this here simply as an example of expert opinion.

29 Markus Gabriel, *Why the World Does Not Exist* (Cambridge: Polity, 2015), and *Fields of Sense* (Edinburgh: Edinburgh University Press, 2015). If you're interested in pursuing further details of the academic debate, see Thomas Buchheim (ed.), *Neutraler Realismus: Jahrbuchkontroversen 2* (Freiburg im Breisgau: Alber, 2016).

30 Gabriel, *Why the World does not Exist*, p. 7.

31 Ibid.

32 Thomas Huxley, *Lessons in Elementary Physiology* (London: Macmillan, 1986), p. 193.

33 For a general critique of the idea that we simply mirror nature, either as consciousness or by means of models, see the influential Richard Rorty, *Philosophy and the Mirror of Nature* (Princeton, NJ: Princeton University Press, 1979). Unfortunately, Rorty got rather carried away with this idea and became one of the main advocates of postmodern constructivism. His error was to infer from our not being mirrors of nature to the thesis that there can be no truth and no secure knowledge of reality. But the one thing doesn't follow from the other.

34 Wittgenstein, *Philosophical Investigations*, §265.

Chapter 5 Reality and Simulation

1 Iris Radisch, 'Was ist hinter dem Bildschirmschoner?' *Die Zeit*, 18 June 2014.

2 Bruno Latour, *We Have Never Been Modern*, trans. Catherine Porter (Cambridge, MA: Harvard University Press, 1993).

3 On this, see the classic text: Jürgen Habermas, *The Structural Transformation of the Public Sphere: An Inquiry into a Category of Bourgeois Society*, trans. Thomas Burger with the

assistance of Frederick Lawrence (Cambridge: Polity, 2008). Habermas charts the emergence of modernity out of the media structures of the Enlightenment.

4 Ludwig Wittgenstein, *Philosophical Investigations*, trans. G. E. M. Anscombe (Oxford: Blackwell, 1974), §255.

5 G. W. F. Hegel, *The Phenomenology of Spirit*, trans. Terry P. Pinkard (Cambridge: Cambridge University Press, 2018), p. 49.

6 Theodor W. Adorno, *Negative Dialectics*, trans. E. B. Ashton (London: Continuum, 1973), p. 99 (translation modified).

7 Radisch, 'Was ist hinter dem Bildschirmschoner?'

8 The exaggerations and fallacies of the postmodern theories that lie behind this madness have been exposed with particular clarity in Paul Boghossian, *Fear of Knowledge: Against Relativism and Constructivism* (Oxford: Oxford University Press, 2006); and Ian Hacking, *The Social Construction of What?* (Cambridge, MA: Harvard University Press, 1999).

9 Jean Baudrillard, *Simulacra and Simulation*, trans. Sheila Faria Glaser (Ann Arbor: University of Michigan Press, 1994).

10 Martin Heidegger, *Bremen and Freiburg Lectures: Insight into That Which Is, and Basic Principles of Thinking*, trans. Andrew J. Mitchell (Bloomington: Indiana University Press, 2012), p. 29.

11 Jean Baudrillard, *America*, trans. Chris Turner (London: Verso, 1988).

12 Baudrillard, *Simulacra and Simulation*, p. 1.

13 Koushun Takami, *Battle Royale*, trans. Yuji Oniki (2nd edn, San Francisco: Haikasoru, 2009).

14 Guy Debord, *The Society of the Spectacle* (London: Rebel Press, 1992).

15 Yuval Noah Harari, *Sapiens: A Brief History of Humankind* (London: Vintage, 2015).

16 Nick Bostrom, 'Are You Living in a Computer Simulation?' *Philosophical Quarterly* 53/211 (2003), pp. 243–55.

17 Nick Bostrom, *Superintelligence: Paths, Dangers, Strategies* (Oxford: Oxford University Press, 2014).

18 Nick Bostrom and Marcin Kulzycki, 'A Patch for the Simulation Argument', *Analysis* 71/1 (2011), pp. 54–61.

19 You can watch his TED Talk 'You are a Simulation & Physics Can Prove It' on YouTube, where it has had millions of views.

20 Bostrom, 'Are You Living in a Computer Simulation?', p. 248.

21 Ibid., p. 243.

22 Ibid.

23 Ibid., p. 244.
24 See Markus Gabriel, *Die Erkenntnis der Welt: Eine Einführung in die Erkenntnistheorie* (Freiburg im Breisgau: Alber 2014; René Descartes, *Meditations on First Philosophy with Selections from the Objections and Replies*, ed. John Cottingham (Cambridge: Cambridge University Press, 2013).
25 Ludwig Wittgenstein, *On Certainty*, trans. Denis Paul and G. E. M. Anscombe (Oxford: Blackwell, 1969), §383.
26 Wittgenstein, *Philosophical Investigations*, §258.
27 Ibid.
28 Plato, *Theaetetus and Sophist*, ed. Christopher Rowe (Cambridge: Cambridge University Press, 2015), p. 170 (263e3–5).
29 Aristotle admittedly believes that there is also a form of thinking that is infallible – namely, grasping indivisible atoms. This idea demands a detailed discussion. Yet he is at any rate clear that, wherever error is possible, synthesis is necessary. In *De anima* (trans. C. D. C. Reeve, Indianapolis: Hackett, 2017), p. 55 (430b26–28), he writes: 'The understanding of indivisible things is found in those cases concerning which there is no falsehood, whereas in those in which there is both falsehood and truth, there is already some sort of synthesis of thoughts as into one.'
30 Bertrand Russell, *The Problems of Philosophy* (Oxford: Oxford University Press, 1998), ch. 8.
31 Descartes, *Meditations*, p. 94.
32 For those interested in the further details, I recommend Jens Rometsch's path-breaking work *Freiheit zur Wahrheit: Grundlagen der Erkenntnis am Beispiel von Descartes und Locke* (Frankfurt am Main: Vittorio Klostermann, 2018).
33 Plato, *Sophist*, pp. 142–5 (245e–247e).
34 See especially, Plato, *Timeaus and Critias*, trans. Robin Waterfield (Oxford: Oxford University Press, 2008), pp. 43f. (51a4f).
35 David K. Lewis, *Philosophical Papers*. Vol. II (Oxford: Oxford University Press, 1986) p. ix.
36 Johann Wolfgang von Goethe, *Faust, Part One*, trans. David Luke (Oxford: Oxford University Press, 2008), p. 15.
37 For more details, see Jan Westerhoff, *Ontological Categories* (Oxford: Oxford University Press, 2005).
38 Plato, *Sophist*, p. 155 (254c).
39 Robert B. Brandom, *Articulating Reasons: An Introduction*

to Inferentialism (Cambridge, MA: Harvard University Press, 2000).

40 Plato, *Sophist* p. 164 (259e4–6) (trans. M. G.).

41 G. W. F. Hegel, *Elements of the Philosophy of Right*, trans. H. B. Nisbet (Cambridge: Cambridge University Press, 1991), p. 20.

42 See Andrea Kern and Christian Kietzmann, *Selbstbewusstes Leben: Texte zu einer transformativen Theorie der menschlichen Subjektivität* (Berlin: Suhrkamp, 2017); and especially Pirmin Stekeler-Weithofer, *Denken: Wege und Abwege in der Philosophie des Geistes* (Tübingen: Mohr Siebeck, 2012).

43 See the monumental Anton Friedrich Koch, *Versuch über Wahrheit und Zeit* (Paderborn: Mentis, 2006), as well as his *Hermeneutischer Realismus* (Tübingen: Mohr Siebeck, 2016).

44 Quentin Meillassoux, *After Finitude: An Essay on the Necessity of Contingency*, trans. Ray Brassier (London: Bloomsbury, 2009).

45 Thomas Buchheim (ed.), *Neutraler Realismus: Jahrbuchkontroversen 2* (Freiburg im Breisgau: Alber, 2016).

46 Jocelyn Benoist, *L'Adresse du réel* (Paris: Vrin, 2017), p. 72.

47 Rainer Maria Rilke, *Duino Elegies and The Sonnets to Orpheus*, trans. A. Poulin, Jr. (Boston: Houghton Mifflin, 1977), p. 59.

48 Thomas Nagel, *Mortal Questions* (Cambridge: Cambridge University Press, 1991), pp. 165–81.

49 Rilke, *Duino Elegies*, pp. 57–9 (emphases in original).

50 Ludwig Wittgenstein, *Tractatus-Logico-Philosophicus*, trans. D. F. Pears and B. F. McGuinness (London: Routledge, 2001) p. 68 (5.6).

51 F. W. J. Schelling, *Philosophical Investigations into the Essence of Human Freedom*, trans. Jeff Love and Johannes Schmidt (Albany: State University of New York Press, 2006) p. 29.

52 Immanuel Kant, 'What does it Mean to Orient Oneself in Thinking', in *Religion and Rational Theology*, trans. Allen W. Wood and George di Giovanni (Cambridge: Cambridge University Press, 1996), p. 7 (8: 133).

53 Friedrich Nietzsche, *Dithyrambs of Dionysus*, trans. R. J. Hollingdale (London: Anvil Press Poetry, 2001), p. 23.

54 Wolfram Hogrebe, 'Risky Proximity to Life: The Scenic Existence of Homo sapiens', trans. Adam Knowles, *Graduate Faculty Philosophy Journal* 31/2 (2010), pp. 219–312.

55 Friedrich Nietzsche, *Thus Spoke Zarathustra*, trans. Graham Parkes (Oxford: Oxford University Press, 2005), p. 27.

56 For a good introduction to this topic, see Andreas Hüttemann, *Ursachen* (Berlin: De Gruyter, 2018).

57 George Ellis, *How Can Physics Underlie the Mind? Top-Down Causation in the Human Context* (Berlin: Springer, 2016); George Ellis and Stephen Hawking, *The Large Scale Structure of Space–Time* (Cambridge: Cambridge University Press, 1973).

58 See also Holm Tetens, *Gott denken: Ein Versuch einer rationalen Theologie* (Stuttgart: Reclam, 2015).

59 Niklas Luhmann, *Soziologische Aufklärung, 3: Soziales System, Gesellschaft, Organisation* (Opladen: Westdeutscher Verlag, 2009), p. 216.

60 Gottlob Frege, 'Begriffschrift: Selections (Preface and Part 1)', in *The Frege Reader*, ed. Michael Beaney (Oxford: Blackwell, 1997), pp. 47–79.

61 Gottlob Frege, 'Thought', in *The Frege Reader*, p. 329.

62 Ibid.

63 Ibid., pp. 327–8.

64 Ibid., p. 342.

65 Sebastian Rödl, *Self-Consciousness and Objectivity: An Introduction to Absolute Idealism* (Cambridge, MA: Harvard University Press, 2018).

66 Michael Dummett, *Thought and Reality* (Oxford: Oxford University Press, 2008), and *The Nature and Future of Philosophy* (New York: Columbia University Press, 2010). On this topic, see also the reconstruction of Anselm of Canterbury's famous proof of God's existence in Markus Gabriel 'Ist der Gottesbegriff des ontologischen Beweises konsistent?', in Thomas Buchheim, Friedrich Hermanni, Axel Hutter and Christoph Schwöbel (eds), *Gottesbeweise als Herausforderung für die moderne Vernunft* (Tübingen: Mohr Siebeck, 2012), pp. 99–119.

67 Heraclitus: *Fragments*, trans. with a commentary by T. M. Robinson (Toronto: University of Toronto Press, 1987), p. 57.

68 Georg Christoph Lichtenberg, *Philosophical Writings*, trans. Steven Tester (Albany: State University of New York Press, 2012), p. 152.

69 F. W. J. Schelling, *On the History of Modern Philosophy*, trans. Andrew Bowie (Cambridge: Cambridge University Press, 1994), p. 48.

70 Sigmund Freud, *The Standard Edition of the Complete Psychological Works of Sigmund Freud*, ed. and trans. James Strachey, vol. XVII (London: Hogarth Press, 1960), p. 143.

71 Friedrich Nietzsche, *Nachgelassene Fragmente 1882–1884*, Kritische Studienausgabe vol. 10 (Munich: dtv, 1988), p. 258.
72 Sigmund Freud, 'Analysis Terminable and Interminable', *International Journal of Psycho-Analysis* 18 (1937), pp. 373–405, here p. 380.
73 Axel Honneth, *The Struggle for Recognition: The Moral Grammar of Social Conflicts*, trans. Joel Anderson (Cambridge: Polity, 1996).
74 Michel Foucault, *Histoire de la Sexualité*, 4: *Les Aveux de la chair* (Paris: Gallimard, 2018).
75 Aristotle, *Metaphysics*, p. 210 (1074b15) (translation modified).
76 Ibid., p. 211 (1074b31).
77 Ibid. (1074b32).
78 Ibid. (1074b33–5).
79 See his essay 'Homer's Contest', in Friedrich Nietzsche, *On the Genealogy of Morals and Other Writing*, ed. Keith Ansell-Pearson, trans. Carol Diethe (Cambridge: Cambridge University Press, 2007) pp. 174–83.
80 Aristotle, *Metaphysics*, p. 206 (1072b26) (translation modified).
81 On this, see the contributions in Robert J. Sternberg (ed.), *The Nature of Human Intelligence* (Cambridge: Cambridge University Press, 2018).
82 On this, see the nowadays unjustifiably neglected Günther Anders, *Die Antiquiertheit des Menschen: Über die Seele im Zeitalter der zweiten industriellen Revolution* (Munich: C. H. Beck, 2002).
83 Immanuel Kant, *Critique of the Power of Judgment*, trans. Paul Guyer and Eric Matthews (Cambridge: Cambridge University Press, 2000), p. 298 (5:430).
84 Plato, *The Symposium*, trans. M. C. Howatson (Cambridge: Cambridge University Press, 2008), 223d4–8.
85 Johann Wolfgang von Goethe, *Faust, Part One*, trans. David Luke (Oxford: Oxford University Press, 2008), p. 10.

Index

269